The world of Chaucer

Derek Brewer

D. S. BREWER

First published as 1978
Reissued 1992 by D. S. Brewer, Cambridge
Illustrated edition 2000

D. S. Brewer is an imprint of Boydell & Brewer Ltd
PO Box 9, Woodbridge, Suffolk IP12 3DF, UK
and of Boydell & Brewer Inc.
PO Box 41026, Rochester, NY 14604, USA

ISBN 0 85991 607 3

The paper used in this publication meets the minimum requirements
of American National Standard for Information Sciences ‑
Permanence of Paper for Printed Library Materials, ANSI Z39.48 1984

Printed in Slovenia

CONTENTS

ABBREVIATIONS

BD   *The Book of the Duchess*
CT   *The Canterbury Tales* (the roman numeral following *CT*
         signifies the number of the Fragment in accordance with
         Robinson's edition)
HF   *The House of Fame*
LGW   *The Legend of Good Women* (*Pro F* = Prologue F; so for G)
PF   *The Parliament of Fowls*
TC   *Troilus and Criseyde*

PREFACE

The year 2000 is the 600th anniversary of the death of Chaucer. Chaucer is after Shakespeare perhaps the greatest and most varied of English poets, whose works remain still accessible and enjoyable. The anniversary offers a fitting occasion to re-issue the present book in the full attraction of its original illustrations, and with some slight revision, including a reversal of the sequence of words in the original title. The text is fundamentally the same, though more up-to-date, and the obligations expressed in the earlier versions remain as warmly felt.

DEREK BREWER

Preface to 1992 Edition

The present book is a second edition with corrections and minor alterations of the text of the first edition of 1978. I am grateful to those friends, scholars and reviewers, including the late Professor M. M. Crow and C. P. Snow, whose kind remarks have encouraged the publication of this second edition.

Chaucer scholarship and criticism have continued to develop since this text first appeared, and different views of various matters will always be possible, but there has seemed to be no need for fundamental revision on my part. The first edition had a number of new points and ideas which still seem valid, and with rare exceptions there has been no attempt to list new bibliographical material. The book remains a serious attempt to describe and analyse Chaucer's life and poetry in close contact with the life of his times.

I am glad to acknowledge again my previous major obligation to *Chaucer Life-Records*, ed. M. M. Crow and Clair C. Olson, 1966. The standard edition of Chaucer's Works is now *The Riverside Chaucer*, ed. Larry D. Benson, 1988, from which quotations are taken (though I diverge from it on p. 193) and this admirable work contains vast amounts of up-to-date bibliographical and other information.

Preface to 1978 Edition

The aim of this book is to give as vivid an impression as possible of Chaucer's life and historical circumstances. No literary criticism is attempted, but the work depends on the premise that he is one of the very greatest English writers, and I have written for a wider audience than specialists.

A list of books consulted is given at the end, and there are notes (easily ignored) to specific points in the text, but I should particularly mark my debt to the edition of Chaucer's *Works* by F. N. Robinson (from which quotations are made); to *Chaucer Life-Records* edited by C. C. Olson and M. M. Crow, which must be the foundation of any discussion of Chaucer's life; and to *The Fourteenth Century* by May McKisack. While I have drawn with great benefit on a variety of other books these fundamental works of scholarship give us the great commonplaces of the subject.

INTRODUCTION

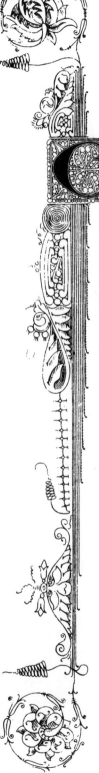

EOFFREY CHAUCER IS THE FIRST LITERARY PERSON-
ality in English, and we know more about the outline of his life than we do
about Shakespeare's. His inner life is recorded in his poems, and he liked to
put himself as a character into them. He was an extraordinary man, a great
poet who was courtier, soldier, learned man, much-travelled minor diplomat.
The range of his experience and interests is amazing, from common life and
bawdy tales to puritanical religion; from passionate love to an equally obsessive
interest in philosophy and science. He knew all sorts of people, not only English
but French, Italian, Flemish, German courtiers, soldiers, scholars, merchant-
financiers, monks, priests, ladies, servant girls, from the highest in the kingdom
down to all except the poor. Yet to judge from what he himself says, what he
most liked to do was to read in solitude. His attitudes ranged from a sentimental
feeling for small children, a deep interest in love, to a sardonic cynicism. Pity is
the feeling he most often consciously expresses, yet he can never keep flippancy
out of his treatment of the most serious matters.

He was fat, he tells us, and not talkative. People felt they could condescend to
him. But he was a wonderful mimic, and in his own way very self-assured.
There was a touch of the devil in this quiet, kindly man that occasionally broke
out in escapades he may have regretted. He was at the centre of English society,
yet also by temperament one who sought the margins and gaps; an official, he
was intensely interested in the unofficial.

England, and Europe, was in his day very different from our urbanized
industrial world, and I devote the rest of this Introduction to an impressionistic
description of Chaucer's England. Like all countries it was entirely dependent
on agriculture. Oats, barley, rye and wheat, cabbages and roots, were cultivated
in large open fields composed of strips held by different tenants, and with far
fewer hedges. Sheep, cows, goats were pastured in commons and wastelands;
fuel, timber and game came from the woods. There were great forests, and
broadly scattered woodlands almost everywhere apart from the moors on the
higher uplands, and the heather-covered sandy tracts of Norfolk, now paradoxically covered with conifers.

Townsmen were almost as close to the countryside as were villagers and
peasants. Chaucer's poetry is full of country images. He travelled constantly on
horseback, exposed to all weathers and seasons, on muddy tracks, meeting all
the variety of medieval travellers, part of the landscape and of the turning world,

OPPOSITE *The basis of all life was farming work*

as all medieval men had to be. The great opening of *The Canterbury Tales* is the immortal expression of that sense of relief and release when winter's sharpness has worn away. Heavens and winds and earth and people are all linked in the spring surge, bird song, animal movement, that includes new life, sexual energies, gratitude, religious devotion, social enjoyment, all together in one overriding image – not mere image, but actual fact – of the English countryside. Something like this appears in dozens of English poems:

> The mirth of all this land
>   Maketh the good husband   [farmer]
> With labouring of his plough.
>   I – blessed – be Christés sand   [message]
> That hath us sent in hand
>   Mirth and joy enough.

The plough goes early and late, through the clay, that makes men sweat, to get barley and wheat.

You cannot enjoy summer if you do not know in Chaucerian phraseology 'the sword of winter, keen and cold', its 'cold mornings', 'wet rains', its dry death of 'woods and hedges'. There was a bitter side to the ploughman's toil, as a fourteenth-century alliterative poet describes it. As he went by the way he saw a man hanging on the plough. His coat was of coarse cloth, his hood torn, his shoes broken, his mittens only rags, and his hands muddy. His four heifers pulled the plough feebly and his wife walked by him with a long goad. She was ill-clad and the ice cut her bare feet, while at the furrow's end was a cradle with a baby wrapped in rags, two more children two years old by its side, and all wailing in misery, while the poor ploughman sighed and said 'Children, be quiet!' Chaucer never shows the plight of the poor so pathetically, though the poor are for him, as for so many medieval poets, the generalized image of humanity. Yet he also portrayed with half-amused realistic sympathy such poor cottages as that of the old widow who owned Chanticleer the cock. She lived a simple life, beside a wood in a valley, with her two daughters, three pigs, three cows, a sheep (all of whom no doubt inhabited the same sooty 'hall' and 'bower'), and had a yard with a cock and seven hens. Milk and brown bread, grilled bacon, and occasionally an egg or two, with no wine, was her diet – a very healthy one, too, as the overweight Chaucer wryly points out. Chaucer does not sentimentalize this, any more than he does the exemplary shepherdess Griselda in *The Clerk's Tale*, with her tangled hair and dirty clothes. It seems to have been natural for him to accept both the squalor and the spiritual dimension. There was no separation between the fact and the symbolic power that gave it value, when Chaucer saw the countryside. And this was because he knew it so well, felt it in his bones, and yet as a courtier and townsman was detached from its miseries and injustices. He felt differently about things he was closer to.

Towns and villages were scattered all over England, and the nucleus of almost every town and village now in England had been established by Chaucer's day – indeed, long before. Before the Black Death of 1348–9, the

ABOVE *Medieval fields (ridge and furrow ploughing) northeast of Padbury, Buckinghamshire*

population may have been as much as three million. Since only five per cent of the population lived in towns, of which only London, and possibly York, had more than 10,000 inhabitants, most of the population were scattered about in villages, hamlets, isolated houses. After the Black Death the population may have been reduced to two million. There were less severe but still terrible visitations of plague in 1361–2 and 1369, and the population by 1400 may have been half of what it was in 1340, which was about the time when Chaucer was born. So riding about the country Chaucer would have seen deserted fields, houses, even villages. All the same in *cultivated* parts there would not necessarily have been even so much solitude as in country parts in England and Europe today. Everywhere there were people working on the land.

Quite other were the great tracts of forest and woodland. The roads skirted these, for nearly all the forest was protected by savage game laws, and pursuit of their rich wildlife was restricted to the king or gentry who owned the forest. Hunting was the constant occupation and recreation of all the gentry. Everything eatable was game, from the little hunted hare, rabbit, to the deer and the mighty, dangerous boar. There were still wolves in the forest, but those were not hunted. Chaucer knew the hare with its staring eyes and expresses the traditional pity for its fear, as it lies weary in its form, pursued by hounds great and small. Generally speaking, though, hunting was loved by all classes. The sport caught the imagination. It was fierce and hot in pursuit, bursting with hope, exulting in the kill, in the bloody disembowelment, the triumphant return home with horns blowing and the carcass on a pole to be roasted at the feast.

There was a hunt of love too, with a triumphant consummation and ambivalent death. This is what interests Chaucer more. The actual hunting of animals is for Chaucer only a part of the background of the courtly life, in contrast with the fourteenth-century poet of *Sir Gawain and the Green Knight*, for whom its actual and symbolic realities are much more central. Chaucer was never interested in food, fat as he was. In *The Book of the Duchess* he is, in a dream, called out to hunt the deer, and we feel the stir and excitement of beginning the chase, but he soon strays away from the hunt and is led to hear the lament of the Man in Black. The hunt is a significant but remote background to the pursuit of love, more tender, equally carnal; and each ends in a death. Chaucer's interest was in the personal feeling, not the physical excitement. For the natural and vigorous

BELOW *A hare for supper. For the poor, hunting was part of a grim business of survival*

fun of the hunt itself, as well as its symbolic force, we must go to the equally courtly, but provincial, northern poem, *Sir Gawain and the Green Knight*.

Like the hunt, the forest as well as being a constant real presence is also a profoundly symbolic, even sacred place, where we lose and find ourselves. This is a little more to Chaucer's taste, as, in *The Book of the Duchess*, he wanders down grassy drives in a well-managed forest, to find the mourning Knight in the depths. For the poets in general the forest is the place of adventure, of meeting the wonderful girl, the golden-haired, fresh beauty who lightens a man's life.

When spring comes, birds sing, blossoms flourish, all the world is joyous. But if the beloved is cruel, or, as in *The Book of the Duchess*, dead, the forest is a place of loss and confusion. All creatures make love, says a poet; women become marvellously proud, and well it suits them: but if I lack my will of that one, I must abandon all this wealth of joys and be a lost man in the wood. As another poet puts it, in a line that echoes Chaucer, 'I must go walk the wood so wild'.

The forest was a place of joy and excitement as well as loss and confusion – legal records are full of men punished because they would not keep out of the forest. And some men had to keep inside it; the outlaws, robber bands, real-life equivalents of Robin Hood (first heard of as a folk hero in Chaucer's time), living 'in hazel-wood, where jolly Robin played', as Chaucer says.

An outlaw had a 'wolf's head', which might be cut off by anyone who could. The female equivalent was a *weyve*, abandoned without protection of law to any fate – poor Maid Marian. Outlaws and *weyves* had no property, no rights. It was such men, members of a gang working in several counties, who

RIGHT *A French ivory mirror case shows the hunt as part of the pursuit of love*

robbed Chaucer on 3 September 1390, at or near 'The Foul Oak' in the parish of Deptford, Kent, only five miles from the walls of the City of London, when he was on one of his innumerable journeys on horseback.

The roads over which Chaucer passed were rarely paved. The usual reference made by the Canterbury pilgrims to the road is as 'the slough', the mud, and so it must have been, in a rainy April, with horses and carts constantly churning it up. Even in modern times I have seen a road in mountains rendered waist-deep in mud from the passage of mules. In the fourteenth century (and as late as the nineteenth) even the nobility might find it impossible to travel because the weather made the roads impassable. In 1339 Parliament had to be postponed because bad weather prevented the barons from arriving on the proper day. Yet there were roads, and even in England it does not rain all the time, so except in really bad weather it was normally possible to travel with some hope of arriving.

In some towns (for example, Southampton and Lincoln) roads were paved, though flint (in Winchester) or gravel (in Oxford) were used, and there were even relics of Roman roads, in England and Europe, whose firm base had wonderfully endured ten centuries' wear or more. Paris was paved, and so were some London streets. One paved road that Chaucer knew very well, the Strand and its extension from Temple Bar, the western edge of the City of London, to Westminster, had become in 1353 so full of holes and quagmires, and the pavement so broken, that it was very dangerous. Each proprietor on either side

In this rather idealized picture, no less than seven roads are being built simultaneously, and into an idyllically ordered countryside

was ordered by the King to make a seven-foot footway on the edge of the paved centre of the roadway. In 1356 the City imposed a road tax to pay for repairs, because the roads were so bad. A French ordinance referring to Paris, a bigger, richer town than London, in 1388, shows how bad things might be. In the suburbs, roads, lanes and bridges were damaged or destroyed by watercourses, big stones, and by hedges, brambles and trees, so that some had to be quite abandoned. In many English towns the level of the road rose steadily with the accumulated rubbish. Fourteenth-century legislation at least shows that someone was trying to improve matters. But nature is strong. In modern England and Europe, many centuries-old lanes and paths have been lost, despite modern technology. In the fourteenth century, with only hands and simple tools, the physical effort needed to keep civilization afloat was enormous. A constant battle had to be waged to keep ways passable, by men who were less utilitarian, far less well fed and well clothed than we are.

Means of transport were limited. The poor, both the actual and the professional, such as friars, walked. Most regular travellers rode, on horses good or bad. You judged a man by the horse he rode, as some people do nowadays by cars. Chaucer's Knight in *The Canterbury Tales* has good horses, though he himself is not flashy in dress. The Monk, on the other hand, is richly dressed and has many a fine horse in his stable – and we draw the appropriate conclusion, that he has what in modern terms would be a very lush expense account, though vowed to poverty. The admirable Clerk, ideal university professor, does not go out for the money and rides a horse as lean as a rake. The equally ideal, humble, hardworking ploughman rides a poor mare. We are not told what the ploughman's brother, the parson, rides, but in his remote parish where the houses are far apart he goes on foot, with a staff. Women normally rode on horseback and astride, though riding side-saddle began to come in during Chaucer's lifetime.

Most goods also went by horseback, but there were carts. They were used for farming – there is a dung cart in *The Nun's Priest's Tale*, and in *The Friar's Tale* a cart full of hay is caught in a deep narrow track. The word 'cart' was also used for 'war chariot' in poetry, but the medieval painters thought of the war chariot as a simple farm cart. Chaucer also mentions a *fare-cart*, one that carried provisions. The great armies and the continuously travelling king's court had large clumsy baggage wagons. When Chaucer was an esquire at the king's court he would have become familiar with the arrangements. Ladies might even have carriages. They had four wheels. Solid beams rested directly on the axles without springs. On these was raised a long semicircular structure like a tunnel. Four or five horses in line pulled them, urged on by a postilion seated on one with a whip. Jarring and inefficient, they were vividly carved and painted outside, with tapestries and embroidered cushions inside, and windows with curtains. Elizabeth de Burgh, Lady Clare, in her will of 25 September 1355, endowed her eldest daughter with her 'great carriage with the couvertures, carpets and cushions'. Chaucer must have seen this when he was page to her daughter Lady Elizabeth, Countess of Ulster, in 1359. The gypsy wagon that survived in England till this century, gaudily painted and often not dissimilar in

LEFT *A great lady travels in her chariot with her damoiselles and retinue*

OPPOSITE *The Pilgrim's Way above Trottiscliffe, Kent*

shape, though lighter, was a direct descendant, still touched with some of the romance of the road, though the medieval carriage lacked the comfort of the gypsy's stove and stovepipe. The covered wagon of the great American treks to the West was probably even closer in design. Medieval carriages were very expensive. Richard II paid £400 for a carriage made for his second queen, the child Isabella, and Edward III had paid £1000 for one for his sister – a truly staggering sum. No wonder they were rare. There were also horse litters, like stretchers between two horses, but again infrequent.

Speeds over roads varied enormously, as today. The two-and-a-half-day pilgrimage from London to Canterbury made by a group of thirty pilgrims, over a distance of fifty-seven miles, could be travelled in one day by a king's messenger using pre-arranged changes of horse. It can be done nowadays, even in dense motor traffic, in three hours or less. That is the measure of a different feel about time and space. England in the fourteenth century was much bigger, in terms of how long it took to get anywhere at any possible speed. It was quieter, except for birds, which were not decimated by pesticides. There were many more wild animals, big and small, than now. It was far more dangerous and uncomfortable.

Chaucer stopped at inns when he travelled, as did almost all but the very highest and lowest. He had to sleep in a room in which there were a number of beds, if he was lucky; if he was unlucky, he had to share a bed, with one or more others. There is a gruesomely comic Italian anecdote written by a contemporary

of Chaucer's, Francesco Sacchetti, about a man who came late to a crowded inn. There were a lot of beds with two men in a bed, all in the same room. Only one had a single sleeper. And he had died the day before. The latecomer, who had a superstitious horror of corpses, did not realize this and got in beside him. Later in the night he thought his bedfellow was taking up too much room, became enraged, kicked him out of bed, found he was dead, and added to the horror of the corpse the thought that he had himself killed him. There are no anecdotes or records that I know about the difficulties of women travellers. (What brave man shared a bed with the Wife of Bath? How did the Prioress keep herself to herself?) Some taverns, especially in London, were brothels, and by a natural conjunction also harboured violent criminals. Chaucer on his journeys probably sent a servant on ahead to book accommodation. Are there bugs or fleas, asked the servant? No, said the host, quite untruly, though there are mice and rats (quite true). On entering the inn Chaucer probably bargained with the innkeeper or his wife – have you a room for me and my men? How much do you charge? people, as always, complained about prices, and laws were promulgated to keep them down, with the usual lack of success. Travellers fed in the common eating room, where, if it was a popular place, would be others, eating, drinking, talking, singing, telling stories, gambling, like the 'rioters' in *The Pardoner's Tale*. The Warden and two fellows of Merton College, Oxford, with four servants, travelled from Oxford to Newcastle in winter in 1331. Their bill for one representative day was as follows: Bread, 4*d.*; Beer, 2*d.*; Wine, 1*d.*; Meat, 5*d.*; Soup, ¼*d.*; Candles, ¼*d.*; Fuel, 2*d.*; Beds, 2*d.*; Fodder for Horses, 10*d.* Occasionally they added eggs or vegetables for a farthing. These men lived very simply, but in winter fruit, for example, was not available, and no doubt cheese was scarce.

In the morning the traveller had a drink of beer, perhaps with bread, or if indulging himself, had cake and spices soaked in wine, and settled the bill, more or less amicably. It was prudent to ask the way, for there were no signposts. Are there any robbers ahead? (And is the innkeeper in league with them?)

The day's travel would in populated parts, like the way to Canterbury, take people past humble alehouses recognized by a bush above the door and perhaps the alewife standing outside to inveigle passers-by inside, as used to happen in Japan until very recently, and must be a widespread ancient custom. John Skelton (1460?–1529) has an amusing poem about such a woman, Elynour Rummyng: her loathly complexion is nothing clear but ugly to see, droopy and drowsy, scurvy and boozy, comely crinkled, wonderfully wrinkled, etc. She caters for tinkers and tailors, for Kate, Cissy, Sarah, with their legs bare and feet very unsweet, their clothes in tatters, bringing dishes and platters, to fill up with beer. William Langland (1330?–1400?) has a wonderful pub scene in London, with Cissy (again), Wat the warrener (though he is with his wife), Tim the tinker, Hick the hackney man, Clarice of Cock's Lane (the local prostitute), Sir Peter of Priedieu (one of the local clergy), their counterparts still to be seen in much the same places today, though rather better behaved. At such a pub, an 'ale-stake', Chaucer's Pardoner in *The Canterbury Tales* insists on stopping for a drink and a bite of bread before he tells his tale. It is all a curious mixture of the

'So was hir [their] joly whistle wel ywet.' A fourteenth-century tavern scene

strange and the familiar. These were low-class places and Chaucer never willingly passed any time in them, hail-fellow-well-met; but it is easy to imagine him, if he had to stop, pleasantly taking a drink, not of ale but of wine, shuddering slightly at its quality (the vintner's son detecting the adulterating Spanish ill-concealed in the only slightly better French), and either listening to the general chat, inconspicuously observant, or as often as not abstracted, thinking of something quite different.

Apart from alehouses, other small buildings on the way were small mills for grinding local grain, the houses of recluses (paradoxically notorious sources of gossip), or the dwellings of hermits. It is not quite that there was a building every two hundred yards or so, as in so much modern English countryside, but at least the larger roads were by no means deserted. Hermits very often occupied a little cottage and repaired the road, or bridges, for such was a well-known work of piety. They might be more retired, though, and the only reference to them that Chaucer makes in his writing is to compare himself jokingly in The House of Fame with a hermit because he goes home every night to read in silence.

The towns and villages of medieval England were not so very far apart and had a definite ratio of size to distance from each other. The favoured size of an English village in the late fourteenth century was around 100 to 150 persons, of a town perhaps 1000 to 2000. Such towns were typically between 25 and 35 miles apart, and the larger villages, or small market towns, lay some dozen miles from the regional centre – half a day's travel, or less. So it was possible to travel, usually, from small town to small town. Towns tend to have about 1.5 per cent of the region's populace. A capital city like London, therefore, bearing the same proportion to the country as a whole, had about 35,000 or a little more in the latter part of the fourteenth century. Even small towns, though an intimate part of the countryside, also set themselves apart, clearly defined by walls, establishing a special sense of relative freedom and innovation, more comfortable and safer, than the country. Country and town begin clearly to differentiate themselves, and surely it was always with a slight sense of relief that Chaucer came to the town. Towns had gardens, but that was nature tamed more effectively, turned to favour and prettiness.

From their prison window, Arcite and Palamon see Emily in the garden weaving flowers 'to make a subtil gerland for hir hede' and singing 'as an aungel hevenysshly'; they both fall in love with her. The picture is taken, not in fact from The Knight's Tale *itself, but from Boccaccio's* Teseida, *which Chaucer used as a source*

As Chaucer approached a town from the country he saw first the cluster of small poorish houses outside the wall. The place to live was inside the wall, and only the poor were outside. The chief exception to this was the procession of grand houses along the Strand between Temple Bar and Westminster. In these nobles lived and one of them, the Savoy, he knew well, as the grandest house in England, belonging to John of Gaunt, Duke of Lancaster. Ordinary suburbs were a different matter, a scrubby growth outside a usually modest wall, with, however, a substantial gate, shut at dusk. (He himself for a while lived in what we would now call a flat or apartment above the gate in Aldgate – a characteristically equivocal position.) London had good walls, while in some towns they were ruinous, but still the wall defined the town, showing its privilege of fortification, and of exacting market tolls; its security, independence, good government and pride. Yet in England, a natural fortress set in the silver sea,

ABOVE LEFT *A city garden of 'virtuous herbs'*

ABOVE *Watering can, fourteenth-century style (earthenware)*

which served it in the office of a wall, or a moat defensive to a house, with relatively good, centralized government there was less need than in less fortunate lands for mighty walls and great urban fortifications. There was in consequence less sharp definition of town from countryside, less intense urban loyalty, less development, except to some extent in London, of special urban consciousness. The difference between town and country was there, but graded and blurred.

Once past the gate, he was at the beginning of the main street, often broad and pleasant, for not all the streets were narrow and winding. Some towns retained the earlier Roman chessboard pattern as Gloucester recognizably does even today. Others had recently been laid out on a grid pattern like New Winchelsea, a royal foundation of the thirteenth century, or Bury St Edmunds, which Chaucer must have known, with its great abbey that became the home of his most prolific disciple, the monk John Lydgate. The main street of a town might be fifty feet broad, for the convenience of setting up a market. Some towns were centred on the market square or triangle, especially if this was sited close to abbey or castle. There were many permanent shops in the streets. When Chaucer rode down the broad High Street of Oxford or Southampton, as he must several times have done, he saw numbers of shops with narrow frontages, rather humbler than his father's house, but of much the same kind. In Oxford the High Street was gravelled, not paved as in London. The shopkeepers lived above and behind the shop, as did his father, and the narrow buildings ran a good way back, with narrow alleys and lanes here and there, still to be seen. In Bristol, although some main streets were fifty feet wide, there were alleys of eight or nine feet wide and a few of six. There was a vast number of trades of all kinds, though each trade tended to group itself in special streets or in quarters. The streets inside the town were sometimes paved, though lanes were not, and a gutter, called a kennel, ran down the centre of streets to carry off water. Big houses had cesspits in the cellar, but there was no general sanitation, except of a fairly simple sort in London (part of whose wooden underground pipes were not finally renewed till the nineteenth-century). There were wells and communal pumps for getting water, streams for throwing it away as well as rubbish. People might empty chamberpots on to the street from windows of the overhanging upper stories of houses, to the merry cry 'Gardy loo!' (*Gardez l'eau*, 'watch out for the water'). Streets and shops and marketplaces were places of social as well as commercial interchange. The churches, bright with coloured walls and adorned altars, were natural meeting places not only for worship but for practical discussions and decisions. There were taverns, respectable and not, where people drank, sang and gambled, and eating houses. On festival days there was a procession to the church in colourful robes, extra booths and perhaps plays in the marketplace, and an influx of minstrels, acrobats, singers and less respectable entertainers. People led hard, insecure lives, but there was many a green isle in the wide sea of misery. The town was insanitary and sometimes smelly, but had human life and activity. There are people even today whose dominant impression of Venice is that it smells; but for those who can look and feel further than their noses, it is a marvellous place. So a medieval town, though not a Venice, was a place of interest and refreshment.

Villages usually clustered along the highway, since traffic was no disadvantage, and had, as now, small houses, a church, a pub of some sort, a village green and a village pond. The village of Pendlebury in Worcestershire, or Cilgerran in Wales, maintains much the same scale now as then, with many fourteenth-century houses. They varied in appearance according to the area. Churches were mostly small but stone-built, it being just before the great boom in parish-church building of the fifteenth century. There is still a wooden church at Greensted, Essex, that was many centuries old in the fourteenth century, but though there were many Anglo-Saxon churches, perhaps most church buildings dated from the twelfth or thirteenth centuries. In East Anglia many were built of flint. Some had thatched roofs, others wooden, a few lead. In villages as in towns the interiors of churches were often decorated with statues that might well be considerable works of art. Village houses had two or three rooms, and the chickens and animals moved pretty freely about the street and house. Dungheaps lay at the front doors. The houses were of stone in the Cotswolds, but were more usually timber-framed, sometimes with the wattle-and-daub infilling whitewashed outside, still often to be seen ('black-and-white' houses), thatched. They were to our eyes charmingly irregular, though the medieval ideal was absolute regularity of height and appearance. The great virtue of such buildings was their human

LEFT *Cruck-fronted cottage at Didbrook, Gloucestershire. This might be the house of a yeoman farmer in Chaucer's day, or even of his Ploughman*

OPPOSITE *The fortified manor house of Stokesay Castle, Shropshire, with its splendid gatehouse, is an image of protective comfort in a countryside still not fully tamed*

scale and intimate relationship with the environment. Since technology was so primitive men had to cooperate with nature. The jarring inappropriateness to the environment of the scale, design and material of agricultural buildings and indeed of almost all buildings today was simply not possible in the Middle Ages. Plumbing, hot water, real warmth, comfortable chairs, were all lacking, but psychological comfort was not. Men built for effect rather than utility. The maddening impracticality of much medieval activity arose because priorities were often different. Hence the placing of so many churches, even perhaps castles, where, by conscious or unconscious intention, they superbly crown the landscape. And we modern utilitarians recognize this as we visit such places in our tourist thousands because we find them interesting and attractive. Even Chaucer, so often realistic and utilitarian before his time, occasionally falls for the sheer glamour of his age, and the poet of *Sir Gawain and the Green Knight*, so often the opposite of Chaucer, revels in it as much as we.

The traveller passed or paused at not only towns and villages but monasteries, manor houses and castles. Sometimes these great buildings stood relatively isolated on their own, sometimes they were the nucleus and dominating element of a cluster of dwellings, and resembled farms with embattlements more than anything else. Sometimes their presence created a town. A vast abbey like that of Bury St Edmunds, whose great size can still be seen from its extensive ruins, dominated the town (with whom it had very bad relations), was a great

landowner and was itself almost a town and farm. It had an extensive vineyard, for example, just outside the walls. A fine sight it made, with its great walls and towers, the clustering outbuildings, the noble church, the library full of books, the scriptorium where manuscripts were written, the stewponds and orchards. Happy the Lydgate who could spend so much of his life there, yet travel to London when he needed to. The towns' people hated the abbey and it was destroyed at the Reformation in the sixteenth century. The monasteries had guesthouses with plain food for humble travellers, who might have to sleep on the floor; ordinary travellers chose inns; great lords and their retinues forced monasteries to entertain them all too sumptuously, as numerous complaints make clear. Chaucer stayed in monasteries as part of the royal retinue; but he is never imaginatively inside the traditional life of enclosed religion, and his monk characters are always travellers outside their monasteries, for good or ill.

Castles are different. The country was sprinkled with them and it would have been reasonable for a gentleman in real life, as so often in romance, to ask at a castle for a night's lodging and be received with courtesy and real pleasure. Such an episode takes place in *Sir Gawain and the Green Knight*, and surely Chaucer might well have found himself asking hospitality when caught by night in unfamiliar countryside. He travelled constantly to great castles, especially when young. During the period that he was with the Countess of Ulster, 1357–9, she, and probably he, as an unconsidered youth in her service, went with ladies'in' waiting, clerks, esquires and yeomen of the chamber, pages, and all those waiting upon them, to Reading, Stratford, Campsey, London (for Easter), Windsor (for St George's Day), Woodstock (for Pentecost), Doncaster, Hatfield (for Christmas), Bristol (for Epiphany), Anglesey and Liverpool. Later in life, apart from official journeys, Chaucer must often have visited his wife who was in service with John of Lancaster's second wife, Constance of Castile, who lived mainly at Tutbury in Staffordshire. John of Lancaster had a superb, ancient, but extensively modernized castle at Kenilworth, where enough still stands, though ruined, for us to admire the large fourteenth'century windows, once perhaps full of stained glass, of the new hall. Walk about Kenilworth Castle and you certainly move where Chaucer once walked, and may re'create in mind the paved passages, the hall bright with glass and tapestry, the parlours with great carved fireplaces where the ladies sat, the vast kitchens with huge fires, the stables, the cobbled court where horses clattered and slipped and carts with iron tyres ground their heavy way. Other magnates built or rebuilt magnificent castles. Berkeley had a new hall; Bodiam was an entirely modern fortress, which even now still dramatically shines above its bright moat. The aim of building was not merely utility but splendour of life, admired by rich and poor, clerical and secular. If God is the supreme splendour, should we not imitate him? Some brilliant compensation was needed for the precariousness of health, wealth, strength, life itself, whose background was heavy toil for almost everyone – including the knight, in his heavy armour, and the cleric with his awkward quill pen and poor light and heat. For everyone, too, there was physical discom'

Bodiam Castle, Sussex. Towers rise glamorously over a moat that was an open sewer

fort of multiple kinds – think only of toothache or constipation, and the absence of scientific medicine. So great houses, like great churches, were adorned with bright torches and candles that imaged the brightness of heaven, with flashing jewels, boldly designed, richly coloured tapestries and hangings, gold and silver plate and goblets, brilliantly coloured stained-glass windows, banners of war, and the richly laden tables of peace. Fortunate indeed was the winter traveller who was welcomed into the private chamber with a fire, was clothed in beautiful robes, to move then to the joyous hall with retainers feasting at the long tables, and merry games and dancing after supper when the tables were removed. The poet of *Sir Gawain and the Green Knight* gives this description to us, and so does Chaucer in *The Squire's Tale* where we get a vividly authentic, though more caustic, glimpse of courtly festival, feasting and dancing, covert flirtation, and the touch of corroding jealousy, all as frame to a story of betrayed love.

Not many peasants or humble travellers were received into such festivities, though the lord's own retainers of quite humble rank had a place. The traveller

ABOVE *Stone carving of a
bagpiper from Beverley
Minster, Yorkshire, c. 1335.
This little figure
is reminiscent of Chaucer's
Miller, who led the Pilgrims
out of town playing his
bagpipes*

BELOW *An assortment of
fourteenth-century instruments*

who earned his *entrée* was the minstrel and entertainer, of whom there were a
variety. There were musicians, singers, storytellers, acrobats, down to those who
made very simple fun indeed, by ranting and gross abuse and breaking wind.
Some of these would even find a welcome in gentlemen's houses; such dwellings were more than cottages, less than manor houses, owned by men of
substance, who were glad of an evening's entertainment from travelling fiddler
or bagpiper or from a man who could tell, or read aloud, an exciting romance.
Such houses as these were more likely to be found in towns, but farmhouses in
the country were no doubt even more glad of such visits. Chaucer must have
heard minstrels in his father's house in London, and in a sense, courtier and
gentleman as he was, he continued their line at a more exalted level, for he was
an entertainer himself.

Over these rough roads, from court to city, town and village, monastery to
castle to farmhouse, over the hills and down to coasts that were deserted but for a
few fishing villages and the ports, travelled a cross-section of the whole population. Since a third of English surnames are place-names, and you do not take a
place-name to distinguish yourself when you remain with a hundred others in the
place you were born in, many quite humble people must have moved about the
country at this time, as one John moved from his village to the monastery twenty
miles away and was thus called John Lydgate after his village. If a man moved
from one village to another others of his family might move too, or visit him. But
these were short and perhaps rare journeyings. More frequent travellers were of
many kinds. All the people in Chaucer's *Canterbury Tale* might have travelled
anyway apart from the excuse of the pilgrimage, except perhaps the worthy
ploughman, and even he presumably regularly visited his local market. Of such a
variety of people, the middling sections of society (not serfs, who were forbidden to
leave their land), *The Canterbury Tales* has given the description once and for all.
Then there were official messengers, as Chaucer often was, and peddlars, soldiers
looking for employment or loot, beggars. At the other end of the scale the traveller
might pass the great train of the king's court itself, with the purveyors far in
advance to buy food or extort it, the marshal also in advance to chalk up marks on
the best houses for the accommodation of the king and courtiers, then the advance
guard of archers, the king himself in glorious array, the ladies, the court officials,
all on horseback, the men-at-arms, the wagons, the servants, camp followers,
troops of hangers-on of all kinds, scroungers, odd-job men, thieves, prostitutes.
Smaller, but similar in quality were the trains of the magnates, including prelates
of the church, bishops and abbots. Slowly they must have moved and wearisome
such a peripatetic life must have been, but the magnetism of the court, the pleasures of change, the force of necessity, the inertia of company and custom, kept
them together and kept them going. Even Chaucer himself, towards the end of his
life, when comfortably settled in Greenwich, remarks a trifle dolefully on his
distance from the court, from the fountainhead of benefits, and of interest.

'The pilgrimage of the life of man' is a powerful medieval commonplace
which Chaucer makes his own Parson in *The Canterbury Tales* invoke towards
the end of the work, calling on pilgrims to seek the heavenly Jerusalem. The

pilgrims as Chaucer shows them are not all devout, and some seem very much the reverse, though we need not doubt their religious intent. The pilgrimage was the climax of travelling in the Middle Ages. Many men travelled out of necessity, from the king down to the humble Parson on foot, whether or not they enjoyed it. On the pilgrimage they travelled by choice. Anxious, uncomfortable and disappointing as it often was, the pilgrimage was a great liberation, a holiday that was also a holy-day. People were able to shake off the rigidity and repetitiousness of ordinary everyday life, which though necessary can become infinitely tedious. On pilgrimage they crossed boundaries, not only of parish and county and coast, but of their own personality and class. Centres of pilgrimage, spiritual centres, are usually on the margins of more everyday centres of power. The two favourite places of pilgrimage in medieval England were Canterbury and Walsingham, both near the coast, far from London. Compostella is on the edge of Spain, Jerusalem on the edge of Europe. Granted that one of the eternal disappointments of travel is that one is still the same person on arrival, the act of change, the transition, is a quickener of feeling and perception, a mixer of elements, a producer of the new. Chaucer apologizes in *The General Prologue to The Canterbury Tales* for not putting folk in order according to their social rank; and in his detailed descriptions of each of the pilgrims in *The General Prologue* he similarly jumbles up the orderly form of description prescribed by the rhetoricians who taught the art of writing. This disturbance of a still strong underlying order of rank or description is exactly right for producing that freshness, that sense of new discovery of the world that we thought we knew. It is exactly right for the pilgrimage, just as it is right that the pilgrimage takes place in spring, the time of new life, new venture, and natural that part of its reason is to give thanks for recovery from past sickness. The pilgrimage goes beyond necessity and utility into the purely human realms of imagination and spirit. The quickening effect of translation from one place to another opens up new views of life. There is much of it in medieval English literature. Sometimes it is felt as a painful sense of transience, but if we want the joy we have to accept the pain. That gladness follows sorrow, as woe follows joy, is one of Chaucer's favourite remarks. Chaucer is particularly the poet of changing states of life, and thus finally of the challenge of death. He never stands still. He must have been a compulsive traveller, always questioning his destination, reflecting on the way. Maybe that is one reason why he is elusive as a personality, just as it must be why he moved through so many different kinds of poem, and left some considerable poems unfinished.

CHAPTER ONE

ORIGINS

CHAUCER, THE SON OF A LONDON VINTNER, WAS born, indeed, but when? He was not sure himself. There were no birth certificates. Even Henry IV, son of John of Gaunt, seems to have been uncertain of his date of birth, and when middle-aged warriors and gentlemen were called upon to reveal theirs, it seems that they often thought themselves a good deal younger than they really were. There are also problems in identifying particular people in the copious but incomplete and sometimes inconsistent records of official payments, charters, lawcourt proceedings, chronicles, from which our knowledge of the fourteenth century has been painfully gleaned by generations of scholars. Surnames were pretty well established by the fourteenth century, though only in the latter part usually fixed and heritable, and they give some help in identification. But, of course, surnames were often shared. Furthermore, some Christian names were very popular and parents showed an astonishing lack of concern for variety, which reveals a much less strong feeling than we have for individual personal identity. Among the Pastons, for example, rich gentry in Norfolk, whose series of letters throughout the fifteenth century gives so fascinating a glimpse of life as it was lived, one John Paston named both his eldest sons also John, and all three became knights. Spelling of names was highly variable. Chaucer appears not only as now spelled, but Chauser(s), Caucer, Chausiers, Chaucy, de Chauserre or Chanserre, etc. Luckily, Chaucer with its variants seems to be a relatively rare name in the second half of the fourteenth century, and Geoffrey not so common a name as John or William.

Geoffrey was born around 1340, in the fourteenth year of the reign of Edward III. The precise date is not in itself very important, but a man's attitude to his own age, and to the activities appropriate to a given age, are of some interest. We only know about Chaucer's date of birth because he gave testimony in a law case, in which many of his contemporaries also appeared, and these testimonies not only give us some information but also bring us close for a moment to the strange society in which he lived. The lawsuit was in the Court of Chivalry and referred to a dispute between the families of Scrope (or Lescrope) and Grosvenor, about the right to display a certain coat of arms, 'dazure ove un bende dor', or in unheraldic language, blue with a diagonal band of gold. This was an important matter of prestige and pride, and also, on the battlefield, of identification – both social magic and real utility were involved. Many gentlemen were called on to

OPPOSITE *A draught of moist and corny ale. One of a very fine series of misericords in the church of St Lawrence, Ludlow, Shropshire*

testify whether and, especially, when, they had seen the arms in question borne by either party. Chaucer testified that he remembered seeing Sir Richard Lescrope armed in the arms in question in France before Réthel on the campaign in which Chaucer was taken prisoner, i.e. in 1359–60, but he also deposed (presumably in English, though the record is in law French), that once in Friday Street in London, as he went along the street, he saw hanging out a new sign made of the said arms, and he asked what inn that was that had hung outside those arms of Lescrope, and someone had answered and said, 'Not at all, sir, they were never hung up outside as the arms of Scrope, etc.', and they had been hung out by Robert Grosvenor. This was the first time, said Chaucer, that he had heard of Robert Grosvenor.

The special interest in all this is that each witness gave his age, and on 15 October 1386, when Chaucer gave his evidence in the refectory of the Abbey of Westminster, he said that he was of the age of forty years 'et plus' – 'and more'. He further remarked that he had been `armed' for twenty-seven years. This confirms that the campaign in France to which he referred was indeed that of 1359–60. But how old was he when first 'armed'? Different people took arms at different times. Edward III's chivalrous eldest son, Edward of Woodstock, the 'Black Prince' of later historians, was sixteen when he commanded one of the front wings in the great English victory of Crécy in 1346. He was perhaps a special case. Other witnesses in the case estimated their own age and the age at which they were armed. This latter would obviously be more easily remembered and checked. Sir Richard Waldegrave said he was forty-eight and had been armed twenty-five years, that is, when twenty-three years old, which seems quite old, though he may have made a mistake, since he was on the same campaign in 1359–60 as Chaucer, twenty-seven years before. Waldegrave, like Chaucer's Knight in *The General Prologue* to *The Canterbury Tales*, had travelled and fought extensively in Europe and in what used to be called the Near East, as far as Turkey. Another man, Nicolas Sabraham, an esquire like Chaucer, not a knight, said he was sixty years old and upwards, and had been armed thirty-nine years, which would make him at least twenty-two in his own opinion when armed. Sir William Aton claimed that he was eighty-seven years old (which can hardly be an underestimate), and said he had been armed for sixty-six years, making him twenty-one when armed. It is clear that the general assumption was that a man was armed when about twenty-one. The merchant's son Geoffrey Chaucer is hardly likely to have been armed when very much younger than these almost professional warriors, and the most interesting point of all this is that Chaucer must have been around twenty years old on his first campaign.

It may be helpful at this point to cast an eye forward for a moment to the outline of his life until he died in 1400. He was about seventeen when first heard of as a member, probably a page, of the household of the Countess of Ulster. He was about twenty on his first military expedition. He wrote his first important poem, *The Book of the Duchess*, in 1368 in his late twenties – an age comparable with Shakespeare's when he produced the equivalent, though less profound, poem *Venus and Adonis*. Chaucer was about forty-five years old when he completed the first great period of his maturity with the long poem *Troilus and Criseyde*, and around fifty when he arrived at his highest originality, greatest maturity, and most inclusive genius, with the distinctive poems and prose of *The Canterbury Tales*. Up to his early fifties he was at the same time engaged in the variously interesting and distracting jobs, or sometimes sinecures, that came to him as a courtier – such as missions at home and abroad, offices in the customs, clerk of the King's Works, member of commissions of inquiry into sewerage, etc. These were all part of the gentleman-courtier's way of making a comfortable though not a splendid living, jobs progressively more lucrative and (except for the King's Works) probably less demanding, the older he grew. There was no money in poetry, but it may have been to his fame as a court poet that he owed his tomb in what was socially the most distinguished church in England, the burial place of kings, Westminster Abbey itself. A nicely paradoxical conclusion to the modest, reserved way of life of the vintner's son. His own son Thomas worthily maintained the line, being Chief Butler to no less than four successive English kings. Thomas was a rich, distinguished man who must have inherited a comfortable if not large patrimony from the poet. Thomas's daughter Alice, the poet's granddaughter, married into the great family of the de la Poles, originally merchants, and thus became Duchess of Suffolk, but the direct male line seems to have become extinct. The Chaucer family in the fourteenth and fifteenth centuries thus offers an exemplary history of steady rise through city and court, with an almost even balance, in the person of the poet, between the two. The origins of this interesting family, in so far as we can trace them, show how, leaving the countryside, people prospered in towns and in the dominant city of London, and arrived at court.

In the late thirteenth century there was an Andrew de Dinnington, sometimes also known as Andrew le Taverner, who lived in Ipswich. The surnames varyingly attributed to him reveal his origin and his trade. There are villages called Dinnington in Northumberland, South Yorkshire, and Somerset, so wherever he came from it was a long way, and perhaps he had good reason to travel. Anyway he was clearly one of the many enterprising countrymen who at all periods, all over the world, leave the country to make, if not a fortune, at least a more comfortable and interesting living in the town. There is always money in food and drink. He set up a tavern, a thoroughly secular and useful service. Ipswich was a flourishing town by the standards of the day, and the county town of Suffolk; it was also a port, with excellent communications with London and the Continent.

Andrew had a son called Robert le Chaucer, or Robert Malin le Chaucer, a citizen and vintner of London, where he was also sometimes known as Robert of Ipswich. He had followed in father's footsteps, continuing his progress, moving from the small town to the great city and raising the level of the family business, presumably, from retailer to wholesaler. The reason why he was called 'le Chaucer' does not appear. English surnames are, apart from nicknames and oddities, of three general types: patronymics or derivatives (like Johnson; Williams; Knights=knight's man); place-name surnames, showing that a

A fourteenth century leather shoe which may be seen in the Museum of London

person has moved from his place of origin (like Andrew de Dinnington or Robert of Ipswich); and trade names, like Brewer or, probably, Chaucer, which show your occupation and that you are neither gentry nor a common labourer. Chaucer seems to be the French name for shoemaker. Robert le Chaucer, if a shoemaker (which was quite a distinguished craft) must also have run a number of lines of other business, like many a successful fourteenth-century merchant, among which that derived from his father the taverner, improved to vintner, was probably the most profitable and with the most social prestige. There appear to have been only two or three families of Chaucers as revealed by the records, and there was probably a loose and far-flung net of cousins in East Anglia and London, connected with the wine trade and perhaps highclass shoemaking, who may have given a helping hand to each other.

Robert le Chaucer prospered. Like so many other fourteenth-century men he married a widow (people died young and marriages were often short-lived). One of the reasons why widows are able to remarry promptly is that they usually have a bit of property, and this was no doubt the case with Robert's wife, who was Mary, widow of John Heron, a London pepperer. Robert and Mary Chaucer were Geoffrey Chaucer's grandparents and had a son called John, who was the poet's father. Chaucer's grandfather Robert did not long survive his marriage. Mary then married a third time, another vintner called Richard Chaucer, about whom nothing else is known, but whom we may suppose was not a poor man. Perhaps this much-married grandmother was one of the proto-types of the Wife of Bath in *The Canterbury Tales*.

John Chaucer, father of the poet, was therefore well established from the first as a member of the vigorous class of prosperous London merchants and freemen of the city who were so significant a force in the general development of civiliza-tion in the fourteenth century in England, and part of a more general European development of towns and capitalism. The town, and specifically London in

England, provided all sorts of at that time new impulses and attitudes, political, economic, social. It was the medieval device that transformed the Middle Ages. If Chaucer so often appears as 'the new man', representing tendencies that devel, oped much further in later centuries, and conflicting with traditional beliefs and attitudes, it is because he was a townsman. The town represented the new spirit of enterprise, endeavour, utility. In it there were no serfs and an escaped serf who could live a year in a town had cast off his bondage. Regularized space and time and a boundary against the country marked the town. London was a special place that in some ways contrasted also against Westminster, the principal seat of the court of the King's Law, his Household, his Chancery and Exchequer. But important as all this difference is, it is equally important to recognize the many links that bound London and Westminster together. The powers of towns, and of the king, grew together. The king's new supremacy over his barons was largely due to the royal ability to get finance or credit from towns. Rich merchants became necessary not only for financing the king but in so doing for running the consequent tax system as 'farmers'. Increasingly in the fourteenth century merchants could be knighted. Michael de la Pole, from Hull, whose grandson married Chaucer's granddaughter, became Earl of Suffolk, though he was an exceptional case. Noblemen readily married merchants' widows and daughters. In terms of class the main class distinction was whether you were or were not gentry. The distinction ran through the town as through the court, though expressed a little differently. Rich merchants were in the fourteenth century gentlemen and they became landed gentry with increasing frequency; the process was commonplace in the fifteenth. A country estate was a sound invest, ment and a mark of gentility, as much as a pleasant place to live. In the Peasants' Revolt of 1381 certain rich merchants were as much the subject of attack as were John of Lancaster, or rich monasteries, or lawyers. The merchant Richard Lyons, whom Chaucer knew, was murdered by the mob. Within the towns, the merchants, and their apprentices, could be lined up with the gentry (as it were, 'the officers') and grouped in ruling oligarchies. Journeymen and workmen were grouped with the 'other ranks'; their attempts to form gilds – early versions of trades unions – were resisted by the masters of crafts. The merchants were well represented in parliament, where the Commons were all gentry of one kind or another, and some had considerable influence at court. Chaucer's origins show him to have been of this class, well established in an environment of relative wealth, significant township, and as a gentleman.

John Chaucer, the poet's father, had a lively life. When he was eleven or twelve, on 3 December 1324, his aunt Agnes de Westhall, sister of his dead father, together with one Geoffrey Stace and others of Ipswich, kidnapped him from the home of his mother and stepfather in order to marry(!) him to his cousin Joan de Westhall, daughter of his aunt Agnes. Evidently the pull towards Ipswich in the family was strong. Aunt Agnes did not at all agree with her sister-in-law and her second husband about the destination of the family property, which was one of the important things that marriage was essentially about. The age of the persons concerned is not very surprising by fourteenth-century standards. Edward III married Philippa of Hainault when they were both fourteen, again as a matter of property and political alliances, though affection also arose. Some royal marriages were made between tiny children. In the case of John Chaucer the marriage was avoided, we do not know how (if made it would have been valid and effectively indissoluble, though forced), but the family was racked for years after by lawsuits concerning his inheritance from his father, which is another sign of gentry status. Legal action was taken against Agnes in January 1326, and the case lasted until October 1327 but eventually Agnes was imprisoned in the Marshalsea for some time, with Geoffrey Stace, and they were fined the huge sum of £250 (perhaps to be multiplied by two or three hundred times for a rough modern equivalent), which was paid to John himself before 26 November 1330. Since John's own personal income from property was at that time only 20s. a year, though there may have been much more tucked away somewhere, he in the end came off pretty well. This little passage may be concluded by noting that when Agnes's husband, the father of Joan, died, Agnes married her collaborator Geoffrey Stace as her second husband. There was even more to the whole affair than a desire to keep property in one part of the family. The ladies of the Chaucer family seem to have been as energetic and determined as the men.

As to Joan de Westhall, having escaped, or lost, John Chaucer, she married Robert de Beverley. He and Joan both came into the service of Queen Philippa and Joan was one of her ladies-in-waiting (*damoiselle*) until she retired in 1359 with a pension. The whole Chaucer family, from grandfather Robert's time onwards, has a steady connection with the royal court.

In 1327 John Chaucer joined the summer campaign of Edward III against the Scots and thus entered to some extent the national scene. It was a period of great disturbance and difficulty and here I must digress for a moment to describe something of the background of principal events of the early part of the century, especially since they were frequently in men's minds in connection with Richard II at the end of the century.

The personality of the king was crucial to national politics in the Middle Ages. He was at the apex of the legal, social and political structure, combining in himself both the immense symbolic magical power of royalty and the practical power of the head of the largest administrative organization in the country. Yet all government is in the end by the consent of those governed. And in the Middle Ages the king in England particularly needed to command the assent, and the services, of the great hereditary barons, the magnates, some of whom were not so much less powerful, in terms of property and immediate adherents, than the king himself. There were about twenty magnates. They believed in kingship; they were no revolutionaries; but they intended to participate in its powers and benefits. The barons had forced Magna Carta on King John in 1215, and Magna Carta, setting out rights and privileges, was constantly invoked in fourteenth-century parliaments.

Edward I, who died in 1307, had successfully deployed both the symbolic and

The delicacy of alabaster gives beauty in death to a spoiled life – Edward II's tomb in Gloucester Cathedral

practical powers of kingship. He was a remarkably able, dominating man, perhaps the greatest of medieval English kings. It is not altogether surprising that his son Edward II resembled him only in a tall and handsome physique, being in all crucial respects the very opposite of his father. Though this son was married to the French king's sister Isabella, who was an outstandingly beautiful and lively woman, and had several children by her, of whom the eldest succeeded him as Edward III, Edward II was by choice a homosexual, with a fatal proclivity for being dominated by attractive young men on the make. Moreover, he was a man of essentially private tastes and hobbies, attractive in themselves, but pursued to the detriment of the interests of the kingdom as a whole. He liked simple people, music, acting, and, as a messenger of the royal household got into trouble by saying, was interested in ditching, thatching 'and other indecencies'. Sympathetic as a man with such innocent tastes for `do-it-yourself' activities must appear among the harsh struggles of fourteenth-century national politics, there is no doubt that he neglected his duty and in so far as he governed, governed badly. Even the charitable Professor McKisack calls him a weakling and a fool, lacking imagination, energy and commonsense. When such a king listens to greedy upstart favourites to the disadvantage of traditional counsellors and the magnates, there can only be disaster. The wonder is that Edward II reigned so long, but the loose organization of a medieval kingdom, the self-contained nature of the predominantly rural society of which it was composed, the difficulties of travel, the slowness and uncertainty of the spread of information, meant that a huge slack had to be taken up to accomplish anything, good or bad. At last, mismanagement and the savage rivalries of different factions culminated in civil war. Edward's Queen Isabella took as lover Roger Mortimer, Earl of March, and in September 1326 they landed in Suffolk with the young prince Edward and an army. General discontent was such that large numbers joined them and after a brief civil war Edward was forced to abdicate. He was imprisoned, horribly and symbolically murdered, and his chief favourites executed. The new King Edward III, aged fifteen, was installed under the guidance of a council of regency which was managed by Mortimer, who soon achieved a dominance resented almost as bitterly by the country as that of the favourites of Edward II (who within a few years, extraordinarily enough, came to be venerated almost as a saint). Mortimer did not last long. In 1330 Edward, now eighteen, by a daring coup captured Mortimer, who was hastily condemned to death by a Parliament called for the purpose.

To return to John Chaucer, such was the violent background of political events during his youth. The campaign against the Scots which he joined in 1327 was the first of Edward III's military expeditions, when he was fifteen, roughly the same age as John Chaucer himself. John Chaucer's early military experience parallels that of his own son, the poet, thirty years later and shows how varied was the experience of gentry of this kind in the fourteenth century, with war, trade, diplomacy, legal affairs all mingled together, in a constant journeying.

John Chaucer was probably involved in other adventures, but from 1337 onwards, when twenty-four or twenty-five years old, he was a citizen, vintner and merchant of London, probably dealing in various sidelines as well as in the varieties of the wine trade. He became a substantial leading citizen and owner of quite a few houses, shops and some land, a freeman of the City and close to the ruling oligarchy of merchants. He stood as surety, that is, as guarantor of money or good behaviour, for various citizens, including the notorious, or at least very wealthy, Richard Lyons, who was also a vintner. In this case John Chaucer and four others gave security in December 1364, that Lyons would not harm Alice Perrers or prevent her going about her own business and that of the king. This is an early reference to the lady, who was obviously even then the king's mistress. There was presumably a conflict of interest between her and Lyons in some business matters. They were not always on opposite sides, for each needed the king for personal profit. Once again we become aware of how the Chaucers moved in at least the outer circles of the royal court. Among a number of other lawsuits of various kinds in which he was engaged John Chaucer was also accused in 1353 by Geoffrey de Darsham of beating and wounding the said

Geoffrey. The verdict is not known and might not be reliable if it were, but such a case is a fair example of the kind of offence a perfectly respectable citizen might commit or at least be thought capable of committing. Crimes of violence were regarded much as motoring offences are regarded by many members of the middle classes now, though violence was often followed by death. It was very well to speak of the king's peace, but there was no body of police to enforce it with impartiality. Impartiality was a concept hardly recognized. The archaic forms of justice, whereby a man's innocence was judged by the warmth of support he received from family and friends, were still prevalent. Hence the acts of surety and 'mainpernorship' in Chaucer's life. More abstract, general, impersonal forms of justice had long been recognized, derived largely from the Church, but it was a long battle to get them accepted.

Round about 1339, John married Agnes Copton, whose family were also well-to-do London citizens. The family house of John and Agnes was in Thames Street, which even today follows fairly closely its fourteenth-century course near the river. It was in the Vintry ward, a ward being one of the subdivisions of the City which elected two representatives to the City council, and so forth. The name tells the occupation of many of the inhabitants. They were well-to-do vintners who had a number of large houses there, due to the fact that wines were unloaded on the riverside quays that formed the southern boundary of the ward. The ward itself spread along the north bank of the river with Thames Street running through it and was close to St Paul's. The whole City covered about a square mile, so nowhere was far from anywhere else.

John Chaucer bought the house before 1343, as we know from the names of owners of the neighbouring houses at each side. Although there was an elaborate system of leases and sales the houses were only identified within the parish boundary by being between other houses whose owners are named, as for example in this case, where the house was between the house of William le Gauger on the east and the house that once belonged to John le Mazelyner on the west, had its front on Thames Street at the south and extended to the Wallbrook stream at the north. There were no street numbers. The Chaucers' house had one clear physical boundary, the Wallbrook, and one boundary which was the street; the other two boundaries are mere juxtapositions. In this house, probably, Geoffrey Chaucer was born.

The house itself had two cellars, built of stone, for storage. The ground floor was built on the cellars, and was reached by a few stairs. In the front there was probably the shop, or at least John Chaucer's main place of business; behind it maybe another small room, then the hall, with a high roof, so that it occupied both the ground floor and the floor above. Behind the hall would be another couple of small rooms, of which one might be the kitchen; or the kitchen might be a separate shack in the yard. The hall was the main living room, and might even have a gallery running round it at the level of the upper floor, reached by a simple flying stair and leading off to small upper rooms called 'solars'. If there was no gallery the solars were reached by loft ladders. Above the cellars all was built of wood. The only heating was a fire in the hall, probably with a stone

chimney, and a well-to-do merchant probably had a sea-coal, not a charcoal or wood fire. The only carpet, if there was one, was a luxury item laid on the table. The floor was covered with rushes, changed as often as the household liked and sweetened by being mixed with herbs that gave a scent when crushed. Furniture in the hall would consist of something like a trestle table and a standing table, a long settle, a chair, benches, stools, screen, fire irons, bellows, basins (for washing hands before meals), cushions, tapestries for the wall. The hangings, cushions, chair covers, curtains, could be very rich and lovely. The walls, where not covered by hangings, might be painted (there are some fifteenth-century wall paintings at the Swan Hotel in Stratford-upon-Avon). The hall was bright with lively colourful decoration of stories and mythical animals or other motifs — as at Longthorpe Tower near Peterborough. In *The Book of the Duchess* Chaucer describes his bedroom as having the story of *Le Roman de la Rose* in stained glass and something like this was quite possible. A rich Southampton burgess who died in the 1290s in Southampton, had in his house glazed windows, a tiled floor, painted roof, a stone drain; he used wine jugs from southwest France,

Wall decorations in the handsome fourteenth-century rooms of Longthorpe Tower near Peterborough, Northamptonshire, showing St Anthony and the basketmaker and below, the Philosopher and his pupil

lustrewares from Spain, glass from Venice, silk from Persia. In John Chaucer's house must have been well-carved chests for linen, clothes and other objects, including possibly one or two books. There were silver dishes and silver-gilt cups, as well as others of pewter, latten, earthenware and wood, often imported and very handsomely shaped. There were knives and spoons but no forks. There were probably pet dogs and cats and at the back of the house a small garden of rough grass, perhaps a gravel walk, and a few fruit trees. Flowers were not grown for ornament till later. Since the property backed on the Wallbrook the family privy was probably, like too many others, built over it, though the house might have had the rarer luxury of an indoor privy and a large cesspit at the back of the cellar. The City constantly promulgated ordinances about cleanliness, since everybody recognized the danger of infection from bad smells, such as arise from household rubbish, or, for example, from rotting entrails (the skinners practised their stinking trade in Wallbrook Street in order to use the stream as a sewer). There were arrangements for refuse collection but in effect the Wallbrook itself was an open sewer, though liable to flood if there were exceptionally high tides in the Thames. A rent of 2s. a year was payable for having a latrine over the Wallbrook. On the whole the City must have resembled a farmyard.

It was a most interesting district for Geoffrey Chaucer to grow up in. Along Thames Street, apart from other large houses, and on the same side as the Chaucers' house, not far away was the great mansion called La Riole. It was owned by Queen Philippa until her death in 1369. Joan of Kent, Princess of Wales and mother of Richard II, stayed there in 1381 and Richard himself in 1386. There were also great town houses or 'inns' belonging to nobles, among them the inn of Sir Simon Burley who was well known to Chaucer.

Things had faces in a vividly anthropomorphic world – two views of a bronze jug of the period, now in the British Museum

Returning to Chaucer's own immediate neighbourhood, we find the house of Sir Nicholas Brembre, grocer, Lord Mayor of London, who became immensely rich, only to be executed by the Merciless Parliament in 1386. He was well known to Chaucer. Another similar house belonged to Sir John Philipot (fishmonger), a notable merchant whom Chaucer must also have known well.

On the opposite side of Thames Street and quite close to the Chaucers' house was the great house that once belonged to Henry Picard, vintner and Mayor of London 1356–7, who had inherited it from another vintner and former mayor, John de Gisors, whose granddaughter Henry Picard married. There was a legend that Picard had entertained five kings to dinner there in 1357. The date is probably wrong, and there could have been no more than three, including Edward III, but true or not the story well illustrates the interpenetration of nobility and the great merchants of London. The house later belonged to John Study, father-in-law of Brembre. Not far away was Ipris Inn where Lancaster, the greatest lord of the kingdom after the king, and Percy, the great northern lord, were dining with some merchants in 1377 at the height of Lancaster's unpopularity with the Londoners. There was a tremendous riot and Gaunt and Percy had to dash out of the back door.

All these merchants conducted much of their business, and kept their goods, in their own houses. At the same time the greatest of them, such as Lyons,

Brembre, Walworth and Philipot, not only dealt in many sorts of goods but were, above all, financial experts who often 'farmed' taxes. That is, when parliament voted a tax, one or more merchants (Lyons was an outstanding example) paid the king a lump sum and collected the tax himself. It was a traditional method, with some risk to the `farmer' and some convenience to the king, but many people felt that the disadvantages lay mostly with the king and the taxpayer, since the `farmers' became rich enough to lend the king vast sums of money at a substantial rate of interest. Lyons was once accused of charging fifty per cent per annum but this seems to have been an exaggeration.

There were also foreign merchants not far from where the Chaucers lived. Foreign merchants are always rich. The Hanseatic League of towns, including Cologne and Hamburg, had their headquarters in the Steelyard (a name derived from a German word meaning a courtyard in which goods were set out for sale). The richest and most advanced of all foreign merchants were the Italians, whose cities and states were far more developed than England in the fourteenth century. Italians were the bankers of Europe, leaders in industry and commerce. Not merely the king but even many abbeys were deeply in debt to them. They consequently received specially favourable treatment from successive kings (as did Hanseatic merchants) though they were not much loved by their native competitors for obvious reasons. Nevertheless people did business with them and the Chaucers must have known them quite well. There was a group of Italians in several towns, including Southampton, where John Chaucer was deputy to the king's Chief Butler 1347–9 and so must have had dealings with them, but they congregated particularly in London where by the fourteenth century Lombard Street marks their centre of activities. Remarkable as appears Geoffrey Chaucer's knowledge of Italian, it cannot have been unique and could easily have been acquired in London.

Another group of foreigners engaged in trade was the Flemings, brought in during the earlier part of the century to practise the cloth-trade. They were never popular, and were hunted by the London mob during the Peasants' Revolt. Chaucer is very casual about it. The shouting of the people when they chase the fox is far louder, he says in the comic *Nun's Priest's Tale*, than Jack Straw and his followers in the Peasants' Revolt `Whan that they wolden any Flemyng kille'. Their insecure place in society is emphasized by the fact that most prostitutes were Flemish. The prostitutes were confined to an area called `The Stews' (i.e. the brothels) outside the City, on the south bank of the Thames.

Between Thames Street and the wharves, as among the larger houses all around, was a network of narrow lanes with tiny houses, shops of all kinds, eating and drinking places. The nearest analogies today are found in those lovely small medieval town centres in Italy, which are often contemporary with Chaucer, but which reveal Italy's then greater wealth and organization by being built in stone; or in some small Japanese town which, with its miscellany of open-fronted shops and arcades open till late at night, its bright signs and bustle, its close juxtaposition of shops, houses, small businesses, trades and industrial firms, retains something of the same quality. In such towns there is crowding,

*An embarrassing moment in a
medieval brothel*

noise, and sometimes the drains leave something to be desired. In the press
tempers may rise. But also such a mingling, for all its tensions, or partly because
of its tensions, is psychologically satisfying to everyone but the natural scholar,
religious recluse or paranoiac. The buildings are on a human scale. There is
variety, vivacity, personal communication, orderliness without undue regimen-
tation. According to Christian story we have lost Paradise, which is a quiet
country place, somewhat underpopulated, but Heaven, where we hope to
arrive, is the Celestial City, the New Jerusalem. The Lady Julian of Norwich,
one of several outstanding mystics who were contemporary with Chaucer, says
that God made man's soul a city in which to dwell, but that since man fell God
must live on bare earth (*Revelations of Divine Love*, chapter 51). A preacher in
Florence in 1304 said in the wordplay of a medieval Latin sermon that civitas
(city) sounds so much like *caritas* (love) because men love to live together.
London had achieved that special 'civilized' quality, in a modest way, that
allows us to compare it with the great cities of western Europe, in Italy, France,
Flanders and the Rhineland, where the new powers commerce, industry,
individual freedom and enterprise, were being forged together. The exploitation
of these powers by Edward III, especially in his reliance (to them deadly) on
Italian bankers, was no small part of his success as King. The interpenetration
of court and city has been part of the argument of this chapter. The king grew
with the City. Yet this growth produced a powerful inner contradiction, for
court and city were also deeply incompatible, with the fundamental incompati-
bility of the archaic and the new. Hence much that is divided in the culture of
the times, and in Chaucer himself. The city survived, the court did not.

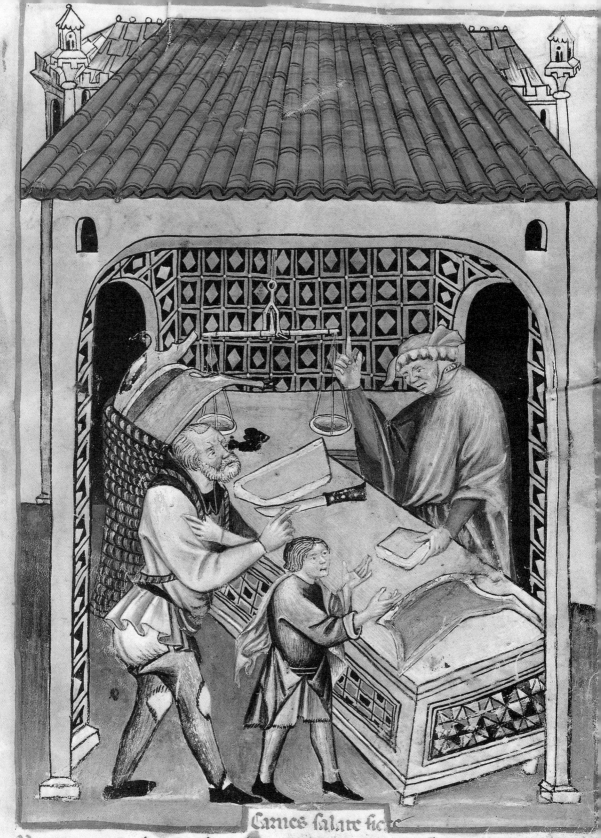

Carnes salate sicce

Ratuc. c. i. x̃. ſ. i. z̃. melior ex eis pingues huĩe. Iuuamẽtũ
luctantibus. et balentes ẽplenones flegmaticas. nocumentũ
colluic. remocio nocĩ. cũ decoquant cũ oleo et lacte.

CHAPTER TWO

A FOURTEENTH-CENTURY CHILDHOOD

HEN GEOFFREY WAS BORN HIS MOTHER AGNES WAS in a big bed, probably in their house in Thames Street, helped by a midwife and probably a woman friend or two from the neighbourhood. The scene in essence is familiar to us from dozens of European pictures painted in the later Middle Ages of the birth of the Virgin. A substantial bed, the cluster of women, the hot water in a bowl, a cat in the corner — all cleanly if not hygienic. The mother is tired out but contented, the women pleased, the newborn child apparently less so, but soon wrapped in the swaddling clothes that so constricted the tiny frail-seeming arms and bent legs. In the upper classes, like those of Chaucer's parents, it is likely that the child was suckled by a wet-nurse, some poor woman who had lost her own recently born child, or was prepared to wean or deprive it for the sake of the necessary money earned by suckling someone else's child. Whether from nurse or mother, baby Geoffrey throve, fed from the breast perhaps till as much as three years old, and fortunately so, since water in towns was far from pure, cow's milk not always available (and not always pure, either) and no other drinks but wine or beer. In pictures of the birth of the Virgin her father, St Joachim, husband of St Anne, is usually shown hovering anxiously outside, for this is a woman's world.

It was strongly felt that the newly born baby was extremely fragile. The vast majority of babies died. He was washed with care, and the current encyclopedia, the thirteenth-century *De Proprietatibus Rerum*, written by the Franciscan Friar Bartholomew the Englishman, recommended using a mixture of roses ground up with salt to get rid of the grease that surrounds a newborn child. His mouth was rubbed with a finger dipped in honey to clean the mouth and encourage him to suck. Great care was taken that the wet-nurse have pure milk. If the child was ill medicines were given to the nurse, not the child. As the child developed so nurse or mother began to give it other foods, chewing up meat in her own mouth. And of course she cleaned him and cuddled him and talked and sang to him, put him to sleep in a darkened place, straightened his legs and tied them tightly in swaddling bands to make sure that the limbs grew straight.

I do not see Agnes as a firm-minded, dominating woman. In Geoffrey's poetry the image of the mother is tender, soft, delicate, more often glad than sorry, always loving. The adjectives that are used in the poems to describe mothers are *dear, sweet, beloved, blissful, generous, meek, kind, woeful, benign, blessed, true, rich, gay*. These adjectives are quite different from those used for the father. Scattered as

Mr Chaucer takes Geoffrey to the butcher's

they are through many different poems they evoke a basic image which is characteristic of Chaucer's imagination and thus, basically, of his experience. In the
kind of story that attracts Chaucer the mother-figure is, if present, loving and
never dominant. Compare with this the often baleful image of the mother in
fairy tales, where she is usually represented by a wicked stepmother; or the highly
ambivalent image of the mother given by most of Shakespeare's plays, or the
image of the mother that is created in Dickens's works, of which the silly, fussy
Mrs Nickleby is the type, or that in E. M. Forster's works, where she is elderly,
dominant, now sterile, yet perceptive. As far as biographical glimpses are given
of medieval men it seems that a number of great spiritual leaders may well have
owed their penetration, intensity of purpose, self-awareness, to dominating
mothers. St Augustine, Guibert of Nogent, St Edmund Rich are examples.
Chaucer's poetry lacks the intensity and spiritual vision given by a dominant,
strong-minded mother. Agnes left him free, yet confident. I imagine her as
young, pretty, loving, playful, highly intelligent, rather passive, occasionally
neglectful and perhaps sometimes neglected. She was pious in an upper-class,
conventional way, and in 1351, when Geoffrey was ten or eleven, she was
allowed to choose her own confessor. He may well have been one of those friars
whom Chaucer mercilessly satirizes. Another image that runs through
Chaucer's work is that of the loving but betrayed and deserted woman. I do not
imply that Chaucer's mother was ill-treated by his father, for I think that the
image of the betrayed woman represents something in Chaucer's own psyche,
not a material event in someone else's life. The capacity to feel for another
person's suffering is in part an historical cultural development, a product of
Christian teaching that was growing strongly in the fourteenth century, but it is
also a product of a particular temperament and environment, and this capacity to
feel for others in Chaucer surely relates to a loving yet undominating mother.
Chaucer's capacity for sympathy and his variety of response to many different
kinds of people seems also to relate to a loving but unassertive mother. On her
husband's death in 1366 she remarried, and fades from history.

His father, if he followed the advice of Friar Bartholomew, our thirteenth-
century Dr Spock, was less tender, though no less loving. He would have gone
without food himself to feed his children, but luckily that was not necessary for
John Chaucer. He was a busy man, but as soon as Geoffrey was weaned he had
him joining the rest of the family at table. After babyhood children were hardly
ever treated as special cases, and certainly the household did not revolve around
them. The family ate together, father in his wooden armchair, mother in hers or
on a stool, Geoffrey on his stool — all, incidentally, wearing their hats indoors as
out, for fear of chills and infections. John Chaucer made sure the boy grew up to
behave properly, and was ready with a cuff over the head, or a harder blow with
his fist, to teach him his place and his manners. He would not be genial in
manner to the child in case the child became conceited, yet he thought continually of his welfare, and much of John Chaucer's profit and purchase of land was
for the benefit of Geoffrey. The more he loved him, the more strictly he treated
him. The generalized image of the father in Chaucer's poetry is *old, wise, spiritual,*

ABOVE *A pair of woollen hats found perfectly preserved in a bog, and now on display in the National Museum of Ireland, Dublin*

fleshy, cruel, ready, argus-eyed, hoary, stern, hard, wretched, poor, jealous, false. He is older than the mother, farsighted, prudent, but a bit grim, and he arouses an apprehensive response in the child. That might mean that the child was over-sensitive rather than that the father was really severe, since children always mythologize their parents. I do not think that John Chaucer was particularly overbearing, though he may have appeared a little stiff, because Chaucer's poetry shows no sign of an imagination bothered by a dominating father-figure. It is very noticeable, for example, that in the long poem *Troilus and Criseyde*, the Trojan hero Troilus is not in the least hampered by his father, King Priam, who is barely mentioned. Troilus is a deeply sensitive, highly inhibited, passionate idealist, which argues a secure, strict upbringing for him, and for his creator, and the difficulties he meets with are those of the world at large, not difficulties caused by internalized family conflicts. The heroine, Criseyde, is also not exactly hampered by the existence of a father. Neither protagonist has to fight a father-figure. Rather the reverse. Criseyde's father is the reverse of dominating, for he is a traitor to the town of Troy, besieged by the Greeks, and has fled to the enemy. It is the absence, the *loss*, of a father-figure, of protective authority, which is so disturbing. This again corresponds to the deep sense of loss and betrayal that I have already noted in Chaucer's writings. Perhaps Chaucer in some obscure way felt let down and neglected by his father, who was, maybe, over-occupied by his business affairs. There is a contrast here, as so often, between Chaucer and the *Gawain* poet. The story of *Sir Gawain and the Green Knight* has as its centre a conflict between the hero, Gawain, and the Green Knight, and it is easy to see that the Green Knight is a father-figure, half genial, half terrifying, who tests the young knight as he emerges from adolescence. The young Lady in the poem, who tries to seduce Gawain, and the malevolent old Lady, who is at the back of the plot by which if he is seduced he will be beheaded by the Green Knight, are clearly aspects of the mother, one tender, one severe, both treacherous. The poem, like so much folk tale and fairy tale, and like so much other literature, is yet another rendering of the ancient family drama whereby the growing child has to throw off, and come to terms with in his own psyche, the father-image and the mother-image, usually in order to achieve an equal relationship with a member of the opposite sex. The comparison with *Sir Gawain and the Green Knight* is interesting because that poem is absolutely contemporary with Chaucer, and yet Chaucer shows practically no signs of the internal conflicts of the family drama. His conflicts lie elsewhere. City families in the late Middle Ages show a notable new interest in family harmony. Probably it was so in Chaucer's family. However remote a city merchant might appear to be, his base was still the family house, he was never encased in solid stiff armour. Prudent, loving, not over-assertive, we may assume Chaucer's father to have been – perhaps a bit abstracted, like many a busy man, but liable to turn on him suddenly. Here we may note that Chaucer, at the very end of his life, condemned all his own non-religious poems. A profound but last-minute severity and hardness appear, which may reflect a basic paternal attitude, normally easy-going, but in the end strict.

As soon as she was strong enough to get about Chaucer's mother was 'churched', i.e. she attended a service of purification for the birth of a child. The child was himself baptized, presumably at the parish church of St Martin in the Vintry. The service took place at the big stone font at the back of the church, attended by friends and relations. The priest spoke the efficacious words, sprinkled the baby with the holy water, or even dipped him in it altogether, and his godfather lifted him from the font and named him Geoffrey, a name for the relative uncommonness of which we may be thankful. Then they all went home and had a feast. On such occasions royalty, as was natural, had a sumptuous banquet. When Queen Philippa arose after the birth of her first child she was given fine robes and furs. It would be natural for John Chaucer, well-to-do young vintner, to give Agnes a fine new dress. And so Geoffrey entered into the great social circuit of activity and ceremony that marked out the stages of medieval life in a way so different from our own. Baptism, the first of the great rites of passage that mark the stages of our lives, entered him into the society of Christians, gave him a name, which is the beginning of personal identity, and a destiny to fulfil or fail in. From then on the course of the year in the city was

BELOW *Walking the dog was a daily chore even in the fourteenth century. A bench end from Ixworth, Thorpe, Suffolk*

BELOW RIGHT *An undernourished greyhound gnaws a bone on this misericord in Christchurch Priory, Hampshire*

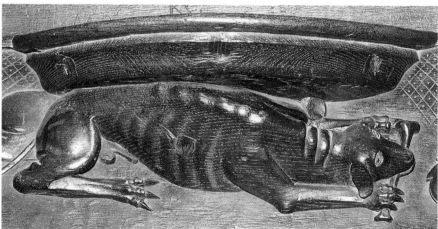

marked in the winter months mostly by church ceremonies to which all the parish went, and in the summer months by civic and secular ceremonies, processions of gilds, the Lord Mayor's Show especially, and maying in the nearby fields on the first of May. The sequence of the ritual years would also bring the once-for-all rites of passage of marriage and funeral, in which society and individual came together for joy and sorrow, festival and comfort.

Until he was about seven years old Geoffrey remained mostly under the rule of women, dressed in long clothes, little constrained except at table when his father was there, on the whole rather indulged. When he could walk and talk he began to be absorbed into the household and went to bed and got up at much the same time as everybody else, which was close to the hours of daylight. As a baby he slept in a wooden cradle, but when he outgrew that, and was dry at night, he probably slept in a bed of his own, for any little brothers or sisters that were born soon died, and he was effectively an only child. It was a job to keep him clean when small, with the muddy lanes outside, and indoors no carpets but only the rushes and sweet-smelling herbs, where he tumbled about with the cats and dogs.

People were not very conscious of age, or of relative differences of age. The baby and the old man or woman were naturally clearly distinguished, but between crawling and crumbling there were only rough-and-ready distinctions. A man was as old, or as young, as he felt, and a woman too. Chaucer was as vague as anyone. His notable hero and heroine, Troilus and Criseyde, can be deduced to be in their late teens, but he treats them as fully adult and pays no attention to their age. It is impossible to be certain of the age of Troilus's friend and Criseyde's uncle, Pandarus. He could be anywhere between eighteen and fifty. Few of Chaucer's characters except the babies and the pathetic seven-year-old child of *The Prioress's Tale*, and obviously old men, are clearly differentiated in age. There was an unconscious unity of treatment of various ages, but no cult of youth or of adolescence, except in so far as all dominant values – valour, loyalty, *joie-de-vivre*, love – in secular medieval society were rather adolescent.

The seven general stages of life, familiar nowadays in Shakespeare's formulation, from muling and puking babyhood to drivelling old age, were a well-established notion by the fourteenth century and to some extent compensated for the lack of a sharp sense of the actual years of life, though the stages varied with different authorities. After babyhood up to seven came childhood till fourteen; youth till twenty-eight; manhood till fifty; maturity till seventy; and old age thereafter. From seven to fourteen it was generally agreed that a child, especially a boy, is naughty and troublesome. He has to be continually checked and snubbed, though he continually escapes like quicksilver. He had better be beaten fairly often. At this stage Geoffrey abandoned the long dress worn by small children and dressed more or less like a man, in a longish tunic loose at the throat and reaching to his knees, and either bare legs and feet, or woollen hose with leather shoes or wooden clogs. For underclothing he might have a smock of coarse cloth and probably nothing else, though he might as he grew older wear a *breche*, a sort of loincloth, as well. In winter a hood kept his ears warm, though young men usually had rather bushy hair and often went without hats.

Man picking his nose (or trying to stifle a sneeze). A misericord supporter in Beverley Minster, Yorkshire

There is a string of English poems, going back to French and Latin originals centuries earlier, about bringing up children, and how they should behave. The instructions are obsessed with manners and repression. Be polite, kneel, don't talk too much, or tell dirty jokes, don't pick your nose, wipe your mouth before you drink, don't spit over the table, don't wipe your nose on the tablecloth, don't be greedy with the cheese, don't wriggle, etc. In a way the very instructions give a hair-raising impression of what children, or people in general, *might* do. There is always a gap between word and deed in medieval life, so one never knows how literally to take the words, what allowance to make for exaggeration, or for the degree to which people simply paid no attention to words. Furthermore, civilized manners take many generations to acquire. But no doubt most mothers, and nearly all fathers, nagged steadily at their children, who soon became as stones over which the constant stream of exhortation might flow with relatively little effect. If you took words seriously, what powerful effects such exhortation might have, even if consciously rejected. Indeed to take literally the oriental hyperbole of the Bible, or even the more ordinary exhortations of parents and preachers, could have explosive effects, either in action of reaction.

I imagine that Geoffrey Chaucer accepted the drift of instruction but was quite a lively child. He must also have been imaginative, even dreamy at times, and surely eager to hear stories and read them for himself. Literary geniuses, or even merely very clever men, usually learn to read when very young, and though the difficulties were greater in the fourteenth century, Geoffrey was hardly likely to be an exception. He would have read greedily. Books were much harder to come by, however, and for much imaginative sustenance he had to rely, like any other child, on storytelling, conversation games and general chat. In the evening the household gathered in the hall, with a wood or coal fire in winter. When it was dark a candle or two, or smoky torches of resinous wood fixed in the wall, gave a wavering artificial light. When he was a young man at court, in bed and alone, but unable to sleep, he called for a light and read in bed; when older he put off going to bed for the sake of reading. At those times he could afford to have a candle or two to himself, as perhaps his father did. But when he was a child it was no doubt a case of listening with the family group or sleeping. There were singing and storytelling and jokes and riddles around the fire, as well the long conversations of adults about business and politics so boring to a child.

The unaffected 'broadness' or ribaldry of some of the chat and jokes might surprise us now, though conventions in this respect have changed so rapidly in the second half of the twentieth century that it is hard to know what is the modern norm. The jokes in *The Canterbury Tales* used, in the latter part of the nineteenth century and until quite recently, to be thought bawdy; yet Wordsworth's sister Dorothy could at the beginning of the nineteenth century read *The Miller's Tale* aloud to him in the evening (as doubtless some of Chaucer's friends had read it to each other four centuries before) without their morals or manners being impugned. On the other hand, the romances in English of the fourteenth century are notably decent, and the brutally shocking, often perverted, sexuality of modern literature was certainly never attempted. At the worst in the fourteenth century it seems rather to have been 'good clean dirt'.

It is quite likely that Geoffrey's father had a book or two, miscellanies of religious instruction, romances, medical remedies, etc. There is a famous manuscript in the National Library of Scotland called the Auchinleck Manuscript which was written somewhere in London about 1340–5 and which has been thought by some scholars to have been known to Chaucer himself. If so, it is an astonishing coincidence. But he certainly knew a manuscript like it, or several small manuscripts which added up to much the same list of contents. The contents are mostly romances written in English in the curious stanza called tail rhyme, which in later life Chaucer mercilessly mocked in *The Tale of Sir Thopas* in *The Canterbury Tales*. Chaucer's early poems, especially *The Book of the Duchess*, reveal quite clearly in diction and rhythm the influence of these tail rhyme romances, apart from the tail rhyme itself, which is a slightly absurd hiccup at the end of the stanza caused by the last, short line. These romances are rather simple and of an unsophisticated pietism strongly associated with the East Midlands and East Anglia. The Auchinleck Manuscript is a big book, a collection of over fifty items, which must have been meant for well-to-do people, and its texts were certainly known to courtiers, for all their simplicity. (The poems are good vigorous stories that can still be read for entertainment.) Chaucer knew these romances very well when he was young. It is entirely possible that his father, with his East Anglian origins, had a book like the Auchinleck Manuscript and that he read it aloud in the evenings in the hall of the family house. When Geoffrey got a little older and could read well, indeed, could read superbly, acting the various speeches with wonderful sympathy, he himself might read these romances to family and friends. What more likely to inspire him to try his own hand at writing? Some of his own poems seem to have been written by him to be read aloud (one might almost say, acted) in his own person. In such cases there was no gap between author, scribe and reciter or minstrel. In general at that time family and group reading were common among educated people. 'To read' was commonly understood as meaning 'to read aloud'. Literature was heard, was part of the warm, social world outside oneself.

Minstrels might be brought in for a special family occasion and make an evening's entertainment in the rich merchant's household, though their more usual place was more public. They told stories, sang songs and played musical instruments. Songs and instrumental playing at home were common. It is quite possible that Chaucer had a stringed instrument, called a psaltery (equivalent to the guitar of the modern student), of his own, which he strummed with pleasure and sang to. This was the case with the student Nicolas in Chaucer's *Miller's Tale*. Or he may have played the flute. The Squire in *The General Prologue* is singing or playing the flute all day long. When he was old Chaucer confessed that as a young man he had composed 'many a song and many a lecherous lay'. He must himself have learned to sing. Song was the most usual mode of music, expressive of joy or sorrow especially in love, though musical instruments also went with joy, feasting, dancing, and were used to accompany the songs.

The boy was not restricted to indoor amusements, even when at school. He

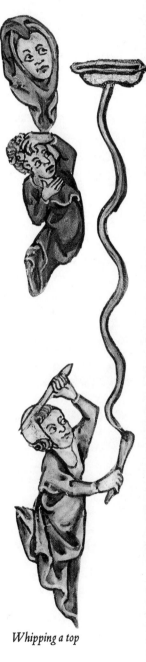

Whipping a top

had the city to wander in during daytime (a curfew emptied the streets at night). He could play at ball in the street, climb over the piles of timber lying about, fool about on London Bridge. Such games could be dangerous. A young man riding his horse too fast down a narrow street hit and killed a child; a tumble on loose timber brought down a baulk to break a tender leg, and in those days a broken limb often led to death. Children fooling about on the bridge could and did fall into the river and drown. In the absence of playgrounds many children must have been playing in the streets, although with such small populations nowhere was densely crowded. There were also less dangerous amusements. Froissart gives us a long list of the games he played as a child and surely Chaucer too dammed little streams and made little mills by them, played with shells and stones (there is an ancient game, known to my childhood as gob-stones, consisting of throwing up one stone and picking up successively one, two, three, four, while the other is in the air, which is perhaps the game meant by Froissart); there were hobbyhorses, playing 'touch', hide-and-seek, follow-my-leader, jumping; there were tops and blowing soap bubbles and making a pipe by cutting notches in a straw. A lively little boy with intense curiosity surely dabbled in all these.

He could have taken part with, or watched, the groups of boys, many the sons of citizens, but drawn also from the retinues of nobles and prelates, who gathered in the fields just outside the city walls, especially on Sundays in Lent, to fight mock battles, sometimes even on horseback, with spears from which the iron warheads had been removed. In the Easter holidays they had naval 'battles' on the river. A shield was fixed over the water, and a boat with a boy holding a lance was rowed full speed downstream to try to hit the shield and not fall in. In summer there was archery practice and bear baiting for boys, and dancing for girls. In winter there was skating on the ice and more mock but rough battles. At Smithfield just outside the city gates there was a horsefair and horse racing, with boys as jockeys. There were football and cockfighting and wrestling matches. Since the fields were near there was always the possibility of coursing, and perhaps even the more specifically aristocratic pastime of hawking. But probably Chaucer's father was rather too busy to take his son out on such sports and Chaucer in his poetry makes little reference to them. All these games were shared by young and old alike, according to taste. Many of them were violent

and martial, but required also some ordering and disciplining. Most were amusements for somewhat older boys. I envisage Geoffrey as a lively interested member of some groups, ready to play his part, but never a leader. He was obviously no simply extrovert hearty, and had a certain detachment, even an occasional withdrawal. A highly sensitive, spirited, rather critical boy.

He saw less violent entertainments which also interested him deeply. There were plays once a year at a place called Skinner's Well, so named because it was there that the Skinner's Gild regularly performed plays from Scripture. The miracle plays were favourites with all, even King Richard II. Chaucer in later life was supercilious about them, as about English poetic romances. All the same he had absorbed particularly their social placing, for the bawdy *Miller's Tale* has one 'hero', a barber and parish clerk, a squeamish, flashy young man, who absurdly enough played the blustering part of Herod, and the plot itself has echoes of the favourite play of 'Noah's Flood'. In public places minstrels could also be found.

'Minstrels', as already mentioned, were a large and miscellaneous class of entertainers, varying from musicians who were in the pay of the king or a great lord to unattached groups or individuals who scraped a poor living by vulgar tricks. Some of them were *gestours* (i.e. tellers of *gests*, which were narrative poems), or *disours*, who perhaps told similar tales, whether of heroes, saints or sinners, and who varied their offerings with jests and dramatic sketches, like the music-hall and vaudeville artists of later times. At a lower level were others whose idea of amusement was to heap foul abuse on each other, which lasted longer in Scotland than elsewhere, called 'flytings'. At a less verbal, though hardly more sophisticated level, were tumblers, sometimes women, whose fascination in days of long dresses and little underwear needs little imagination; and the `podicicinists', the breakers-of-wind, an activity which not only many of our ancestors, including Chaucer (in *The Summoner's Tale*) found irresistibly funny, for the last practitioner of this dubious art, one Poujol, performed in the early twentieth century in Paris. There was plenty of interest going on in London streets, and the boy was easily moved to laughter as well as repulsion.

Geoffrey also saw many a civic procession winding its way through the streets, led by dignified citizens, including his father, all splendidly dressed in robes of red and blue and white, and religious processions, led by mitred and gloved bishops,

Children's games.
OPPOSITE *Blind Man's Buff*. BELOW *Punch and Judy*

or priests, resplendent in copes, with bells and books and candles. There were also festivals of Church and home, notably Christmas, Twelfth Night, Easter. These were all part of the continuity of explicit religious and social rituals, which helped to hold society together, stabilized it against the tremendous uncertainties, the precarious brevity of individual life, gave colour and above all, meaning and significance, to lives that had to endure so much boring, laborious work, so much physical discomfort and personal sadness. These ceremonies and festivals were almost swept away at the Reformation in the sixteenth century; but we cannot but notice that to Chaucer himself they also lacked interest. Like the Reformers his eye was turned much more inward, towards individual personal feelings. His friendship with the Lollard knights is an example in later life of his natural sympathy with the anti-formal elements in his society. Of course he was not an anarchist or nihilist. He had to start from the general level and interests of his own society, so much more identified with the external world than we are, or than he was. There is still much of his own society in Chaucer, and his intensely absorbent, sympathetic tone of mind, his capacity for imitation – themselves aspects of a more self-conscious, inward-turning spirit – allowed him to reflect a good deal of society, and encouraged his sharpness in portraying the realistic visual scene. All the same, he usually refuses to describe ceremonials, feasts, the public life, in his poetry, or does so in a curiously negative way. As a child and youth he cannot be imagined absorbed into the cheerful mindless heartiness of sports, or rapt in contemplation of civic processions. He was aware of their glamour, especially of chivalric ceremonial, yet could not help noticing the individual jealousies and reluctances under the surface of ritual social unity.

He was moved more by the newer rather sentimental piety of the age which found its chief expression, for him, in the worship of the Virgin Mary, which I imagine reflected a domestic tenderness in his own life, and the new urban development of bourgeois family affectionateness, which was still not common in those harsh times. It was a private, inner devotion, like that of the child in *The Prioress's Tale*, that he felt.

The child in *The Prioress's Tale* dies. The fourteenth century was necessarily much concerned with death. *The Book of the Duchess*, Chaucer's first known big poem, is a consolation poem addressed to John of Lancaster on the death of his young wife, mother already of five children. *Troilus and Criseyde* and *The Knight's Tale* are romances where death becomes as significant as love. In *The Pardoner's Tale* death is madly sought by three de-bauchees. This is not to say that there is a morbid obsession with death in Chaucer's poetry, and so in his life; merely that he, like each of us, had to come to terms with death, and that death could not be disguised in the fourteenth century as it often is in the twentieth. Probably all children knew death in the fourteenth century, but as a child Geoffrey knew it with peculiar horror and frequency, for in his seventh or eighth year, perhaps when his serious schooling had just started, in 1348, England, like the rest of Europe, sustained the heaviest natural disaster it has ever known, from that occurrence of bubonic plague which has become known as the Black Death, though contemporaries called it the Great Pestilence.

The course and effects of this catastrophe are well known and have often been written about. Starting in the east, a peculiarly virulent combination of bubonic and pneumonic plague moved steadily west, causing an immense number of deaths, and reached the west of England in August 1348. The great medieval doctor, Guy de Chauliac, gives a clear account of the dual form, based on his observation of the outbreak at Avignon in 1348.

> The said mortality began with us in the month of January and lasted for the space of seven months. It was of two sorts: the first lasted two months, with continuous fever and expectoration of blood; and men died of it in three days. The second lasted the remainder of the time, also with continuous fever and with external carbuncles and buboes, chiefly in the armpits or the groin, and men died of it in five days.

Recovery was rare. Altogether it is thought that between 25 and 35 per cent of the population of England died in the period of about fourteen months that the plague spread through the country. It is needless to speak of the individual horror and distress. Our nearest personalized impression in English of what it could be to live through such oppression is given by Pepys's first-hand description of the Great Plague in London, 1665, but there is plenty of contemporary European testimony as well, especially from Italy. The gruesome stories of mass graves, of the stench of rotting flesh, of parents burying their children, of children bereft of parents, the macabre collection of corpses, the gloomy tolling of bells, the desertions, all make solemn reading. Many pious people felt that the plague was the judgment of God on their sins, and in Italy there were huge donations to churches. There is evidence for the moralist's condemnations in England, but any records of donations have perished. Less pious people reacted in a devil-may-care attitude, wonderfully well illustrated by Chaucer in *The Pardoner's Tale*.

The deadly black rat realistically drawn by Giovanni di Grassi, a fourteenth-century Italian artist

It is remarkable with what resilience European society recovered from the cataclysm. Italy is best documented, but in England, as elsewhere, there was no general panic, no general flight from the worst spots, only a brief dislocation of trade. The historian's general view is that the effects were to intensify social tendencies already at work, rather than to introduce some totally new element.

The same may be said for the psychological and general cultural effects. A widely spread predominantly rural population, if it does not achieve great heights of culture, has also great power of survival. People already knew death and suffering well enough. The normal darknesses and contrasts were heightened by the plague in England, but the fundamentals were not changed. Neither Chaucer nor his age show remarkable pessimism. They knew things were bad, complained a great deal, and thought that things in this world would get worse. This in itself was quite natural. But they also had built into their culture, independent of vagaries of personal belief, a concept not only of the terrors of judgment after death and the possibility of an eternity of just punishment, but also of the hope of heaven. They were committed to belief in a fundamentally good and morally just governance of the universe which extended beyond mortal existence. Life could, therefore, never become meaningless. National life as a whole was not disheartened; there was crisis, but not despair.

Although Chaucer could not have been conscious of such considerations when as a child he lived in a London terrified by plague, they conditioned the response of those around him. People must have been full of dread and anxiety to an even greater extent than normally, but his father and mother survived, and if a number of more distant relations died they enriched the living with their property. There were further visitations of plague in later years including 1369, when Queen Philippa died, but these were only intensifications of the incidence of common mortality. Life at court and city seems to have gone on uninter

ABOVE *Plagues must have been partly responsible for the preoccupation with themes such as* The Triumph of Death. *On the far left of this fresco three elegant young men out riding are confronted by the sight of their own corpses. The fresco is in the Campo Santo, Pisa*

ABOVE RIGHT *The Courtier may wish to pursue the ideals of the Monk but the lifestyle of the court, its preoccupation with appearance, status and the acquisition of wealth, exposes him to the prickings of the Devil's fork*

rupted: after all, what else could people do? The Great Pestilence of 1348–9 and its sequels may have halved the population between the mid-century and 1400, and this weakened many economic and social structures, profoundly affecting many lives, Chaucer's among them, but it had no detectable personal effect as such upon him. In his poetry it received only the rarest passing allusion.

It would seem likely that going to school would have had as great, or even greater an effect, upon a very young child, than the national calamity. We have imagined him quick, sensitive, highly intelligent, indulged, eager to learn. For such a child a medieval school would be a mixed blessing; new horizons and adventures for thought and feelings, but much mechanical repetition and brutal punishment. It would sharply contrast with home. Before he went to school he might stay in bed late in the morning, awakened by sunbeams, and lying easily between sheets, looking up at the coloured great beam and the rafters of the roof, and perhaps have breakfast in bed. Once school started, whether as a boarder or day boy, it was up at five a.m. by candlelight in shivering winter.

Geoffrey's father as a merchant probably saw several possible careers that were not for his son, as well as several that were. The Church was not for him for he was too disdainful of ritual and, though not exactly disobedient, too evasive of discipline, too much interested in the world, the flesh and the devil to take to a monastic career. Also, he came from rather too well-off a family to become an ordinary parish priest, and his origins were not sufficiently aristocratic for him to be placed immediately high up on the ladder of advancement in the Church.

Nor was Geoffrey longing to be a knight and carve out the basis of his fortune by first fighting in France as did a number of his later associates, like almost all the Lollard knights, who came from the lesser gentry. So Church and chivalry being out, the future might see him as either a merchant, like his father, or a lawyer, or perhaps some sort of courtier and administrator – the career he eventually did take up, which was only now becoming possible. Knowledge of Latin was the basis of all education beyond the most elementary. Presumably the boy might acquire French at home, since his father would have used French for business dealings. In some way the boy learned the difference between Continental French and the home-grown variety. He would also have to acquire arithmetic for accountancy and business studies. John Chaucer was perhaps sufficiently farsighted to be in touch with modern developments. Even in England as early as 1280 one John of Oxford had produced tracts on business methods, and from 1350 to 1410 there was a well-known teacher, Thomas Sampson of Oxford, who taught these subjects, and a school attached to Merton College at Oxford.

Geoffrey's father must himself have been intelligent and well educated. Even in England the families of merchants at this period were by no means all nests of philistines. Sir William Walworth, for example, the extremely rich and energetic fishmonger and financier who as Lord Mayor of London struck down Wat Tyler with his dagger during the Peasants' Revolt in 1381, left nine religious works and a number of law books in Latin at his death. Our best evidence for the education of merchants in Europe in the fourteenth century comes from Italy. England was not so advanced, but the stirrings can be felt in the middle of the fourteenth century in England of what would come to birth in the fifteenth century, and which had cousins already alive in Italy. Thus the basic arithmetic book for merchants in Europe was written by the Italian merchant and mathematician Leonardo Fibonacci of Pisa very early in the thirteenth century. By the end of the thirteenth century there were a large number of private lay schools in Italy, besides the ecclesiastical ones. In Milan in 1288 there were eight teachers of the higher grammar and *sixty* teachers of elementary grammar. The lay schools in Italy in the fourteenth century changed to a more practical syllabus than the ecclesiastical schools. The latter had always taught a range of subjects, including what we now call arithmetic, but the lay schools concentrated on providing a practical, commercial education. This meant that after learning 'grammar', i.e. to read and write Latin, boys went on to the 'abacus', that is, to practical training, largely arithmetical. The abacus was a simple but effective calculating machine as anyone who has seen its frequent use in shops until very recently in the efficient modern Japan of today can testify. In the Middle Ages it was constituted of counters set out on different lines on a board or cloth which signified units, tens, hundreds, etc., or it was (as now in Japan) made of rings on wires to the same effect. In 1338 there were six 'abacus' schools in Florence, containing 1000 to 1200 pupils. Other Italian cities followed suit. Pupils usually stayed at the abacus school till about twelve, or even later, then completed their education by becoming apprentices. Moral and general education was not neglected, and bore good fruit, but there is no doubt that the technical education began to

Boys at school

modify men's outlooks equally strongly. From this general mercantile educa‚ tional environment proceeded some of the greatest literary and pictorial art of the fourteenth and fifteenth centuries – for example, the works of Boccaccio and Piero della Francesca, to mention only two. In England the system was not so elaborate, but by 1415 a manual of commercial French written by William Kyngesmill can incidentally claim that a twelve‚year‚old boy in three months has learned to read and write, cast accounts and speak French – where else but in William Kyngesmill's hostel? From early in the fourteenth century, in fact, English merchants of the wealthier type (like John Chaucer) had often sought for their children a good education, including Latin, which included utili‚ tarian, though not only utilitarian, benefits. So it is quite reasonable to suppose that Chaucer went from an educated household to school.

The word 'school' in the fourteenth century covered everything from the most elementary song school to the university; hence the expression 'schoolmen' for the middle‚aged professional theologians and philosophers who formed the core of the universities. Just as there was in the general culture no precise distinction of age, so the idea of the school and the material of learning were not graded into stages suitable for children of different ages or capacities. Men seem to have set out to learn at very different ages. Classes were very miscellaneous, though there were no girls. (Such education as girls got came from home, or little unofficial schools, or nunneries.) But for present purposes 'school' means the elementary and grammar schools a child might attend at ages between seven and fourteen.

There were three known grammar schools in London when Chaucer was a boy, all at churches: at St Martin-le-Grand, at St Mary Arches, and at St Paul's. The last also had a more elementary school, called a song school, attached to it. Of the three schools, St Paul's was nearest and was and is best known. Let us suppose that he went to the song school first, about seven years old. At the age of seven he was able to run through the cold streets, not without fears of wicked men, to get to school by six a.m. The most vivid picture that we have of the seven-year-old at school is, as one might expect, by Chaucer himself in *The Prioress's Tale*. The 'little clergeon' (scholar) eager to read, eager to please, readily knelt before the image of Christ's mother that he passed set in a wall on the way to school, and said his 'Hail Mary' with innocent devotion, as taught by his mother. On arrival at the song school he was registered, for which he paid 2*d*. or 3*d*., as well as 4*d*. to 6*d*. per term as fees. The schoolmaster was a clergyman, helped by an usher or two. He ruled with tongue and rod over a large but crowded room of up to a hundred and fifty boys of ages from seven to fourteen or older, at different stages of learning. The pupils were, however, divided up into three blocks and separated by curtains, the fourth quarter of the room being reserved for the chapel. The beginners were in one block, the more advanced in the other two. It was not easy to learn, since a lot of what was learned was singing the Latin church services, and such an 'open-plan' arrangement was very noisy. On the other hand, if bored with one's own work, one could listen to the songs or the sobbing from the other class behind the curtain. There was also a fair amount of restlessness, asking for permission to go to the privy and so forth. The master sat in a high chair and held the symbol of his office – not a book but a rod – in one hand. Boys sat on forms around and were called out one by one to read. Woe betide them if they could not! It was miserably cold work in winter. They were chiefly warmed by the beating. From about six a.m. to eight they toiled,

BELOW *A good thrashing. A misericord in Sherborne Abbey, Dorset*

RIGHT *Concepts such as that of the Seven Deadly Sins were by no means vague or abstract, but sprang readily to life in graphic 'horror pictures' like this one of Avarice, designed to terrify the impressionable into virtue*

then broke for an hour or two, to take breakfast. Then back from ten till noon, another break for dinner for an hour or two, and back again to school for a long four hours. Chaucer's 'little clergeon' stayed at school all day, either taking his food, or feeding there with the boarders, and Geoffrey perhaps did the same.

He first learned to read English with a little book, a primer. First he crossed himself, then read through the alphabet in big and small letters. All this could have been done at home. The primer was only about twenty small pages written out by a scribe in Gothic letter, rather smudged by greasy little fingers and salty tears. After the alphabet followed a host of brief items: the Exorcism; Lord's prayer; Hail Mary; Creed; Ten Commandments; Seven Deadly Sins; Seven

Principal Virtues; Seven Works of Bodily Mercy; Seven Works of Spiritual Mercy; Five Bodily Senses; Five Spiritual Senses; Four Cardinal Virtues; Seven Gifts of the Holy Spirit; Sixteen Conditions of Charity (I Corinthians 13) going straight on to the Beatitudes (Matthew 5); continuing with five points from St Augustine; then seven hindrances that prevent men coming to Heaven; and lastly four more instructions from St Augustine. This is admirable stuff in itself, a blue-print in its way for a decent, orderly, modest, loving life. Lapses apart, that was the life Chaucer led. On the other hand, such dry lists are neither interesting nor significant to a child. Hardly anyone in education was concerned enough with practical utility to see if the means employed would actually achieve the ends proposed. As early as the early twelfth century Guibert of Nogent in his autobiography commented on the cruelty and impracticality of medieval teaching methods, and there must have been humane and sensible teachers who devised better methods of their own, but the general attitude and tools remained unchanged for many centuries. This mechanical rote learning fired no imagination and made no concession to childish interests. There was no grading of material, no sense of development in the growing child. He was treated as an inadequate adult.

Even here, however, in the latter part of the fourteenth century, there was the famous change of the language of instruction to the mother tongue. Chaucer's 'little clergeon' is assumed to learn in it, as no doubt Chaucer did. The development of the English language in the fourteenth century is a fascinating subject that can be only briefly touched on here. The effect of the Norman Conquest had been to downgrade English, and in the twelfth, thirteenth and early fourteenth centuries the court and upper classes spoke French, while Latin was the language of learning, religion, law. But English though down was never out. Old English lost all its grand words for government, art, general thought, but absorbed huge numbers of new words to replace them from the dominating languages and classes. It also lost most of the multiple endings of words and in some ways it simplified its word order. The continuously developing language that emerged is now called Middle English, though at the time every one of course just called it English, as they had before the Conquest. From quite soon after the Conquest most people except the very highest had spoken English as their cradle language. It worked its way steadily up the scale until, as Chaucer's poetry shows, it became the dominant language of the English court, though French retained its snob value. In Aquitaine the Black prince spoke English to English knights and French to the French. The French spoken in England, Anglo-French, was by now only a dialect, and Chaucer himself was patronizing about it, mocking his Prioress in The Canterbury Tales for her 'French of Stratford-le-Bow' (a district in London). Chaucer's English is full of words adapted from French and Latin, of which he is quite often the first recorded user. His English was very fresh, up-to-date, sophisticated. It was the English of London and the court, which became the main dialect of English and so the ancestor of modern standard English. Scholars have reconstructed it and you can hear it on records of Chaucer's poetry.

The dialects spoken in other parts of the country varied considerably, and in the north and east differed from other forms of English in containing more of the Scandinavian words brought in by Danes and Norsemen who conquered and settled in those parts before the Norman Conquest. So Chaucer in English again appears in the forefront of developments, using the newest and most fashionable language. By contrast much English poetry, and the most 'English' of it, was that great body of alliterative poetry which is so much neglected now, apart from Langland's *Piers Plowman* and the works of the *Gawain* poet. In his poetry, as in other respects, Chaucer is less typically English than he is often said to be.

He was no doubt also less typical in that he received any schooling at all, but if he really did go to school, rather than having a private tutor, he must have gone through something of the usual grammar grind. We may imagine him now going off to school in his grey robe, stockings and shoes, with his penner (sheath for the quill feathers, or pens), penknife to trim them with, and inkhorn (a cow's horn with stoppers, to hold ink), all slung at his belt. At school wax tablets and parchment were provided for writing on. In winter he had to take a wax candle with him for light. After the English primer he was put to the short elementary Latin grammar, the *Ars Minor* of Donatus, called in English the *Donet*.

After the Donet came the versified grammar of Latin in Latin called the *Doctrinale* by Alexander de Villa Dei, who had written it about 1200. It is 2650 hexameter lines long, and the boys chanted it in class to learn it off by heart. There were dictionaries, too, but they were little more than word lists, and although they were divided into sections by initial letter they were not alphabet-ized within the sections, so that it was no easy job to find a word. Dictionaries of Latin words giving corresponding English words seem not to have existed when Chaucer was a boy. It is not surprising that the general standard of Latin was low.

All the same grammar must have been enjoyable, because it opened up a world of vast intellectual and especially imaginative interest, since 'grammar' included studying the great Latin classics, notably Virgil and Ovid, and also practising the art of writing. St Paul's school was extraordinarily well provided with books. An earlier schoolmaster, William de Tolleshunt, in 1328 bequeathed his personal library to the school. There were grammar books, including the advanced book of Priscian, etymological dictionaries, books of logic, sermons for the boy bishops (who were elected at the Feast of Holy Innocents for a day of school festivity), books of science and law. They were not books for children, but could feed the mind of a schoolmaster. More significant for Chaucer is the collection bequeathed to the school in 1358 by William Ravenstone. This included many more of the same kind of books as bequeathed by the first William, but there were also the excitingly imaginative books of the Latin poetry that appealed to Chaucer, of which the traces are scattered through his own poetry. Chaucer's favourite Latin poet was Ovid, so lively in material, delightfully ornate and fanciful in style. His *Metamorphoses*, great storehouse of stories, about love, sex and death, and the book that Chaucer represents himself as reading at the beginning of *The Book of the Duchess*, is here. So is the *Thebaid* by

Parents taking their son to school. A stained-glass panel in the Victoria and Albert Museum, London

Statius, a version of which Criseyde is found having read to her by one of her ladies, in a group, in Chaucer's poem. Juvenal, the coarse and violent satirist, whom Chaucer refers to by name a couple of times in his poetry, is here in two copies. So is Claudian's *Rape of Proserpine*; Maximian's *Elegies*, echoed perhaps in *The Pardoner's Tale*; the Eclogues of Theodulus, a popular schoolbook for many centuries, of which a stray memory occurs in *The House of Fame*; and the celebrated Cato's *Distichs*, another schoolbook, which is a collection of wise sayings in Latin verse, immensely popular, or at least, continuously used, for many centuries. I like to think that the well-read William Ravenstone was Chaucer's own schoolmaster and allowed him to borrow books. William seems to have gone to neither Oxford nor Cambridge, and his literary tastes were not indeed those that were fostered in fourteenth-century universities.

Chaucer's knowledge of Latin must not be exaggerated. Many of his references to Latin literature and schoolbooks could have come from a few anthology volumes. He never read Latin fluently, or very accurately, and he turned to French or even Italian translations whenever he could, even for Ovid. But especially in his earlier works he obviously likes to use his Latin and to work with its immense prestige and richness. Something of this he must have got from school and from a sympathetic schoolmaster.

Another subject he learned, which I suspect his father was keen on, and which he liked enough to use a great deal, though in an unexpected way, is more mysterious – arithmetic. The direct evidence that he was taught arithmetic is even slighter than for his other schooling, but the indirect evidence is overwhelming, revealed by Chaucer's constant use of astronomical lore in his poems and in his scientific treatise on *The Astrolabe* (which is an instrument used in astronomy). You cannot do astronomy without being able to handle numbers. Perhaps his father intended him, as a lawyer, to build up a lucrative conveyancing practice, like that Thomas Pinchbeck, a great figure in the legal profession, whom he mildly satirizes in his portrait of the *Man of Law* in *The Canterbury Tales*. Instead Geoffrey turned his knowledge of arithmetic into more scientific channels, especially to the study of astronomy. But this lay in the future.

A little more should be said about arithmetic in general, for the term is more confusing than at first appears. *Arithmetica* survived the collapse of classical civilization as one of the Seven Liberal Arts into which intellectual activity was codified in the fifth century AD, and which formed the basis of university education until the seventeenth century. But this *Arithmetica* was really treatment of the theory of numbers, a highly abstract study which had little general cultural effect. There was a need for the art of practical calculating, or reckoning, counting, and it was in this that Fibonacci, early in the thirteenth century, as already mentioned, made important advances, and which was significantly developed in Italy. The development of arithmetic in fourteenth-century education is an example of new thought, being part of the developing capacity for abstract, analytical, general thought, which aimed at a rational, overall consistency, and was also related to the growth of cities and of commerce. For centuries arithmetic had been little known or used by the generality of people except in the

Early fourteenth-century wall tiles show two scenes from the Apocryphal Life of Christ. LEFT *Jesus is playing making holes on the bank of the River Jordan when a bully destroys them with a stick – and falls down dead.* RIGHT *The Virgin admonsihes Jesus who restores the boy to life, apparently by kicking him. In this way a domestic realism made the life of Christ vivid even to illiterate peasants.*

most primitive forms. It was even treated with suspicion by ecclesiastically minded devout persons. The story was told of St Edmund Rich, Archbishop of Canterbury (1234–40), that when he was a young master at Oxford and 'read arithmetic' his dead mother appeared to him in a dream and drew three circles on her right hand, indicating the Trinity of God the Father, God the Son and God the Holy Ghost. 'Son', she said, 'Study thou in *these* figures after this time.' The interest in arithmetic, and especially in calculation, was fuelled by secular interests. Arithmetic is a powerful social weapon. As late as the nineteenth century in England there were upper-class people who would allow teaching of reading, or even writing, to poor boys, but not arithmetic – they might get to know too much about wages. Arithmetic is a privilege of secular upper-class education, an instrument of power, control, advance. Chaucer's interest in arithmetic was in the forefront of intellectual and social advance.

The word *abacus* as used in Italy was hardly known in Chaucer's day in England. The English word was *augrim*, or algorism, which descends from the Latinized form of an Arabian mathematician's name, which itself appeared as Algus or Argus. What is now called a 'line abacus' appears in *The Miller's Tale* as the 'augrym stones' which the lecherous student Nicolas possesses, along with an astrolabe and a psaltery and a lot of books. The augrym stones were the counters which had to be placed on a cloth or board marked with lines, or sometimes squares, which signified units, tens, hundreds, etc. This method was well established in England. The cloth or board with squares or checks came to be known, from the French, as an *exchequer*. Its use to calculate the king's revenues led to the naming of that department of state with that responsibility as

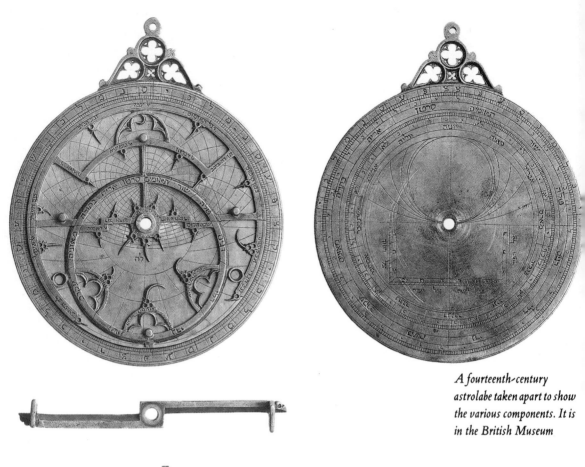

*A fourteenth-century
astrolabe taken apart to show
the various components. It is
in the British Museum*

the Exchequer. Nicolas in *The Miller's Tale* is significantly an Oxford man, for
it was at Oxford, and particularly at Merton College, that mathematical, scientific and astronomical studies were strongest in the fourteenth century.

There is a scattering of arithmetical terms throughout Chaucer's work, but
they are naturally densest in his *Treatise on the Astrolabe* which was written for a
ten-year-old boy whom Chaucer calls his son, Lewis. *The Treatise on the Astrolabe* is meant to teach little Lewis 'sciences concerning numbers and
proportions', because the boy has particularly asked to be taught to use the astrolabe, an astronomical instrument. Chaucer explains that as the boy knows little
Latin the work is in English. So even by 1391, when the treatise was probably
written, it was hard to find a teacher for the astrolabe, other than father himself,
who had perhaps started to learn arithmetic also about the age of ten.

School was not all work. There were plenty of holidays for religious festivals,
and when the London schools celebrated the day of their patron saint they staged
elaborate verbal exercises. The boys from each school were pitted against each
other in debates. Some invented topic was proposed and the more advanced

scholars showed off skills in logic and rhetoric, either imitating the popular methods of university disputations, full of technical logic (for which, in the fourteenth century, the English universities became famous), or deploying the fuller speechifying recommended by the teaching of rhetoric, with its elaborate descriptions, apostrophes, richly varied language, figures of speech and thought. There were also verse competitions; quiz competitions on grammar; and also (what medieval festival could be without it?) derisive, ribald, mocking satires, in verse, by the boys, directed not only against the masters but greater men known to the school – no doubt mainly the higher clergy, archdeacons, deans, bishops. Here we may imagine that the quick-minded, fluent, observant, highly strung, sharp-tongued, Geoffrey was in his element. No torrents of vulgar abuse for him, nor surely the slovenly butchering, tortuously logical and theological disputation. He would have practised the copious rhetorical manner, ready to persuade on either side of a question, and with a touch of the devil in him that encouraged him to use all his skill to make the worse appear the better reason. I envisage a smallish, slight, smooth-cheeked boy with a certain poised manner for all his quietness and occasional intensity, whose insinuating ambivalent effrontery could always be defended, might be defended as naïvety, yet might be broad enough in its implications. There were spectators for these verbal sports as for others, and all his actor's verve would be indulged before grown-ups whose tastes were often as childish as his own. The range of audience was wide and included men of culture as well as others who, whatever their knowledge of the world, were already outdistanced in reading and information by the boy. There were ladies present, too; admiring mothers, and pretty girls who sometimes did not know whether to laugh and blush, or pretend they had not understood.

Around the age of fourteen it was time for a change. The ambitions of the family, the mixed tastes of the boy, with all the oscillating moods and passions of intense adolescence, eager for knowledge of the world as well as for books, all now pointed to that well-established line of advancement for a gentleman's son, a place in a great person's court. Chaucer's father was in a position to get him one. Geoffrey became a page of Elizabeth, Countess of Ulster.

Exactly what game these children are playing seems rather obscure – perhaps it is 'catch'

CHAPTER THREE

A PAGE AT COURT

THE NAME OF GEOFFREY CHAUCER FIRST TURNS UP referring unquestionably to our unheroic hero in a fragmentary record (written in Latin as usual) of a household account that was only preserved because someone tore it up in the fifteenth century and used it to thicken the binding of a volume of poems by Lydgate and Occleve, Chaucer's two principal disciples. The account is that of the household of Elizabeth, Countess of Ulster and covers parts of the years from 1356 to 1359.

The record states that a certain 'paltok' maker in London was paid 4s. for a paltok given to Geoffrey Chaucer by the countess on 4 April 1357. A paltok by this time was a fancy jacket of silk. For a pair of something red and black (the word is illegible but is thought to mean breeches) and a pair of shoes, 3s. were paid. The breeches, or hose, would be one leg red, one black, tied to the paltok with laces. One John Hinton, who is called yeoman in 1359, was given a cloak on 12 September costing 8s. 3d., and a page called Thomas at some time in 1359 received one costing 6s. 8d. This shows that Geoffrey was in a junior position, since such gifts tended to be measured according to the status rather than the size of the wearer (see below, p. 71). He was also paid 2s. on 20 May at London. He was given 2s. 6d. also at London, on 20 December, for necessaries for Christmas, which the countess spent in Hatfield that year. (This would be in addition to his usual daily pay, which was probably around 3d., plus rations.)

Elizabeth's court was in itself a relatively small *familia*, with two or three ladies-in-waiting, one or two clerks, one or two esquires, three or four yeomen of the chamber (*valetti*), two or three pages, and a chaplain; in all, ten to fifteen people, perhaps, not all present all of the time. Her court would usually be with her husband's household, as they moved about together from one great castle to another, either their own or those of relatives. The castle at Hatfield, for example, belonged to John of Gaunt, who was there for Christmas 1357. He was little older than Chaucer; they could not have become friends, but in their acquaintance would have been a mixture of familiarity (because both were gentlemen and a medieval court was a jostling crowd that brought all degrees close together), and remoteness (because of the great social distance between the blood royal and commercial minor gentry). When he became a page Geoffrey had to learn the rich and elaborate pattern of manners and conventions, of what you could and could not do or say or be, that made courtly life so fascinating.

'Upon my trouthe I sey you feithfully, | That ye ben of my lyf and deeth the quene.' Four suitors compete in presenting the most elegant pleas for mercy on this early fifteenth-century Arras tapestry

Ye have bene seke I dar myne hede assure
Or late fed in a feynte pasture
lyft vp your hede be glade take no sorowe
And ye shale home ryde with vs to morowe
I sey when ye rysede have your fylle
Aftur sowpere slepe wyle do none ylle
Wrap welle your hede with clothes rounde aboute
Stronge notte asle wole make yone to roule
Take a pilowe that ye ly not lowe
Off nede be spare not for to blowe
To holde wynde by myne oppinion
Wole engendre collica passyon
And make men to grouen on there ropys
When they have fylled wele per cropys
But towarde nyght ete pou semele sede
Anyys comyne or coryandre rede
And lyke as I power have and myght
I charge yow ryse not at mydnyght
Though it be so the moone shyne clere
I wole my selff be youre orlogere
To morowe erly when I see my tyme
ffor we wole forthe percele afore pryme
And company payde shale do yone glade
What loke vp yonk for be lokes blade
Thowe shalt be mirye who so that sy nay
ffor tomorowe anone as yt is day
And that it ryme in the Este to dawe
Thowe shalt be bounde to a newe lawe
At goynge oute of Caunterbury Toū
And lay asyde thy professyon
Thowe shalt not chees ne thy sylff withdrawe
yff ony myrthe be founden in thy mawe
like the costume of this companye
ffor none so hardy that dare me denye
kaught ne knawe Chanon prest ne nonne
to tel a tale playnly as they konne
When I assynge and se tyme oportune
And for that we oure purpos wole contynue
we wole homwarde the same custome vse
And thowe shalt not platly the evcuse
Be nowe welle ware studye wele this nyghte
But for al this be of hert lyghte
Thy wit shal be the sharper and ye bet
And we anone were to sypere set
And payde wele vnto oure plesaunce
And sone aftur by glade governaunce
Vnto bedd gothe every mane wyght
And towarde gorowe anon as it was lyght
Every pilgryme bothe bet and worse
Than bad oure Hoste take anone his Hors
Whan pe somme rose in the Este ful clere
ffully in purpos to kom to oure dyners
howe the mouke in pe pilgremes departyde from
Buē Ostrynge and broke ther oure fast ¶Cauntbry
And when we wern fro Caunterbury past

Vlot the space of a bowe draught
Oure Ooste in haste hath my brydele raught
And to me seyde as ye were in game
Kome forth davū John by yo Cristen name
And let vs make some manere myrthe or play
Shete youre porelwes Atwenty devyle way
It is no disporte so to pate and so seye
It wole make youre lyppes wonder dreye
Tele some tale and make theroff no iape
ffor by my rounye thow shal not escape
But preche not of none holynesse
Gynne some tale of myrthe and of gladnesse
And nod not so with thy hevy beek
Tel vs some thinge that draweth of to speke
Onely of yoye and mak no lengere lette
And when I sanghe it wolde be no bette
I obeyed vnto his byddynge
And as the lawe me bounde in alle thynge
As I konde with a ful pale chere
My tale I ganne anone as ye shal here

❧ Explicit prologus ❧

❧ Prima pars ❧

Here begynneth the Segge of Thebes ful
lamentably tolde by John lidgate monke of
Bury annexynge it to pe tallys of Caunbry

S Irs quod I sith of youre Curtesye
I entrede am in to youre Companye
And admytted a tale for to tele
By hym that hath power to compele
I mene oure hoste governere and gyde
Of youre esheone rydenge here by syde
Thogh my wit bareyne be and dulle
I wolle reherce a story wonderfulle
Touchenge the segge and destruction
Of worthy Thebes the myghty royale Toū
Bilt and bygonne of olde antiquite
Vpon the tyme of worthy Iosue
By diligence of kynge Amphion
Cheeff cause first of this foundacyon

Geoffrey's older contemporary, the Hainaulter Jean Froissart, fluent poet and chronicler, gives us a complacent, idealized account of his own early life in his poem *Espinette Amoureuse*. How he loved play as a child, he says, and as young as twelve years old longed for dances – the round and figured dances of that age, performed by groups, with singing as well. He longed to hear minstrels and was very fond, rather oddly, of those who loved hawks and hounds. He was fonder still of the little girls, and gave them gifts of pins (prettier objects than we have today) and apples and pears, and longed for the day when he should really fall in love. And though he had to learn Latin, and was frequently beaten by his master (the constant educational note!) and fought with other boys, he was always ready to give chaplets of flowers to girls, and was very happy. When he learned to read he loved to read romances. He gives a charming account of how eventually he fell in love with a beautiful fair-haired girl in springtime, whom he met reading a romance by herself. (Young ladies could usually read, despite their deprivation of education. Writing was a different matter.) He and she took turns in reading the book. She later asked to borrow another romance, and in lending the book to her he slipped in a love poem addressed to her. At times they were in a group of five or six, laughing and talking and eating fresh fruit. But in the end, it came to nothing. He finishes sententiously and sincerely, however, with the reflection that to be in love is a great improvement for a young man, and a very profitable beginning to life, for all joy and honour derive from fighting and love. Love makes a man courteous and able, and changes his vices to virtues. Such was the doctrine of the time.

Another French author, much younger than Chaucer, Antoine de la Sale, born about 1386, a courtier and tutor to a prince, wrote a prose romance called *Le Petit Jehan de Saintré*. The romance has all the strange Gothic mixture of apparently incompatible tones and attitudes. Chaucer brought this juxtaposition of incompatible elements of the 'style of the age' to a fine art of ambiguity, while de la Sale is simply awkward, but *Le Petit Jehan de Saintré* has as its core a quite realistic-seeming and charming story of a courtly widow's teasing attempt to seduce a young page, little John himself, though it concludes with her betrayal of him and her wildly indiscreet love affair with an abbot who reminds one of Chaucer's Monk in *The General Prologue*. The story of Saintré gives a picture that allows us to construct some possible detail for Chaucer's life. Saintré was a very keen, very naïve page, who served every one at table with all his zeal, but especially the ladies. At thirteen years old he was, though small and thin, skilled in horsemanship, singing, dancing, running, jumping, playing at tennis. He was remarkably gentle and courteous. The young widow wanted to make some young squire into a famous man for love of her, and eventually selected little Saintré. She called him into her room and, sitting on the foot of her bed, placed the boy, who was feeling more and more nervous, between her and her ladies. 'Now tell me', she demanded, 'when did you last see your beloved?' He had never thought of such a thing, and his eyes filled with tears. All the ladies teased him to answer, but he stood twisting the tassel of his girdle around his fingers and could say nothing. Eventually in desperation, little Saintré confessed – 'The

Pilgrims on the road to Canterbury, from Lydgate's Siege of Thebes, *which is presented as a sequel to* The Canterbury Tales *about the pilgrims when they return to London. The columns show the intended regularity of the verse, though the absence of punctuation allows some fluidity of emphasis and interpretation*

lady that I love best? It is my mother, and next to her, my sister Jaqueline!'

'O recreant knight!' said the Lady, and went on, pretending to be angry, to ask how could the famous knights Lancelot, Gawain, Tristan and many others, have accomplished their great deeds and won such fame if they had not been seeking to serve love and find favour with their beloved ladies? At last the boy was allowed to escape, in deep embarrassment and sorrow, and the ladies could indulge their laughter. The story proceeds with the Lady instructing Saintré in love, which allows the author to put out quite seriously a very extensive set of solemn instructions on courtly behaviour, including the Ten Commandments, and the need not to be violent and bloody. `He who lives by the sword shall perish by the sword' is quoted only a few pages away from exhortations to be a brave and valiant knight. It is a most curious amalgam. The Lady, being now in love with little Saintré, though she calls him `fair son', gives him money to buy clothes with: a doublet, two pairs of hose, red and brown, four pairs of fine linen shirts, four kerchiefs, and shoes and pattens.

This sort of thing went on for three years, until he was sixteen, and the Lady thought he ought to be promoted from page to squire, since he could now carve well, and they met frequently in secret for talk and kisses. So the Lady asked the Queen for Saintré's promotion, and the Queen asked the King, who hearing of the boy's worthiness, granted the request and told his Seneschal, who told Saintré to begin at once as the King's Carving Squire, allowed to keep three horses at the king's expense, and two servants. When Saintré went along to bed that night in the room which he shared with the other pages, the Master of the pages, an Esquire, congratulated him heartily, and pointed out to the others how well he had done in contrast with them – brawlers, card players, dice players, haunters of taverns, that they were. It was in vain that he had them whipped, they would never improve.

Saintré could hardly sleep, because the Lady had sent him a large sum of money to buy horses with, which he longed for as much as a modern boy a motorcycle. The Lady continued to favour him with kisses, money, and copious advice; to behave properly in court, to read histories, especially of the military triumphs of the Romans, to wear a bracelet for her, and so forth. And he loved her in return. Then she advised him, and supplied him with the necessary money to give a great party, with dancing and singing followed by supper, and rich presents. To this party came lords, ladies, knights, esquires, burgesses of Paris and their wives. Eventually Saintré went off on his travels to seek jousts in honour of his lady, where we need not follow him, for such ways were far from Chaucer's.

This strange yet popular romance even in its lack of artistry gives us a real sense of court life. The group of pages among whom we may place Geoffrey, with their duties about the court, their free time, their amusements, were a group of boys aged from twelve to their late teens, partly servants, partly pupils, partly equals. They were apprentices to the courtly life who could expect to move up a ladder of promotion and be themselves courtiers and knights one day. The tone of the court, as of no other medieval institution, was affected by the presence of ladies, and sexual love was inextricably intertwined with motivation for acquiring promotion, honour, success in war, religious merit, financial profit, and good manners. However, when the Lady eventually falls in love with the Abbot and they have sexual intercourse, this is only slyly intimated; whether she and Saintré are lovers in the fullest sense during the sixteen years of their love is never even hinted. Good manners are here the point, rather than good morals. Sexual love was like a magnetic force, all-powerful but invisible. The Lady combines in herself several possible roles that could exist separately. She is patron, friend, paramour, though she never thinks to be wife.

I am not suggesting that Chaucer was so fortunate or unfortunate as Saintré, but that romances such as these, with Froissart's reminiscences, enable us to recreate something of the inner tone and fascination of courtly life. The Countess

'Ful craftier to pley she was | than Athalus, that made the game | First of the ches . . .' A French ivory mirror case in the Victoria and Albert Museum, London

Elizabeth did not attempt to seduce him, but she was in some sort a patron. There were other ladies about, and promotions must have proceeded by personal recommendations in ways very similar to Saintré's.

Geoffrey was a far more complicated character than Froissart or Saintré. His schooling and the intellectual and literary tastes that he had developed burned in him with a far fiercer flame. He had also acquired a deep, though perhaps intermittent, and quite conventional piety. The constant dinning-in of religious concepts to such a receptive mind could not but provoke both action and reaction. If *The Book of the Duchess* is in some ways remarkable for the purely secular and courtly way in which it treats death, it is also roughly contemporary with Geoffrey's other poem, *An ABC*, an ingenious and pious composition, translated from the French, of devotion to the Blessed Virgin, in which each stanza begins with a successive letter of the alphabet. Though its piety is conventional there is no reason to doubt its sincerity. Courtly life itself was very pious in religious observance and in sentiment, especially towards the Virgin.

There was therefore every possibility of great strain in courtly life, at any rate for less superficial characters than Froissart and Antoine de la Sale. The imagination that responds to the beauty of holiness will often respond just as passionately to the holiness of beauty. Yet holiness and beauty were often opposed. The beauty of women conflicted with the dangers of sex. The love of language was equally suspect. The history of the Church shows us deeply devout men of genius who repudiated their love of words, from St Jerome and St Augustine onwards. The interesting and unusual autobiography of Guibert of Nogent, who lived from 1053 to 1146, repeats the same story. He tells us of that devotion to his mother so often seen in spiritual men, and also of how much he loved learning of all kinds, especially literature, and how eagerly he read Ovid. Here it might be Chaucer – or Milton – speaking. Guibert wrote love poems in his youth – obscene words, he now calls them, as he writes his autobiography, condemning his youthful outpourings as worthless and immodest writings. The courtly Froissart, though he was a clerk in Holy Orders, was not so anguished. The tension between the love of beauty and the love of holiness seems greater for those who have given up beauty than for those who, like Froissart, give up holiness. The pain, and perhaps the reward, seems greater for those who give up the beauty of the world. They have the richer, if more sorrowful, song, if they continue to sing at all. Guibert says that a sword pierced his soul because of the poems he wrote, and he abjured the folly of useless study.

Such rigour was less easy in the fourteenth century, and impossible for Geoffrey Chaucer, who was so firmly set in this world. In his youth, by his own account, he composed 'many a song and many a lecherous lay'. His

Tho myghtist thou karoles sen, | And folk daunce and mery ben | And made mony a fair tournyng | Upon the grene gras springyng

contemporary, the worthy John Gower, in 1390 called Chaucer the poet of Venus, who in the flower of his youth had composed poems and glad songs with which the land was quite filled. For the young Geoffrey the story of love was glad, and the loveliness and joy of love had to be tested, and no doubt tasted. And even when that was done, a whole variety of worldly interests were to be explored, including the scientific, historical, philosophical journeyings of the mind, more enriching to the poetry than the constant journeyings of the body of which they were a counterpart. It was to all these desires for fulfilment, for enjoying the beauty and the wonder of the world, that the court appealed, as well as to the ready respect for honour and the longings for glamour. Where else could Chaucer have sought a career but at court? He could not, with his inter-ests, choose the church, the law, the army, or the shop, even though all those were close enough to the court. Yet he could not choose the court with simplicity either; ambivalent as ever, in his courtly observances love was tinged with philosophy, sex with sardonic comedy, beauty with loss and suffering. He could not scorn delights and live laborious days – not until, that is, at the very end, when in his Retractation at the end of *The Canterbury Tales*, and at the end of his life, he condemns, like Guibert, his glad songs and lecherous lays.

He presumably entered the court at the age of fourteen or fifteen, in 1354 to 1356, along with that rather dull fellow, as I invent him to be, Geoffrey de Stukeley, whose career ran parallel to his own for a good many years. It was quite usual for rich merchants' sons to find a place in court, where a taste for luxury, literature and ladies might be indulged, at the expense of a little work and an occasionally uneasy conscience.

I imagine Geoffrey Chaucer to have been a small sprightly lad, varying between quietness and liveliness, not without his moods, but rarely surly. He was very sharp, when he was not thinking of something else; a reader of romances in English and of the latest French poems by Machaut and Froissart, as well as soaked, like them, in *Le Roman de la Rose*. He could ride quite well, though he was not keen on the painful sport of jousting or the humiliating one of the quintain, whereby you had to hit from horseback with a spear a target at the end of a rotating beam, whose other end then whirled round and hit you on the back unless you were very clever. Nevertheless he shared the general respect for chivalry and the panoply of war. There was a fount of joyousness in him, a ready response to the charm of women, and a vigorous sexuality. At first, probably, he was a young Saintré, zealous and friendly and innocent, rather than a young Troilus, who was innocent indeed, but with a shy schoolboy's mocking fear of love and ladies. This friendliness might still go with a quick temper, at a time when no one in court thought much of keeping a stiff upper lip.

Ladies were constantly present, yet rarely alone, and the elaboration of manners, for the sort of boy I imagine, with some streak of idealism, would also keep him at a distance from intimacy. Distance in imagination with closeness in actuality is a sure recipe for a passionate falling in love with some pretty girl. It is impossible to imagine that Geoffrey did not fall heavily in the end and turn his glad songs to sadness. Perhaps he fell in and out of love several times – a quicksilver, even inconstant temperament. More likely there was a steady obses-sion in the end, something like that of Troilus. No one could write as Chaucer did of Troilus's misery without knowing its depths himself. In his earlier poems he represents himself as unsuccessful in love. This was a poetic convention of the times, but it is common enough in life. He even extends the pose in later poems, like the *Troilus*, to presenting himself as a complete outsider from love. That, too, can hardly be true, but the psychological truth of the unsuccessful lover seems too consistent to reject. Maybe he loved his wife, both before and after he married, but most people, and Chaucer most of all, are a bundle of persons in one skin — we have many lives, many attitudes, not all compatible with each other. But surely Geoffrey learned both the joys and sorrows of love.

As to sex apart from love, men in the world of the court were hardly expected to be chaste, though ladies were. There were prostitutes in plenty, and no doubt plenty of silly girls, as well as young men eager to take advantage of both. Yet Troilus, like so many heroes of romances in English, is chaste until he falls in love with, and wins, Criseyde. When he is her lover he regards himself as her husband. He is recognizably obsessive, faithful to death, intense in passion; Chaucer, however chameleon-like we may imagine him, must have had something of Troilus in him when young. It is hard to think of so sympathetic an imagination as belonging to a brutally promiscuous man. Yet Chaucer also has much in common with Byron — sardonic worldly humour, sympathetic feeling for sorrow, brooding melancholy — and we know Byron to have been such a man. Chaucer does not appear so demoniac as Byron, so passionately egotistical as Shelley, but these ruthless young aristocrats may well represent an element in Chaucer that his writings, so long before Romanticism, lacked the conventions to express. The sexual morals of the court were loose. The king and the king's sons all had mistresses before marriage, and often afterwards. The obsessive and elevating loves of the great Italians, Dante for Beatrice and Petrarch for Laura, did not prevent them from having bastards by other women.

Probably a better comparison than Byron to Chaucer is Pepys, in the seven-teenth century. Pepys was also a gentleman, though of somewhat smaller kind, who steadily moved from the outermost margins of the king's court to a position of some confidence with the king in respect of Pepys's special responsibilities in the Navy Office. Pepys's *Diary* is a most remarkable view of the English court while it was still essentially of the medieval kind, seen through the eyes of a man whose desire for efficiency, ability at accounts (arithmetic again!), interest in history and in science, realism, intense curiosity and self-consciousness, made him very much a modern man. The similarity of the character of Pepys with so much of what we can deduce of Chaucer is remarkable, although the energy that Pepys put into his office work and diary Chaucer put into his courtier work and poems. Pepys was shocked by the corrupting lechery of Charles II, and attributed much of the further lechery and corruption in the court at large to Charles's gross neglect of his duties for sexual self-indulgence. Yet Pepys himself, who when he married his wife felt literally sick from love of her, when he was married pursued shop girls and actresses with shameless, if secret zest. He was very highly sexed, extremely susceptible to female charm, and records in his diary how he overcame the reluctance of one of his earlier mistresses `half by force'. We may remember the accusation of rape from which Chaucer himself in early middle age was released. Yet Pepys himself as a boy and a young man seems not to have been debauched, and Chaucer probably was not. Nor can one see him as one of those pages who was a constant brawler, dice player, card player, haunter of taverns – only as occasionally taking part in such relaxations.

The position of page was traditionally conceived of as an educational one. He was being trained, in theory at least, as well as giving service, just like an apprentice. There is a famous description in one of the very earliest of English romances, *King Horn*, of how a boy should be educated in the court. The King's chief officer, the Steward, is instructed to teach Horn skill in hunting and hawking; to play the harp and sing songs, to carve before the King at table, and serve him with his cup. This is in the thirteenth century, but `the education of a page' (or of a squire) at court becomes a commonplace in romances, until *Le Petit Jehan de Saintré*, written nearly two hundred years after the French original of *King Horn*, is a romance almost entirely *about* education. In the earliest works the emphasis is almost entirely on physical outdoor skills, hunting, hawking, jousting (as practice for actual battle), and on the indoor acts of courtly service, carving before the king or lord, serving him with his cup. By Geoffrey's time there comes in an emphasis on *courtesy*, the virtue of courts, an instruction in good manners, in a certain deference that had to do with feeling for others and was not conceived of as obsequiousness. The sons of great men were at this period themselves constrained to offer their parents and elders in the court this kind of service. Pages were bound also to make themselves useful in other ways, to fetch and carry, set out the chess tables, run errands.

In the fifteenth century in England the sort of instruction Chaucer received as a page and squire was written out. The notable work is John Russell's *Boke of Nurture*. He begins piously and proclaims it his aim to teach virtue and skill to ignorant but willing youths. He then fables how 'in a merry season of May', he walks to refresh himself in a forest. There he meets a thin young man and falling in talk with him discovers that he is miserable because he cannot get a job. Russell offers to teach him – 'Do you want to be a servant, ploughman, labourer, courtier, clerk, merchant, mason, artificer, chamberlain, butler, pantryman or carver?' Out of this extraordinary variety nothing will please the young man more than to learn the skills of the last three. The worthy Russell immediately swoops in after a brief exhortation to the young man to love God and be true and obedient to his master with such details as that a butler must have three sharp knives, one to chop loaves with, the next to trim the slices, the third to smooth and square the slices. (The slices, called trenchers, were used as side plates before being eaten. Four-day-old bread, says Russell, should be used for trenchers, though the King should always be given new bread.) The detail is fascinating, and in some ways brings one closer to the texture of late-medieval life than many a more ambitious treatise. Russell's concrete detail makes his work vivid, rich, immediate. There is a great deal of advice, almost all totally erroneous, about

A serving knife with enamelled handle, decorated with the arms of Philip the Good, Duke of Burgundy

which foods cause constipation. Geoffrey would have been told some of this. He must have been to some extend instructed in how to make Ypocras (a richly spiced wine), how to lay cloths and the table; he was told, yet again, as children were told, not to scratch, nor pick his nose, let it drip, blow it too loud, put his hand in his hose to scratch his private parts (Russell is blunter), nor tell lies, hiccup, nor clean a dish by licking it, nor yawn, belch, groan, stamp, wiggle his legs, pick his teeth. He must always prevent his hinder part from gun blasting, etc. He was given instructions how to carve and serve various sorts of foods, then on how to serve up a banquet, given tips on the subtleties, which were artistic devices, made of paper, etc., with elaborate mottoes. He would have heard the duties of a chamberlain; his courtesy is to be diligent, clean, well dressed. He must look after his master, dress him carefully by the fire, make his bed, fold and brush his clothes, at night undress him, comb his head, turn the sheet back, draw the curtain round the bed, drive out dog and cat, set the commode and chamberpot ready, arrange the night light carefully, and be ready to come whenever called.

I think Chaucer must have found all this sort of thing very boring. He was a reading, thinking, travelling, sociable man, not a folder of clothes and an emptier of chamberpots. All this detail is fascinating to us (or at least to me) for the immediacy with which it brings one kind of ordinary everyday life of the past to the imagination, and I think Chaucer himself would have enjoyed reading about it, as a text descended from the past. But there are more interesting things to do than perform the daily round and common task. It is much more likely that Chaucer preferred such instruction in Latin and astronomy as he might be given by a chaplain, or guidance in reading the modern French verse of Machaut by the esquire in charge of the pages, or indeed by some well-read lady about the little court. This was not necessarily the last stage of his education, but we can attribute to it Geoffrey's remarkable knowledge especially of the poems of the French clerk, poet and musician, Guillaume de Machaut.

Part of the instruction Geoffrey received that went deeper than domestic duties was both practical and symbolic. This was the ordering of people's position in hall according to rank. Highest is the Pope, then come kings, archbishops, etc., down to knights, priors, mayors or ex-mayors of London, serjeants-at-law, masters of arts, parsons, merchants and rich artificers, down to gentlemen and gentlewomen who rank level with squires. There are a good many subtleties and complications, and some variations, but what is interesting is that clear traces of this ordering remain in the order of the list of pilgrims given in *The Canterbury Tales*. The Knight begins the list and we end with decidedly low characters, last of all being the poet himself. He apologizes for not putting folk in their degree, but he, and his first audience, trained as they were, knew well that the order was no more than refreshingly, piquantly, amusingly, disturbed. The marshal of the hall might be an esquire, like the marshal of the hall who orders the rich and substantial establishment of the knight January in *The Merchant's Tale*, so Geoffrey needed to know these things; but once again I do not see him as a vigorous, positive man of action, firmly if tactfully organizing people. No doubt he would do it if he had to. The type of the marshal, as Chaucer sees him, is bluff Harry Bailly, the Host of the Tabard Inn in Southwark, who organizes the tale-telling competition of the pilgrims on their way to Canterbury. He is a big man with bulging eyes, wise, well educated, or at least, literally well taught, very manly and jolly – more positive than a butler, more genial than a serjeant-major, but with something of the nature of both. Chaucer in fact rather patronizes and gently mocks Harry Bailly even though the poet represents himself, on the same journey, as somewhat retiring of nature and socially a 'dull man', probably with some truth. By middle age the fires were mostly within.

The boy Geoffrey with his quick, sympathetic intelligence absorbed courtly instruction readily enough, if with some detachment. It would have been difficult for him to take entirely seriously the solemn pernickety detail of a John Russell. It must have been a relief, when he was off duty, to read the English romances, the French poets, Ovid's elaborate, sensationalist poems, histories, and such scientific works as he could come by.

He also found pleasure in writing poems. Many pages, yeomen and esquires did this, for it was a recognized accomplishment of the courtier to compose songs and sing them. His talent must soon have become recognized. At first his songs were probably in the simpler English idiom that he later mocked in *The Miller's Tale*, and he may have invoked such traditionally phrased refrains as:

> An hendy hap ichabbe yhent
> ichot from heuene it is me sent;
> from alle wymmen mi loue is lent
> and lyht on Alysoun.

(A gracious chance have I obtained – I know it is sent to me from heaven; my love is taken away from all women and has come down on Alison.) But he soon realized how provincial and old-fashioned such diction was. *Hende* and *Alison* are both used derisively in *The Miller's Tale*. He also soon realized that the style of the English romances was often absurd. The French poems he read and sang had a much more splendid vocabulary and an altogether much more sophisticated attitude. Yet the obstinate streak in him made him stick to English, though others of his contemporaries still wrote in French. He read a lot of English poems still, and their influence stayed with him. In the huge English poetry anthology, for example, put together about 1400 and now called the Vernon Manuscript, are poems that Geoffrey must have read in earlier versions. There is a poem giving the dialogue between Jesus and the wise men of the Temple when he was brought by his parents to Jerusalem at the age of twelve. Jesus teaches the arrogant teachers their own ignorance, beginning with the reason why A is now our first letter. That A is our first letter crops up in *Troilus and Criseyde*, written by Chaucer in his forties. So Chaucer, using yet mocking the English tradition, developed a typical ambivalence towards it. This was both cause and effect of his inability to stay serious for very long. He must have been at times a wonderful mimic, and I imagine the small group of his fellow pages were entertained in their room at night (when the esquire in charge of them was out of the way) by wonderfully funny take-offs of their elders and betters. And he could no doubt

The magnificence of a king –
the effigy of Edward III from
his tomb in Westminster
Abbey. It is interesting to
compare this 'official' portrait
with his death mask (p. 104);
the eyes, nose and mouth are
recognizably the same, but
this portrait seems clearly
idealized

tell a story better than anyone. In any big fourteenth-century court there were jesters to make jokes; minstrels to tell tales or sing songs and play instruments; heralds to relate histories (and occasionally, like the Herald of Sir John Chandos, to write them as Chandos Herald did the life of the Black Prince). Geoffrey was no fool, and no chronicler, but he combined in himself much of the jester and the minstrel. The official touch of the herald he abjured – he was too much of a private person. But he was ready at least occasionally to put himself forth in public, though with defensive joking, as an unsuccessful lover, bad poet, dull-spirited man. As a young man, approaching nineteen, he must have shown this paradoxical adventurousness of imagination.

More than adventurousness of imagination was now called for. A period of truce in the Hundred Years War came to an end, King Edward III was assem-bling a vast army for the invasion of France, and Duke Lionel, husband of Chaucer's Lady Elizabeth and son of the king, was going to go with him. It was high time the young man with his taste for books and ladies' company should learn what the real business of a gentleman was – war. So Geoffrey came to the wider and even more violent, exciting, dramatic events of his times, and the excitement and glamour of it all moved him with admiration. Never in all his poetry does he mock honour and the chivalric life, weary as he may sometimes feel of strife and treachery, struggle and suffering.

The court, as an institution, was many things: a household, a *familia*; a place of leisure, sport, culture, love; an administrative unit; but in origin it was the Anglo-Saxon king's *heorth-werod*, his hearth-troop, his chosen warriors, with whom he would lead his people, and who would – or should – die with him. The roots go down into feelings deeper still of the sacredness of kingship, which even in modern times find popular echoes not only where traditional royalty survives but in the mystique that surrounds presidents and leaders of all kinds. Since it is with power that we are dealing, and power depends in the end on material force, even brute physical strength, an associated mystique is that of the fighting man. 'Every man', said Dr Johnson in the eighteenth century, `thinks meanly of himself for not having been a soldier, or not having been at sea.' In our day the underlying truth of this has been variously illustrated by the preva-lence of dangerous sports, the cult of violence in modern literature, art and film, and the general tendency towards student and mob violence in times of peace. Edward III, who unlike his father and grandson instinctively understood this primitive truth, successfully reigned for half a century. The courtesy, the gentle-ness, the very presence of women in the court, paradoxically depended on the court's primitive fighting ability by which, in the end, it justified itself and sustained itself in being. Even its deep sacredness was partially militant. Christi-anity has never been a pacifist religion. Fourteenth-century Christianity was as ready to bless the knight with the sword as the recluse with a hair shirt.

From the point of view of the individual much of the general value set on war can be summed up in the sentiment of honour, common to traditional societies in the West from the Mediterranean to Iceland; mighty now, and mightier then. The notion of honour is often confused, nobly but erroneously, with moral rectitude. Honour is only incidentally a moral quality, in that it implies having a good reputation, and therefore some goodness will be called for. The essence of honour is a more fundamental, less moral, `goodness'; it is that fundamental integrity in a man which is physical bravery, with the social glory derived from it. Honour is, so to speak, the biological virtue of being a man. The corresponding integrity and biological virtue for a woman is chastity, or, if married, faithfulness to her husband. It was recognized that men and women are different and have different roles. Consequently a man's unchastity and a woman's fearfulness do not lose honour. Equally, a chaste man and a brave woman do not, as such, gain it. Monks and priests are outside the honour system. Joan of Arc was burned as a witch, rather than admired as a brave enemy or ally. Honour is supreme social magic, and was particularly strong on the Continent of Europe, as in Iceland. The English have always had a utilitarian bent which makes such magic less

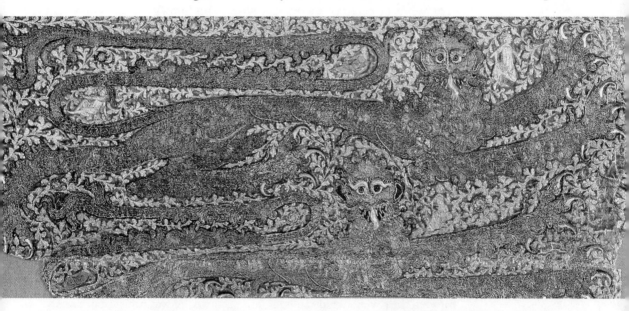

The leopards of England — with their sharp claws. 'Opus Anglicanum' embroidery on a royal banner

strong, and there were even fourteenth-century condemnations of honour by clerics in England. Chaucer does not much mention honour, but nevertheless his perception of its power underlies very much of what he writes, and he never condemns it — rather the reverse. If it was strong for Chaucer, how much stronger it was for more conventional, less thoughtful and learned men.

Add to honour the glamour and excitement that so easily stirs the hormones of young men — the gleaming sword and lance, the dramatically fierce self-display of armour, the comradeship of danger and debauchery. The excitement of war is symbolically and actually sexual, just as sex (for men at least) is symbolically and actually aggressive. Add further to that the discovery of rich lands to loot, the pleasures to young men of sheer destruction, slaughter and rape, the actual profit with which to comfort body and mind in dignified anecdotal middle age. Edward III's youngest son, the unamiable Duke of Gloucester succinctly expressed the appeal of war in 1393, in a conversation reliably reported by

Froissart. Gloucester invoked the glories of Edward III and contrasted with that king the sloth of Richard II, who did not want war. `He (Richard) careth for nothing but for meat and drink, and rest and dallying with ladies and damsels: this is no life for men of war that will deserve to have honour by prowess of deeds of arms. The men of England desire to have war rather than peace, for they can better live in war than in peace.'

In 1359 these feelings and ideas were strong. There was real hope that Edward could consolidate the previous glorious victories of Crécy and Poitiers, capture Paris, and seize the very crown of France. Something of the wider scene will be told in a later chapter. Here we need only follow briefly the outline of the campaign as far as we may guess that it affected Chaucer.

He was probably thrilled by the story of the Black Prince's successful ravaging through France in 1355 to 1357 and his great triumph at Poitiers in 1356, when he captured the French King John himself. Geoffrey now saw the great preparations made for Edward's supreme effort against France. As usual we are ignorant of all sorts of details and can only, helped by the facts in the *Chaucer Life Records*, imagine a plausible account.

Geoffrey's lady, Elizabeth, did not of course go to war, but her husband Lionel did and Geoffrey presumably served with his rather small contingent of seventy men, plus *valetti*, or 'yeomen', among whom Geoffrey was probably numbered. Like everyone else from high to low he was indentured as a soldier and paid, or at least promised, daily wages. Whereas the Black Prince received 20s. a day, Geoffrey was paid 6d. in addition to rations. The horse-archers, with whom lay so much of the English success in set-piece battles where the French knights used to rush into their lethal hail of arrows, were also paid 6d. a day. Welsh foot soldiers were well-off at 2d. a day. (For comparison, a ploughman was usually paid about 12s. – 144d. – a year, with no hope of loot.)

As we know from Chaucer's evidence in the Scrope-Grosvenor case he was 'armed' in this campaign. As a *valettus* or 'yeoman' his equipment was roughly that of an esquire, and there can have been little or no difference in practice between the two notional ranks. If, as I suppose, he was nineteen or twenty, we may think of him as a squire, and he probably wore slightly less heavy armour than a knight. There would be an iron helmet, with protection for the face given by the hinged vizor; body armour of a mixture of chainmail and plate, worn over a thick padded *habergeon* of cloth or leather; iron gauntlets. He would have carried sword and knife, and possibly a spear for his knight.

The campaign was slow to get under way. A huge amount of supporting provisions had to be assembled because the north of France had been so harried and wasted over the previous years that it was no longer possible for an army fully to live off the country. Eventually King Edward gathered at Dover the largest army that had ever left England, composed of men between twenty and sixty years old, says Froissart, together with the Black Prince, Lionel (with Geoffrey Chaucer insignificantly in his train), John of Gaunt, little older than Geoffrey, and the king's young son Edmund. The great host crossed to Calais, and an exciting and confused sight it was in those autumn days of 1359, with all the hundreds of little ships bobbing up and down by the shore, the loading of 6000 carts, all the horses for them (four horses to a cart) and for great numbers of knights, squires and mounted archers, and all the provisions. Hand mills for grinding flour and ovens to bake bread in, were taken, and even portable leather boats, not as assault craft but for fishing in rivers, so that the king should have enough fish next Lent; for the king had vowed not to return before he had made a sufficiently favourable peace, or died in the attempt.

Calais was already terribly crowded by free-lance troops who had come, unasked, to join Edward's army. They had eaten up most of the supplies and pawned their own armour while Edward was slowly gathering his forces and were in no very good temper. The princes of the blood would have had good accommodation taken over for them. Geoffrey would be lucky to find a heap of straw in a corner.

After a short pause they moved out from Calais, and it was joy to see the splendid array, well disciplined and organized, gleaming armour, rich banners, as with Theseus in *The Knight's Tale*,

> Thus rit this duc, thus rit this conquerour [rides]
> And in his hoost of chivalrie the flour.
>   *CT* I, ll. 981–2

In the vanguard were 500 armed knights and 1000 archers; then came the king's division, 3000 men-at-arms, and 5000 archers, all mounted, and in good order. After the king's division came all the baggage train, which stretched out over a distance of six miles. After this, and thereby enclosing the vulnerable provisions section in a steel guard, came the Black Prince's division, which included his brothers (thus Geoffrey too) and comprising 2000 'spears'. The whole vast train moved about twelve miles a day. When out in the open country the order of battle changed somewhat and Edward deployed his usual three-pronged attack, with himself commanding the central main division (which presumably included most of the baggage wagons), the Black Prince another, probably with his young inexperienced brothers, and Henry, Duke of Lancaster, who had gone ahead and now joined the main force, probably commanding the third.

They covered the ground like locusts, and though well managed, it was a dismal campaign. The countryside in early winter was already desolate, and in many places land had not been ploughed for three years. Apart from a few obsti-nate, stupid, optimistic or unlucky people the population retreated to garrisoned towns, some of which were taken and looted with savage zest.

One can reconstruct in imagination a diary of a representative day for Geoffrey. Horns blow at dawn, or soon after. Get up from sleeping fully dressed in a half-ruined cottage. Pull on stiff, cold, soggy boots. Shivering, light a few sticks of firewood either by blowing on warm ash from last night's fire, or by laboriously striking flint against steel to make sparks fall on tinder or dry moss. Warm some wine and spices and put together some stale bread for the knight's, or Lionel's, breakfast and call him. Help him to dress, or go outside and make sure the grooms are getting the horses harnessed. Look at the harness, worry

about one of the horses' loose shoes, or the touch of lameness. Make sure own
horse is all right. Dodge back in, out of the almost continuous rain, into the
dreary house, now bare, with doors and even structural timbers pulled down by
the soldiers for fire. A couple of hours have now gone by. Still raining. Mud very
sticky. Get into the line of march, with much shouting and cursing. Wait for an
hour before starting. Men begin to stray away. Sent to round them up, and take
the opportunity for half an hour's canter to warm the blood and see if there is any
forage to be found the other side of the big wood. Chased and nearly caught by a
group of French men-at-arms, and badly frightened. Lucky the horse (father's
present) is so good. Return to the division, to find it slowly moving. Move at the
pace of the slowest cart. Ride past with averted eyes a couple of ragged old
peasants weeping and begging. Their equally ragged daughter lying by a bush a
few yards off with a queue of soldiers. Each throws a coin by her side as he leaves
her. The last gives her a clout under the chin, collects up the coins and reports to
his laughing comrades. Slowly ride on. Column of smoke on left – farmhouse
burning, some figures moving in the wood. After a while pause, rest the horses;
some bread and wine and a mush of bread and cabbage in hot water, with a
knob of meat. Start again, a bit warmer and the rain stopped. Soldiers sing and
chat. One or two tell ingeniously dirty comic stories. But it is difficult to hear on
horseback over the jingle of harness, creaking and grinding of carts, slopping or
clatter of hooves on the wet or stony tracks. In the afternoon sent to scout ahead
and around a bit to look for a place to stay at night. Under the guidance of a great
man from the Black Prince's household several squires find a small abbey. They
enter, tell the monks to get out. They can have the sheds outside as a concession
(though eventually the archers will dispossess them of that); allow the abbot a
small room; divide the better rooms up for the prince and his brothers; get the
servants to bring up the abbey's stores. A better supper than usual. In the evening
some songs – those haunting medieval modal tunes – comic or sad, of love rather
than good life. Tales, too, of the great battles, especially recent Poitiers, from the
veterans, recalling the shock of onslaught, the whistle of arrows, the thrusting and
chopping, utter confusion, shouts and screams, and afterwards the pillagers,
stripping the dead and even the wounded – unless the heraldic colours of the
latter showed them to be worth ransom. A boy's heavy sleep ends the day.

In the general course of the campaign, here and there a sharp attack is made,
some English killed, some French men, more French women and children. The
army follows the line of the rivers and eventually the three divisions invest
Rheims, dominated by its huge cathedral. But the citizens have had plenty of
warning, the walls are good, and Edward knows that he cannot take it by storm.
It is 4 December, cold and wet. Clothes wet, or at least damp, all the time. But
natural cloth and fur are still the best for such conditions, and Geoffrey is well
kitted-out by the countess and his father. Nothing to do but make oneself as
comfortable as possible. Lionel goes hawking and hunting most days with his
father and the nobles. Geoffrey sometimes goes with him. Did he but know it,
Guillaume de Machaut, his most admired poet, now an elderly cleric, is shut up
in Rheims. But he doesn't know it, and could do nothing about it if he did. He

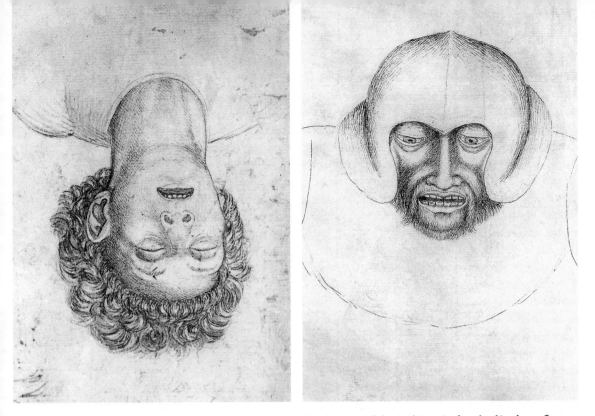

Two faces of war, sketched by Pisanello

turns over verses, his own and other people's, in his mind as he lies by a fire, or huddled in a cloak. One must endure. This is war, but in the end, not very interesting. Geoffrey's first trip to France shows him something very different from the sunny May mornings of French literature.

As we know, Geoffrey got captured, though we do not know how. Froissart gives several vivid accounts of how it could happen which also give a flavour of the war. In some such skirmish was Geoffrey knocked down and picked up. On about 1 March 1360 the king paid £16 for his ransom. It would appear that Geoffrey was captured some time after the king had lifted the siege of Rheims on 11 January and had forced his way into Burgundy. Prisoners were ransomed during the course of the campaign. Richard Sturry, a king's esquire some ten years older than Chaucer, was ransomed about 12 January for £50 (assuming that the king's contribution was the whole sum required and that the delivery of the prisoner came soon after the approximate date of the grant). George *vallettus*, or yeoman, of the Countess of Ulster; Nicholas Falconer (who may have been a yeoman or squire in charge of falcons); William Verder, described as valletus to the queen; were all three similarly ransomed by the king at £10 a head. Geoffrey was worth much more than these, and twice as much as the chaplain John of Champagne who was released for a mere £8. A squire of the Burgundian knight Sir William de Grauntson was, however, worth £20. Geoffrey's status measured by these amounts looks like that of a junior squire.

Also on 1 March were ransomed two *garciones* who had been captured by the enemy. Their status was perhaps that of a page or some junior servant, and they were jointly worth only 52s. The name of one was Thomas of Chester, and though this must have been a common name it does happen also to be the name of the otherwise unknown poet of the poem *Sir Launfal*, a short so-called Breton lay, which shows signs of having been influenced by Chaucer's *Parliament of Fowls*. It seems also possible that Thomas of Chester may have written two other romances, *Libeaus Desconus and Octavian*, poems in the 'tail-rhyme' form which Chaucer enjoyed in youth and mocked when mature. It would be agreeable to think of Thomas of Chester as a very junior marginal member of the courtly circles to which Chaucer more closely belonged. This would explain both his knowledge of Chaucer, and a certain roughness and naivety of his style. It would put these romances as contemporary with Chaucer and show Chaucer in his fifties satirizing through *Sir Thopas* an author perhaps slightly known to him from early days on campaign in France. Chaucer's own audience knew these tail-rhyme romances quite well, as Chaucer's allusions show, and many of his hearers probably took a more unsophisticated pleasure in them than he did.

We have a splendid idealized portrait by Chaucer himself of a twenty-year-old squire in *The General Prologue* to *The Canterbury Tales*, written some thirty years later. He is a lusty young man, nimble and very strong, with hair as curly as if the curling tongs had been used, high-spirited, and singing or playing the flute all day long. He wears a fashionable short gown embroidered with white and red flowers like a meadow, and with exaggeratedly long and wide sleeves. He rides well, jousts well, dances well, writes well, and can both make and write songs. All this is typical of the type, though Chaucer also adds the unusual detail that he can draw well, which I do not think occurs in any other account of a squire's accomplishments. Up to this point, though the spirit of the portrait must surely suit Geoffrey himself, we cannot be sure how far it is a self-portrait of himself in youth even though he was in 1359–60 about the same age. He must have jousted, but it is hard to see him as a frequent and very successful tournament hearty. But the drawing, so unusual a talent, might well fit a more contemplative man who often shows in his poetry a particular interest in pictures, a sharp eye for vivid realistic detail and, later, a practical interest in the cost of colours. If Geoffrey sketched he would not have sketched landscapes or mood pictures but vignettes of the kind we find in the contemporary Pepys's Sketchbook, such as those of birds, or the kind of sketches we find round the margins of manuscripts like the so-called Queen Mary Psalter, or the vignettes and grotesques of the East Anglian manuscripts of the fourteenth century. It is in such marginalia that a secular worldly element entered into a primarily religious world. The Squire of *The General Prologue* has also, like Chaucer, been on campaign in Artois and Picardy, and has done very well, although in so short a time, in the hope of standing high in his lady's favour — we are not told whether this might include being captured by the enemy. He is anyway an ardent lover, who spends many a sleepless night. He is courteous, eager to serve, and carves before his father at table. He is altogether a model young man in the courtly ideal, such as Geoffrey might well have wished to be. And the whole portrait shows a profound acceptance of the values of the courtly life, with no hint of rebellion or discontent or criticism. Loyalty, love, service, valour, beauty: these are the graces of courtly life. They are the glamour of life, they feed the imagination, they are non-utilitarian, often

The hauberk, made entirely of steel links, was an essential part of a knight's equipment during the Hundred Years War. Since each link had to be attached by hand, a small army of craftsmen such as this one must have been needed to meet the total requirement.

Der vor bruder der do starb der hieß heintz
und was ain Salbüret

'unrealistic' and 'impractical'. They are the essence of the 'magnificence' that medieval kings sought to express in their courts. These values and graces need no special defence or commendation, because even in our apparently utilitarian world they are what normal men and women legitimately desire. They appeal as strongly to natural feeling now (see the advertisements in the glossy magazines) as they did in the fourteenth century, or in ancient Egyptian dynasties. They are primitive or archaic, in that their appeal is a human constant.

This primitive or archaic (not old-fashioned or out-of-date) quality of the courtly values which were deeply engrained in Geoffrey by his own desire contrast with the other more modern feelings and interests, equally deep in him, which were much more practical and intellectual, connected with the city, where love, valour and loyalty – in a word, personal relationships – might seem irrelevant, or at best an agreeable decoration, not an intrinsic virtue. There was a certain potential clash here which we can detect in Chaucer's ambivalent and ironic or simply detached attitudes to many things that he also appears to value.

Courtly values were also constantly criticized from another base, less different but more obviously hostile, that of religion. The Church, in the name of other-worldliness, constantly attacked courtly values as worldly. Love of self and of others was idolatry when it came before the love of God. Carnal delights, from sex to fighting, the whole gamut of deadly sins from pride to sloth, destroyed the spirit. Christianity also attacked such courtly worldliness on the basis of a more profound Christian yet practical worldliness which without denying the obvious fact that men are unequal, that talents and duties are diverse, that some men must obey others, also proclaimed the need for justice in the distribution of worldly goods, for fair rewards for labour, fair solution of disputes, for peace and prosperity for all. The Church's attack was confused and often ineffective not only because of normal human corruption but also because of the tangled historical situation whereby the Church to survive at all was part of the system it partly condemned, and was itself bound to be worldly in both good and bad senses. But many preachers, like the admirable Thomas Brinton, Bishop of Rochester 1373–89, whom Chaucer must have heard preach before the court, though he venerated the Black Prince, unweariedly castigated the vices of the courtly class and their exploitation of the poor. Even if courtly values were good in themselves, they might merely give a gloss to gross cruelty, self-indulgence, injustice and exploitation.

Yet it was still possible for the Squire's father, the Knight, as described in *The General Prologue*, to be devoutly Christian as well as courtly. The implicit contradictions were there, but could be bridged, after a fashion, as with the father, or ignored, as with the Squire. At the age of twenty Geoffrey, like most of us, was probably ready enough to ignore them, and quite sensible for a time to do so. The other sides of his nature, other interests of his mind, would come out later. Meanwhile, he remained in the service of either the Countess Elizabeth or the earl, for he carried letters for Lionel from Calais to England some time in October. After that there is a break in the records for five and a half years.

In the fourteenth century stained glass (of which this is an outstanding example) there is a movement away from stiffness and stylization; instead, one can detect a growing realism and delicacy of feeling – as here in the intimacy which the artist has conveyed between mother and child. The development was one which took place in the visual arts and literature alike, and, at least in England, the work of Chaucer is its most brilliant manifestation.

BEGINNING A CAREER

E CAN BE FAIRLY CERTAIN THAT IN 1360 CHAUCER was in one of the Ulster households since he carried letters for Lionel from France to England in October 1360. The next record is from 1366 and finds him on a journey through Navarre, which at least testifies to steady progress and increased responsibility in his career as courtier/civil servant. The previous five and a half years remain a blank. The theory that at least part of this time could have been spent as a student at one of the Inns of Court is now discounted because the supposed Inn, the Inner Temple, did not at that time exist.

Although Chaucer as a youth or young man was at least important enough to be ransomed by the king after his capture to the not inconsiderable tune of £16, as noted above, he was not important enough to figure in any record of the period in question that survives – of course many records have disappeared. The great historian of medieval English administration, T.F. Tout, argued that Chaucer's whole career centred on the households of the king and his sons. He was convinced that 'the excellent education which Geoffrey undoubtedly received was the education which the household of a king, or one of the greater magnates, could give to its junior members' (Tout (1929) 382). The implication is that Chaucer in this period served in a great household where he received further training. Unfortunately we have virtually no detailed information about how such training was given, but the king's court was the archetype of the great magnate's household in which Chaucer most likely served.

The earlier part of the decade of the 1360s was perhaps the most brilliant period of Edward III's reign, when he was at the height of his prestige. Although the campaign of 1359–60 had not achieved its intended aim of capture of Rheims and then Paris and so the establishment of Edward III's claim to the French throne had indeed compromised to the extent of relinquishing That claim – it seems to have been felt at the time that the Treaty of Bretigny with which it was concluded was satisfactory. The English court was of course centred on the king and his personal household, which was the peak of the political, social, administrative affairs of the kingdom. It attracted men of high calibre of all kinds from great nobles to ecclesiastics with all their associated following, engaged in politics, administration, ceremonial (the very important outward sign of what was felt to be an inward invisible grace) and festivity, a combination in which it was difficult to say where one activity began and another ended. It was

OPPOSITE *'It hath and schal ben evermor | That love is maister wher he wile . . .' (John Gower)*

often equally uncertain where a man's ultimate allegiance might lie – to his immediate lord, whether lay or ecclesiastical, or to the king, or indeed to his own interest, which could be determined by which great lord he backed. Nor must one forget the considerable merchant element whose money was vital to Edward, concentrated in the great men of the City of London. These men, like Chaucer's own father, a prosperous wine merchant, often had close personal relations with the king's household, to the extent, in the case of Chaucer's father, deputy butler to the court, of attending the king on his long foreign trips to the Netherlands between 1338 and 1340. Edward III's genius as king partly lay in his ability to hold together the waning factions of this inherently contentious society, striving for power and for honour as both reputation and profit. Edward III's success was underlined by the failure of his grandson, Richard II, to hold the centre. Then things fell apart, despite the powerful mystique of royalty.

If we suppose Chaucer to have been about twenty years old in 1360 he would have been very acceptable to the royal or some baronial or princely household. Such households replicated on a smaller scale the household of the king with a similar mixture of elements. It was a hierarchical society where powerful and weak, rich and poor, young and old lived cheek by jowl, rich robes by dirty smocks. Service in such courts offered the possibility of some upward social mobility by the very nature of apprenticeship, by developing practice, and thus eventually achieving a position based on aptitude. A number of records tell of the steady upward progress especially of clerics, whose careers are more easily traced. Tout saw a slow development in the fourteenth century whereby some especially of the middle rank of household officers became to some extent servants of the state – the beginning of something like a modern British Civil Service – rather than the followers and servants of some great man, even the king, to whose fate they were bound. This development became clearer at the end of the fourteenth century when almost all 'household' officials easily transferred their service from Richard II to Henry IV. The transition was no doubt made the easier by Richard's alienation of almost all classes except the small group of his particular favourites, but one is nevertheless conscious that there was a 'machinery of government' whose loyalty was to the state, or to put it less anachronistically, to the king, whoever he was, rather than to the person of the current king. This attitude was the stronger in that the king himself was always felt to be subject to the law, based on a powerful set of notions of customary law derived from natural law. Chaucer was surely part of this movement.

The multitude of servants in a great household, especially the king's, were divided up into departments, which in the royal household became the great departments of state. Within these was a multitude of devolving duties and responsibilities and it is natural to suppose that Chaucer was given further training in some such department. This would not have been simple clerking in an enclosed office all the time. He was still a courtier, and it would seem likely that he was entrusted with such other tasks as that on which he was recorded in October 1360 in the accounts of Lionel's household. His colleagues would have been similar to those when he was a page. Their everyday speech was English, but he

'A Sergeant of the Lawe, ware and wys . . .'

would have become accustomed to the Anglicised French and Latin of the official documents. He would have acquired 'a wide acquaintance with official forms and precedents, the traditions of his office, the corresponding formalities and traditions of foreign courts and offices, skill in the art of dictamen or literary composition and form, and a good knowledge of law, municipal, civil and ecclesiastical. How was all this knowledge obtained? Mainly, I feel convinced, by apprenticeship under a master, the method in which all knowledge was acquired in the Middle Ages. The junior official copied forms under direction, until he was skilful enough to write them on his own responsibility. Ultimately he became in his turn, the master, the instructor and director, of his juniors.' (Tout (1929) 368). In later life Chaucer made a jesting comment on this situation when, in *The Nun's Priest's Tale*, he wrote a mocking parody of that master of rhetoric, from whom Chaucer had indeed learned much, 'O Gaufred, deere maister soverayn' (*NPT, CT* VII, 3347) – 'Gaufred' being Geoffroi de Vinsauf, author of a famous treatise on rhetoric and poetry, the *Poetria Nova* written in the thirteenth century.

We may perhaps add to the formidable list of accomplishments needed by the lay courtier/civil servant the practice of accounting, since that is what Chaucer later had to do, at least part of his time, when appointed, as noted below, to the Controllerships of the Wool Custom and the petty Customs (Chapter Eight). We should also recall that such learning was not systematic but practical, touching on what is of immediate use. It could not be hugely extensive. It left time for other activities. In the famous passage referring to Chaucer's own work The Eagle supposed to be transporting him remarks that he is a dull man who after he has made his 'rekenynges' (*HF* 653) that is, his accounts, presumably at the Custom House, goes home and reads another book until his eyes are dazed. But before this, somewhat inconsistently, the Eagle has remarked that for a long time Chaucer has 'served Venus and Cupid' without reward by making 'bookys, songes, dytees, / In ryme or elles in cadence' (*HF* 622–3). Whatever is meant by 'cadence' – probably rhythmic prose – it is clear that Chaucer has also been writing poetry and literary prose, almost certainly in English, not accounts or formulaic business letters or the like. There may well have been a tension between the two activities all his life. Chaucer had to keep his accounts in order to continue his career and receive an income as a proto-civil servant when he would much rather have been reading and writing other books. The point is that both official and literary activities would have been fostered by his life as a young man in a great court. There were a number of literate men about the courts. The most famous example is John Froissart the chronicler, poet, and nominally in Holy Orders, who was attached to the service of Edward's Queen Philippa 1360–7. Chaucer leaned heavily on his verses when writing his earliest known great poem *The Book of the Duchess*, for which a plausible date is late 1368. He must have surely known Froissart, who mentions Chaucer in his *Chronicles*, though as a minor diplomat, not poet.

We may note that much of Chaucer's reading was in French – That is, continental French, in which was written the fashionable poetry of his day, like that of Froissart. His only use of Anglo-French seems to have been much later, for *The*

Man of Law's Tale. He probably also read Italian. His culture, like that of all educated men, was European, where the *lingua franca* was French. For all that, his own bent was for the English language, without the chauvinism of some generally lowerranked Englishmen, like Minot, composer of boastful warsongs.

So Chaucer's unrecorded years were presumably, in the light of slightly later evidence, spent learning the skills both of civil servant and courtier, bearing in mind that both kinds of activity were interrelated. The emerging literate layman, of whom Chaucer was a leading example, needed financial support unless, like Gower, most unusually, he was a landowner of private means. By contrast with the civil servant who was a cleric, in however minor orders, the layman could not be rewarded with church offices which provided an income and the opportunity to place a deputy or no one at all to fulfil the duties. For the literate layman a courtier's appeal and the support of patrons were essential. The king had many paid offices at his disposal, as, to a lesser extent, did great barons. Offices were obtained by petition and service. The services were by no means nominal, though the rewards differed greatly. The great men about the king received huge grants of lands and other perquisites. To them that hath shall be given. Men of less state, like Chaucer, received less, but throughout his life, as will be seen, he obtained a stream of respectable appointments.

Possibly The reference to a lack of reward in that passage of *The House of Fame* already referred to (*HF* 614–60, specifically 1.619) besides being ostensibly a disclaimer of success in love, also obliquely calls attention to his need for something more solid as well.

Besides the practice in administration, the courtier's skills in song and conversation in French and English, his own reading and writing in English, which was rapidly becoming the dominant language of courtly society, Chaucer's time was taken up with missions such as the earlier letter carrying. We can be sure of this because he surfaces in a remarkably indirect way as the bearer of a safeconduct (an official letter declaring that the bearer must not be molested) issued by the King of Navarre in February 1366 to Geoffrey Chaucer with three unnamed companions, to allow him to travel through Navarre, which bordered the south of Aquitaine, ruled since 1360 by the Black Prince. It is by no means unlikely that Chaucer served some time in the household of that paragon of European chivalry, eldest son of King Edward. The The document is now in the archives of Navarre in Pamplona. No evidence for his journey has been found in England, and the purpose of his journey is not stated in the safe conduct. Navarre comprised what is now the northern part of Spain, the country of the Basques. It was independent of the principal Spanish kingdom of Leon and Castile, and was ruled by the appropriately named Charles the Bad.

English links with the kingdoms of Spain were in the 1360s close, continuous and complicated. Spain was not in the English mind a little faraway country with which English interests were not concerned. It was possible to sail from Bristol to Compostela in a week with reasonable weather. By land, what was important was that the English had long held the fief of Gascony or Aquitaine (called by the French Guienne) which extended from north of Bordeaux to the

A ship in a storm: St Nicholas rebukes the tempest. An early fifteenth-century painting by Bicci di Lorenzo, in the Ashmolean Museum, Oxford

border of Navarre. Aquitaine was very important because it was so rich. The French king claimed overlordship (not possession) of Aquitaine, and dispute over this was a principal cause of war between England and France, which brought in the Spanish kingdoms. The English garrisoned Aquitaine continuously, but the 1360s, when Aquitaine was ruled, or misruled, by the Black Prince, saw continuous crisis. The English holding was whittled down by French action to a strip of land from around Bordeaux southwards, till it came to the kingdom of Navarre, which bordered to the south on the Spanish kingdoms of Castile and Aragon. Navarre's King Charles the Bad (1322–87) played fast and loose with both French and English. The neighbouring kingdom of Castile was particularly important, since it possessed a highly efficient permanent navy, which if allied with France could and eventually did penetrate to the English Channel, give France and Castile control of the seas, capture shipping, and raid and burn English south-coast towns. From 1350 to 1369 the King of Castile was Don Pedro, referred to by Chaucer as the noble, worthy Pedro, glory of Spain (Monk's Tale CT VII, 2375) and by his enemies as Pedro the Cruel. Pedro was inclined to the English side, but in 1367 was ousted from his throne by his half-brother Henry of Trastamara, who was supported by the French. The Black Prince had been made Duke of Aquitaine and had held a magnificent court in Bordeaux from 1362 onwards. He invaded Spain in support of Pedro in 1367 and won the famous battle of Najera near Pamplona, thus enabling Pedro to regain his throne. The Black Prince, however, either for chivalric or economic reasons, would not hand Pedro's captured enemies over to him (in which case they would certainly have been murdered), but eventually released them; so that within two years they murdered Pedro – hence Chaucer's lament in The Monk's

A palmer seeking a strange land – St James of Compostella as a pilgrim, with his scallop-shell badge

Tale. Pedro had failed in his promise to pay the Black Prince for his military services, and the prince returned to oppress the Gascons with heavier taxation in order to pay his army. He had also contracted the wasting disease that stultified the last ten years of his life. Castile allied with France. Navarre oscillated.

There were thus a good many Englishmen in Navarre at various times in the 1360s. It was also on the overland pilgrim route from France to the popular shrine of St James of Compostela, in northwest Spain, which the Wife of Bath had visited, and where Chaucer might conceivably have been going to in 1366. But Geoffrey Chaucer when young, for all his piety, does not strike one as a devout pilgrim, and it is far more likely that he was on some sort of official business, of a kind that frequently occupied his travels in later life. It was not unusual for esquires to move about from service in one royal household to another, and it is quite possible that when the countess of Ulster died in 1363, Geoffrey moved over to the Black Prince's court in Aquitaine. Throughout his later life he is associated with that group of soldiers, administrators and courtiers, the Lollard knights, who had served with the Black Prince in Aquitaine and Spain. They had close ties with his wife, later widow, Joan, the Fair Maid of Kent, mother of Richard II. The foundations of this life-long association might have been laid by service with the Black Prince in Aquitaine any time from 1362 onwards. The trip to Spain might then have been a normal minor diplomatic mission of a familiar kind from the Black Prince's court to that of Navarre, or, passing through Navarre, to the court of Pedro. Some personal knowledge of Pedro would account for the very unusual way in which his fate is sincerely lamented in The Monk's Tale by a poet who makes extraordinarily rare reference to contemporary affairs. But it must also be added that Chaucer's wife became lady-in-waiting to Pedro's daughter Constance of Castile when that lady married John of Gaunt as his second wife, so Chaucer had other reasons at least to know about Pedro and to feel on his side.

There is no sign that Chaucer knew anything of Spanish literature, though the most famous fourteenth-century Spanish poem El Libro de Buen Amor by Juan Ruiz, Archdeacon of Hita, is a very 'Gothic' work which recalls Chaucer's work in general, with its mixture of serious and flippant styles, multiple points of view, puns, proverbs, traditional stories, realism, satire, and a serious ending. There was scope for temperaments like Chaucer's in the fourteenth century.

The journey through Navarre would presumably have started in any case from Bordeaux. Either Chaucer was at Bordeaux already, with the Black Prince, or he sailed there from England, a journey that might take about ten days. It would have been familiar to him already at least in name, not only because of the war but because of the wine shipments that his father made from this most famous of the wine ports, where so much claret came from. When Chaucer described the Shipman in The General Prologue it is from Bordeaux that he says the Shipman brings the wine that he filches on voyage. The Shipman also knows every creek in Brittany and in Spain, and has a range from Hull to Carthage, which would include the whole of the Spanish coastline. Spain, including what are now called the Straits of Gibraltar, is referred to some dozen times in

Chaucer's works, France being mentioned a little more often and Italy much more often. The wine merchant's son took a poor view of Spanish wine, which was often used to adulterate good Bordeaux claret. From Bordeaux he rode along the flat and sandy coast with his three companions, their servants, baggage, riding horses and packhorses, taking, as necessary, guides from village to village, staying the night in inns, or occasionally at monasteries or private houses. In February it would not have been weather for sleeping out if they could avoid it, especially as they might have moved through the western end of the Pyrenees. These splendid mountains made no impression at all on Geoffrey's poetic imagination, anymore than did those on the way in his later journeys to Italy. One of the three passes through the Pyrenees that he might have used is Roncesvalles, where Roland fought his last battle against the Saracens, too proud to sound his horn to call for help; Chaucer refers to the story as early as The Book of the Duchess, and partic ularly associates it with the death of Pedro in The Monk's Tale. But the human drama, and the personal betrayal, interest him, not the scenery. South of the pyrenees the land sloped downward through forests of pine, beech, oak and chestnut, interspersed with pastures, and rich in game, even bears, and rivers and streams full of fish. Pamplona was the only considerable town. It would have been an interesting journey, but in general it may be said that though Spain was decidedly a part of Chaucer's imagination, its warring kingdoms gave him no special imaginative stimulus. Spain was as marginal to the French and Italian core of European culture in the fourteenth century as was England.

The possibility that Chaucer spent some time in Aquitaine is strengthened by his marriage, for we now hear of his wife. She was Philippa, and on 12 September 1366 she is recorded as a ladyinwaiting to Edward's Queen Philippa, receiving for her duties an annuity of ten marks, £6. 13s. 4d. By this time the king's and queen's households were amalgamated. Philippa was almost certainly one of the daughters of Sir Giles Roelt, a herald who was Guienne King of Arms, that is, King of Arms for Aquitaine. Perhaps Chaucer met Philippa out there, and they both returned to England after his February trip through Navarre. She seems to have been in the queen's service before Geoffrey got his job with the king. And she was undoubtedly a lady, since her father was a gentleman. Heralds were very characteristic medieval courtly officers, with numerous ceremonial tasks and duties, responsible for the important business of allotting distinctive arms to those judged entitled to them, the seriousness of which can be judged from the proceedings of the ScropeGrosvenor case. Heralds were also organizers and umpires of tournaments, and envoys in times of war. Geoffrey was marrying right into the centre of traditional courtly ceremony.

Sir Giles was a Flemish knight with lands in Hainault where Queen Philippa had come from. For some time he was one of her knights, and had also been the master of the household of the Empress of Germany, who was Queen Philippa's sister. He was, in other words, a career court officer, who moved between related royal households. It was not too difficult for him to get both his daughters jobs in royal English households. Philippa became ladyinwaiting to the queen. His other daughter, Katharine, became governess to John of

*'And pleyinge
entrechaungeden hire
ryneges . . .*

Lancaster's children by Blanche. Sir Giles was more usually called Sir Payne, which seems to be a nickname meaning, in French, either 'peacock' or 'pawn'. Perhaps he was rather a flashy, boastful, cocky little man. We know no more about him, except that he died in England, and was buried in Old St Paul's.

As to Philippa there is a steady sequence of payments of her annuity (usually collected by her husband when he collected his own) up to 18 June 1387. He drew his alone on 7 November, so Philippa died that autumn. They had just over twenty years of married life, and may be considered lucky to have had so much. Even so, Philippa was probably only in her forties when she died. They lived much apart, because Philippa became lady-in-waiting to Lancaster's second wife, Constance of Castile, whom he married in 1371, and who spent much time out of London, while Chaucer was mostly in London when he was not travelling abroad. They had at least two children.

It was not unusual for squires to be married to ladies-in-waiting and the Chaucers were a typical pair of courtiers. Philippa and Geoffrey are both found in a list of the king's household of 1368 showing those to whom robes and allowances were granted for Christmas 1368, and in another list of 1369 showing those to whom mourning was issued on the death of Queen Philippa. In 1368 Philippa Chaucer is one of thirteen ladies and in 1369 one of a group of sixteen. In 1368 she comes in a group immediately after the wives of the great men, but in a longer list of 1369 she is a little lower. In this second list we may observe a symbolic detail very characteristic of courtly society. The granddaughters of the king, the little children of John of Gaunt, and some ladies equally high in rank, are each issued with twelve ells of black cloth, and the Countess of Brittany indeed gets thirteen. The sister of the dead queen gets twelve also, plus furs. Other not quite so great ladies get nine ells, with furs; two more, eight ells, without. Then follows a large group, clearly ladies-in-waiting, who are less distinguished, of which Philippa Chaucer is one, and they get only six ells 'long'. In the next group of ladies inferior in rank again, each gets six ells 'short'. Then we turn to important knights, who get nine ells 'long'. The officers of the king's household vary between twelve and nine.

The length of cloth was determined not by practical considerations of size, or of number of suits needed, but mainly by rank. All the gentlemen of the king's chamber, including Chaucer, got three ells 'short'. The system is not quite simple, because to Walter Norman and his forty-one companions, 'noz Bargemen' in the 'French', and to one hundred and twenty-four grooms, are granted four ells in black and one en laeur, for some reason I do not understand.

The queen died on 14 August 1369. We next find Philippa Chaucer mentioned when she was granted in August 1372 an annuity of £10 for services to John of Gaunt's new wife, Constance of Castile, daughter of Don Pedro, to whom a daughter was born in 1372, and a son in 1374 who died in infancy. As far as can be seen Philippa remained in attendance on Constance fairly steadily all her life. Constance herself died in March 1394. Constance was 'a pattern of orderly and devout living', who spent half her not very long life in England. She made little impression on the English court, and neither tried nor was encouraged to identify herself with English life. Hers was a political marriage, and no doubt her heart remained in Spain partly because Lancaster in marrying her hoped to succeed to the Spanish throne; but also because Philippa Chaucer's sister Katharine, wife of Sir Hugh Swynford, became Gaunt's mistress round about the very time that Gaunt married Constance. Katharine's position was openly acknowledged not only in Gaunt's splendid palace in the Strand, the Savoy, and his castle of Hertford, but even at great court ceremonies such as the Feast of the Garter, and at Westminster. She received many handsome grants from John of Gaunt and must have become rich. When Constance died the adultery was openly acknowledged in seeking (and receiving) the pope's dispensation for it when Gaunt married Katharine and legitimized their four bastards, already high in places of honour and profit in church and kingdom.

It used to be thought that with this close family connection through his wife Chaucer himself could be regarded as under the patronage of John of Gaunt, but such was not the case. Philippa herself may have benefited to the extent of receiving gifts, such as the six silver-gilt buttons and the 'buttoner' she received as a New Year's gift, 1 January 1373. A buttoner was a strip of material with buttons attached to it, and since it could be embroidered with roses and pearls it could cost as much as ten marks, which was the amount of the annuity granted to Philippa by King Edward III. So it was not an inconsiderable gift. On the other hand, that and the silver-gilt hanap, or goblet, which she, like three other ladies-in-waiting, received as a New Year's gift in 1380 and other cups given in 1381 and 1382, though valuable, are quite comparable with gifts to other courtiers and show no special favour at all. There are no records of other gifts or grants. On 19 February 1386, Philippa was admitted to the fraternity of Lincoln Cathedral. The fraternity was a group of lay people who were associated with the canons who (under the dean) ran the cathedral and its services, and it was very much a Lancastrian family interest. The brothers and sisters of the fraternity received spiritual benefits, such as those of the thirty or forty masses celebrated every week in the cathedral by the resident clergy. These accumulated merit that would shorten the soul's stay after death in purgatory (which is where, at best, one can only imagine the souls of courtiers went). So the fraternity was worth belonging to. John of Gaunt was a member. On this particular family occasion were admitted John's eldest son Henry Bolingbroke, Earl of Derby, now aged nearly nineteen, the future King Henry IV; John Beaufort, John's bastard by Katharine Swynford; Katharine's own grown-up legitimate son Thomas Swynford; and one Robert Ferrers now aged thirteen, who was to marry Joan Beaufort, Katharine's bastard daughter. It must have seemed only fair to bring faithful if 'illegitimate' Aunt Philippa in on such a family party. Probably Katharine was already a member. The only one left out would appear to be John's own legitimate wife, poor neglected devout Constance herself.

This glance ahead has already shown something of the life at court which was Chaucer's environment for the next twenty years. His annuity was granted 'for good service' done and to be done by 'our beloved *vallectus*' (in the Latin) or 'esquier' (in the French) and though these writs and patents are all written in a highly conventional style it may be that Chaucer had some earlier service as well in the king's household. The way it worked, broadly speaking, was that the king, or more likely the steward or treasurer of his household, agreed to employ Chaucer either at his own petition or at that of some friend or relation with influence. The steward or treasurer sent instructions to the Keeper of the Privy Seal, one of whose clerks made out a letter patent in French to the Keeper of the Great Seal, the Chancellor. A clerk 'enrolled' a translation into Latin of the letter patent in the roll for the year, and issued a copy to Chaucer. When Chaucer wished to collect his money he also had to have an authorization or mandate, sometimes called a *Liberate*, which he had to present at Easter and Michaelmas each year in order to collect the money in two instalments. Often enough he did this on Philippa's behalf as well. The system was relatively elaborate and efficiently maintained. Sometimes Chaucer borrowed in advance and occasionally was abroad when he should have collected; occasionally payments fell into arrears or were collected by somebody else on his behalf. But in general he and Philippa received their salaries quite regularly. Usually the payee could collect in cash from the Exchequer, but sometimes money was paid by 'assignment'; that is, the payee was told to collect his money from someone else who owed money to the king. Sometimes the debtor could not or would not pay, in which case the payee had to go back to the Exchequer and more complicated accounting proce-dures would take place, usually involving a fictitious loan by the payee to the king, which would then be 'repaid' in cash, leaving the original accounting details of the unsuccessful assignment unchanged on the general record (the Issue Roll) though cancelled on the Receipt Roll, when these rolls were entered up after intervals of daily accounting. There were also further auditing and control-ling devices. These are some of the sinews that lay under the surface of courtly magnificence and indeed made much of it possible. The offices and clerks were part of the more general network of hundreds of people about the king's court and elsewhere who carried out the middling sort of jobs, and received the middling sort of sinecures, that fell to Chaucer. We meet many names of such people again and again in the *Life Records*. Above them were the greater gentry and prelates who were leaders in policy, faction and administration, culminating in the magnates, and bishops who were so often chancellors, the stewards of the household, who also gathered into their circle the great merchants. It is difficult to form a clear idea of the numbers involved, but when, for example, an order was made to the Clerk of the Great Wardrobe to deliver robes for Christmas 1368, which included both Chaucer and his wife, both king's and queen's households, the list begins with the royal dukes on the left, their ladies on the right, and so on downwards through knights, clerks, esquires, serjeants-at-arms, other serjeants, esquire falconers, heralds, minstrels, various 'boys', and the whole list ultimately extends to the number of more than six hundred persons. Somewhere in the upper echelon of this crowd we must locate Chaucer's friends, his primary audience, and his first readers. If we take the top level there were about thirteen ladies to forty-odd men, so that Chaucer's immediate audience had, as we might guess from his poems, a fair if not large proportion of ladies.

It is not known if the robes were all of the same kind. Robes were valuable and the cost must have been considerable. Also implied is a large number of subsidiary servants, not only the tailors required here, but the servants of most of the six-hundred-odd people given robes. And all these people needed food and accommodation. This varied mass of people who were strictly graded and conscious of rank, who yet necessarily lived in close and familiar proximity with each other, must have provided a fascinating and attractive spectacle to a highly imaginative man. It often provided his primary audience. Yet the stresses and strains of court life must have been almost equally repulsive. It was an arena for struggling ambition, treachery and lust. Chaucer was divided in himself between sympathy and a caustic cynicism, or religious disgust. 'Flee from the press [crowd] and dwell with soothfastness' is the first line and general theme of one of his rare poems of personal expressiveness.

He was eager for courtly life in one part of himself. Nearly a year after Philippa Chaucer was appointed Geoffrey himself is found on the roster of the king's household 20 June 1367 awarded an annuity of twenty marks.

CHAPTER FIVE

AT THE COURT OF EDWARD III

CHAUCER's ANNUITY WAS AWARDED IN JUNE 1367 FOR good service done and to be done by our beloved vallectus (in the Latin) or *esquier* (in the French). *Vallectus* is usually translated 'yeoman', a grade lower than 'esquire', but the French versions of these contracts are less precise than the more official Latin. In November 1368 and May 1369 he is described as an esquier and in September 1369 as an esquire of 'less degree', all of which signifies an assured position in the household, not menial, but not in the inner circle of the king's *secreta familia*.

The court, that potent though to us mysterious amalgam of the sacred, the glamorous, the utilitarian, and the sordidly selfish, complicated as it was, revolved round the personality of the king, who gave it its characteristic tone and style. It was Edward III's strength and weakness that he seems almost completely to have realized, until he became prematurely aged, the fourteenth-century English ideal of a king.

His earliest independent act, in 1330 at the age of eighteen, was to capture Roger Mortimer, his mother's lover and effective ruler of the country. Mortimer's tyranny had become as oppressive as that of the favourites of the murdered Edward II, and he became as much hated. Edward was the centre of the plot to remove him, helped or at least encouraged by the elderly Duke of Lancaster, and by Richard Bury, later Bishop of Durham, who was keeper of the Privy Seal. More vigorous support came to Edward from his friend of the same age, William Montagu, a yeoman of the king's household. By a daring stroke Edward with a group of young friends surprised Mortimer at Nottingham Castle, and a few weeks later Mortimer's peers in parliament sentenced him to the gruesome traitor's death of hanging followed by disembowelling while still alive. He was the first to be executed at Tyburn and the king ordered his body to be left on the gallows for two nights and days as a lesson to all men. But there was no general persecution. Edward treated his mother generously and though she had to give up the great revenues she had acquired, she was allowed to retire, still only thirty-six years old, to Castle Rising in Norfolk (now a noble ruin) with £3000 a year, to while away her time with hawking, romances and piety.

Edward established excellent relationships with the magnates and others who helped govern the realm. The Duke of Lancaster took little part in public life after Mortimer's fall, but his son and eventual successor, Henry of Grosmont,

OPPOSITE *St George, patron of the Order of the Garter. Detail of a retable by Jacques de Bauze in the Musée des Beaux-Arts, Dijon*

one of the finest men of the century, remained for a generation Edward's friend. The savage rivalries of Edward II's reign were healed by Edward's behaviour, which was simply the unforced expression of his character and tastes, so typical of the nobility. Sir Thomas Gray, Edward's contemporary, both knight and chronicler, refers in his *Scalacronica* with approval to Edward and his friends leading their young lives in pleasant fashion. Edward had the knack of doing what everybody thought were the right things for a medieval king, making war, distributing largesse, and in peacetime indulging in tournaments, hawking, hunting, churchgoing, making love, encouraging those about him to do the same. This is the honourable courtly life. But war was of its essence.

There is no need here to discuss the complex beginnings and conduct of the so-called Hundred Years War, which dragged on intermittently from 1339 to 1453. The French king was undoubtedly provocative. Edward had some possible legal right. There was ancient hostility between France and England, as between Scotland and England, and there was a dangerous alliance between Scotland and France. There were French and Scottish acts of piracy in the Channel and complicated feuds and alliances between the various kingdoms and duchies of northern Europe. But in the end the nub of the matter is made plain by Froissart, that the king, who was then in the flower of his youth, desired nothing so much as to have deeds of arms. War was the function of nobility, and his counsellors told him of the rich loot to be had from undefended Normandy, where the people were not used to war.

Edward knew when to take advice. He was also an admirable military commander. He grasped and held firmly on to a principle of three-pronged attack or defence, combined with the maintenance of a tactical reserve, which stood him in good stead time and again. So the English harrowed Normandy, with much success, the soldiers attacking towns, killing the men, raping the women, looting their goods, and burning what they could not take away. A cruel war, even Froissart says. But it was the deplorable practice of the times. It seemed natural to rise before dawn in the bright summer weather, as the king did on 26 July 1346, hear mass before sunrise, and then lead an army into the good town of Caen, full of drapery and other merchandise, and rich townsmen, noble ladies and fair churches, especially two great and rich abbeys, and to kill and rob, though Sir Thomas Holland rode into the streets and saved many ladies and nuns from defouling; for, says Froissart, the soldiers were without mercy. The king became very angry – because the townspeople defended themselves so vigorously and killed or wounded more than five hundred Englishmen. He was only persuaded not to make a total slaughter of the townspeople because he would lose more men who would be needed later. Sir Thomas Holland (who was distinguished by having only one eye) had had a good day. Besides saving many ladies he had captured the Constable of France and the Earl of Tancarville, and Edward bought these valuable commodities from him for 20,000 nobles, that gold coin first minted in his reign, worth 6s. 8d.

This particular *chevauchée*, or in Chaucer's word, *chivachye*, of the kind which he himself, and the Squire in *The Canterbury Tales*, made in Picardy and Artois,

Looting a house

was distinguished by the battle of Crécy, by which Edward and the Black Prince confirmed their European fame, and Edward's character is glimpsed. On the Friday night, 25 August, the king gave supper to his chief lords, and when they departed entered his oratory to pray that he might conduct the next day to his honour (rather than victory). Edward went to bed about midnight, but was up early to hear mass, and with his son and most of his company was confessed and shriven. Then he ordered everyone to the chosen place of battle. He made excellent dispositions with a fortified place by a wood for the baggage train and horses, having dismounted his knights. He divided the army as usual into three 'battles' or divisions, and commanded the third division himself, as a tactical reserve. The first division was commanded by Edward of Woodstock, eldest son of Edward, who was made Prince of Wales, and was now a boy aged sixteen, known to historians, though not to his contemporaries, as the Black Prince.

The course of the battle is no part of Edward's personal character, though it witnesses to his genius and luck as a commander. The French were in disarray, the English archers shot with their accustomed fierceness and accuracy, the half-naked little Welshmen in Edward's army with their long knives hamstrung horses and killed knights lying helpless in armour on the ground. The French greatly outnumbered the king's force and fought bravely, so that the front division led by the Black Prince was hard pressed. It is here that the revealing anecdote comes, whatever its basis in actual truth. Those around the prince sent a messenger to the king asking him to bring up his reserve. According to Froissart (in Lord Berners's translation) the king asked,

'Is my son dead or hurt or on the earth felled?' 'No sir', quoth the knight, 'but he is hardly matched; wherefore he hath need of your aid.' 'Well', said the king, 'return to him and to them that sent you hither and say to them that they send no more to me for any adventure that falleth, as long as my son is alive; and also say to them that they suffer him this day to win his spurs; for if God be pleased, I will this journey [i.e. day of battle] be his and the honour thereof, and to them that be about him.'

So the knight returned and the men around the prince were much encouraged.

Froissart alone tells the story of the burghers of Calais but there seems no reason to disbelieve it and it reflects Edward's character. As the king's siege of Calais pressed the town harder and harder the captain of Calais sent all the poor people, men, women and children, out of the town to save pro⁄ visions, to the number of 1700. When these miserable refugees approached the English they were asked by the English what they were about. When he heard of their plight Edward ordered them to be given a meal and two pennies each as alms. Such inconsistent generosity slightly modifies the horror of war, but what could have been the subsequent fate of such destitute people, bereft of everything? It seems not to have occurred to those who pitied them that they had caused their distress.

When the defenders of Calais were reduced by starvation they wished to discuss honourable terms of surrender. But Edward, once again angered by resist⁄ance, demanded unconditional surrender, with the chance that he would put many to death. His captains remonstrated; so according to Froissart, he required six of the chief burgesses of the town to come out bare⁄headed, bare⁄foot and bare⁄legged, in their shirts, with halters about their necks, with the keys of the town and castle in their hands, and to yield themselves entirely to his will. The actual humiliation with its expressive, demonstrative, and as one may say, artistic symbolism, is typical of the man and his age. All the English who saw the burgesses, the most distinguished men in Calais, wept for pity, but the king looked savagely at them and ordered their heads to be cut off. Not even Sir Walter Manny's interposition could save them. Then Queen Philippa, great with child (as usual) knelt to Edward, and he relented. There is a close analogue to this scene, which has never been noted, in Chaucer's *Knight's Tale*, when Duke Theseus out hunting finds the young knights Palamon and Arcite fighting. One has escaped from Theseus's prison, the other has been banished on pain of death. Theseus shakes with anger and will have them put to death, but his queen and her sister implore him to spare them. Eventually he reflects that 'Pity runneth soon in noble heart' and relents. It is hard not to feel that Chaucer had in mind many of the traits of Edward III in his prime, when he was drawing the portrait of the fiery, magnanimous, chivalric Theseus in *The Knight's Tale*.

Edward was loved because he no more spared himself than his people or his enemies. He was prepared to take romantic risks. In April 1331, when only nineteen years old, and soon after his successful coup, he had a secret meeting with Philip of Valois, King of France, at Pont⁄Saint⁄Maxence to which he travelled disguised as a merchant. His companion, only a couple of years older, was Henry of Grosmont. There is reliable documentation for the episode but it sounds like an episode from the *Arabian Nights*, or medieval romance. Edward held tournaments three or four times a year in great splendour. On 9 April 1348 there was one at Lichfield, in which the king himself took part wearing the arms of Sir Thomas de Bladeston. The principal participants were given blue robes with white hoods, and the king's daughter Isabella, six ladies of high rank, and twenty-one other ladies, presumably damoiselles, ladies-in-waiting, like Chaucer's wife later, wearing coats and hoods of a similar kind, with visors and masks in addition, were prominent in the festivities. Ladies again in masks entered the city of Canterbury in procession with the jousters in 1348. These joyous festivals seem to have continued with little regard for the Black Death.

Still more like romance, and illustrative of another side of Edward's character, is Froissart's story of how he fell in love with the Countess of Salisbury. Like so much of Froissart's history this is gossip raised to the level of art; but there may be some basis of historical fact, and the story is emblematic of love-sentiment in Edward's court. The episode is said to have occurred in the Scots war of 1341, when Edward was about thirty years old, married fifteen years, and father of several children. The Scots were besieging a castle (perhaps Wark Castle) which belonged to the Earl of Salisbury, himself a prisoner in France, and defended by his countess. The Scots withdrew at Edward's speedy approach,

A lady of Edward III's court

much to his chagrin, though his men and horses were tired. He took over the Scots' quarters and visited the lady and castle. She came out to greet him richly dressed, 'that every man marvelled of her beauty and could not cease to regard her nobleness, with her great beauty, and the gracious words and countenance that she made. When she came to the king, she kneeled down to the earth, thanking him of his succours, and so led him into the castle to make him cheer and honour, as she that could right well do it.' It is not surprising that the king 'was stricken therewith to the heart with a sparkle of fine love that endured long after'. So they entered the castle hand in hand. At last the king went to a window seat and remained silent and abstracted. Everybody tried to cheer him up, and the lady delivered a loyal speech. 'Ah, fair lady', said the king, 'surely the sweet behaving, the perfect wisdom, the good grace, nobleness and excellent beauty, that I see in you, hath so sore surprised my heart, that I cannot but love you, and without your love, I am but dead.' Who could resist so direct an assault from the brave, young, cheerful and handsome King of England? But the lady did, according to Froissart, referring to her husband in prison. They washed and went to dinner, though the king could eat little and say less. His knights were astonished at his glumness, it was so unusual; some thought that it was because the Scots had escaped him. For the rest of the day love battled with honour and truth in Edward, but in the end he departed, 'all abashed', to chase the Scots.

This is 'fine love', not lechery, which, perhaps, Froissart would not have condescended to notice. The lady has been tentatively identified as Joan of Kent, the king's first cousin, who certainly at one stage of a chequered married life was Countess of Salisbury though as she was born about 1328 she would only have been thirteen or fourteen years old at the date attributed to this incident. However that was the age of Shakespeare's Juliet and Miranda, and we should think of Chaucer's Emily as about the same age. So young an ideal femininity

*'Offrande de Coeur', an
Arras tapestry in the Musée
du Louvre, Paris. The knight
is actually holding in his right
hand a heart, which he is
offering to the lady*

accounts for much in the attitude to heroines. It is noticeable that although the
lady is implicitly praised for resisting the king's advances, and no bones are
made by the cleric Froissart that his love was contrary to honour and truth, the
king is not at all condemned for his attempt on her virtue. Such is the nature of
honour. One of the many festivities Edward organized was that of 1342 when for
fifteen days, according to Froissart, nobles from England, Germany, Flanders,
Hainault and Brabant took part in tournaments in honour of the Countess of
Salisbury. On this occasion Edward wore a velvet tunic embroidered with trees,
birds, the king's arms, and tiny figures of Saracens made of gold and silver, each
containing a jewel with the king's motto.

The king has a reputation for excess in his middle years to which his prema-
ture senility is often attributed, but war and love traditionally go together and are
the product of the same carnal energies. The king was amorous, and considered
himself entitled to take his pleasures like a gentleman, without much regard for

the consequences. The traditional attitude for centuries before and after was succinctly expressed by the much admired sixteenth-century gentleman and poet, Sir Thomas Wyatt, who in the speech written to be delivered at his trial wrote, 'I grant I do not profess chastity; but yet I use not abomination', by which latter he appears to mean prostitutes. Edward no doubt felt the same. He is not likely to have made a practice of seducing the wives of the barons with whom he achieved so harmonious a relationship, and they would in general have had much the same attitude as he – and many modern people – though he destroyed himself and damaged the country by his self-indulgence. A prolonged flirtation with his beautiful cousin, the countess, Joan of Kent, the most charming woman in England, is possible, but eventually it was his son the Black Prince who married her, when both were in their early thirties. No chronicler however eager for scandal suggests that that prince married his father's mistress.

The countess is associated with Edward's creation of the Order of the Garter, which seems to have been his own idea, and which was so typically successful in uniting the great men (apart from the clerics) of the kingdom. The under-lying historical mythology was that of the Arthurian legend, often invoked at tournaments since the thirteenth century. It was generally believed until the middle of the seventeenth century that when Troy was destroyed by the Greeks and Aeneas had escaped to found Rome, a grandson of Aeneas, called Brutus, had discovered Britain and founded both London and a line of kings of whom Arthur was the greatest. He was thought to have lived in the fifth century AD, succeeded after his tragic fall by Constantine and then eventually by the Anglo-Saxons. Both English and Anglo-Normans by the fourteenth century accepted Arthur as their great precursor in England, possession of the land being more important than succession by blood. Arthur himself was reckoned one of the Nine Worthies – that recapitulation of the medieval secular notion of European civilization, comprising three Old Testament warrior heroes, three heroes of classical antiquity, Alexander, Hercules and Hector, and three great medieval kings, Charlemagne, Godfrey of Boulogne, and Arthur. Edward unaffectedly cast himself in the role of Arthur, and his magnates as Knights of the Round Table. The exact date of inauguration and the detailed organization of the earliest stage of the order are not quite clear, but the idea took shape around 1340, when Chaucer was born and the king was in his middle thirties, and the order was perhaps formally inaugurated on St George's Day, 23 April 1348. The making of the great round table now hung on the wall at Winchester Castle dates back even to the thirteenth century (repainted in the early sixteenth) and may have encouraged the king's enthusiasm. As at other festivals there were great jousts, which Edward loved, and feastings and dancing, and the order was publicized throughout Europe. At some stage perhaps really did occur the incident, picked up by sixteenth-century historians presumably from courtly folk tale, of how at a ball given to celebrate the fall of Calais in August 1347, the Countess of Salisbury, now a mature nineteen, dropped her garter as she danced. Edward picked up the blue ribbon and bound it round his own leg (garters being non-elastic and tied just below the knee). The gesture is gallant,

An exquisite ivory comb from the Victoria and Albert Museum, London

flamboyant, amusing, with a touch of poetry; symbolically yet delicately expressive of how the lady has fettered the knight with a light yet unbreakable, lovely bond. A private attachment is publicly though not grossly expressed in a gesture both spontaneous and ceremonious. Edward was a poet of actions rather than words, but he capped his poetic gesture with a splendidly sententious, superbly apt courtly phrase, Honi soit qui mal y pense – 'Evil to him who thinks ill of this'. It is grand, generous, and with a touch of humour. The phrase is nicely balanced between internal and external considerations: independence of public opinion is not carried to the extent of total disregard, while regard for public opinion does not lead to abandonment of personal authority. The gesture and motto are a rich symbol of Edward's gift, until his physical decline, for managing and expressing in his behaviour the dominant values of his society. He was not so much original as climactic. That the Order of the Garter was secular goes without saying, but equally inevitable was its religious dedication, to St George as the patron saint of England, and to St Edward the English royal saint. Religion and a sense of nationhood can hardly be separated, and their conjunction explains to some extent how those outside the nation (for example, the French) or those who rejected the natural hierarchic structure within the nation (for example, rebellious peasants or even earls) put themselves outside the rules of pity, justice and mercy which were supposed to operate inside the religion and the society that gave it expression. We may note that the order was also to provide for the needs of twenty-six poor fighting men, and that this original intention seems to have come to nothing.

The order, like any good club, was highly exclusive, being limited to twenty-six knights, including the sovereign. Yet within it all were equal. It is common to emphasize the hierarchical structures, the graded ranks, of medieval society, and right to do so, but it is also important to recognize areas in medieval society where men, and in some cases women, were reckoned as equal, or perhaps one might better say, since equality was not an admired concept, where rank and hierarchy were disregarded. These were areas of war and religion, though both activities were simultaneously hierarchical. Equality in a strongly structural hierarchical society may either occupy a place within the structure or from outside offer a serious challenge to the whole society. A hierarchical society that can accommodate some equality within it is clearly more flexible and complex than one that cannot make accommodations. Edward's genius was to make the accommodation without giving away essential control, at least in his own lifetime, and the Order of the Garter illustrates this. It was his grandson Richard's tragedy that he could not accommodate but must be absolute. Edward took as a basis the secular, natural, equal interest among men in fighting, and the Order of the Garter institutionalized that partial equality of comradeship that arises from war, the fundamental activity of knights, even if peacetime friendship was also envisaged. Comradeship in war, whereby men of very different ranks and temperaments share danger, hardship, and mutual support, is a profound and complicated emotional relationship not easily appreciated by modern literary intellectuals. He brilliantly symbolized it by the institution of the Order of the Garter, among his own court. Plain knights (if the term may be allowed for great captains, who acquired great wealth, like Sir John Chandos) were members, along with magnates like the Earls of Worcester and Warwick, and the king's own sons. The order may also reflect to some extent the general feeling that there is an equality among the gentry, and that the king himself can be no more than a gentleman. It also invokes that part of the family model of society, so strong in the fourteenth century, which is brother-hood. In Chaucer's most courtly poem it is notable how often Pandarus, who is not related to Troilus, and is socially inferior, calls him 'brother'. There may be a great deal of variety within the equality of brotherhood. To sum up, the Order of the Garter presented the virtues of war, hallowed by religion and nationhood, as a unifying force, with all the glamour of courtly life. The brutal, selfish, utilitarian elements in war were forgotten and in the jousts, feastings and dancing, a courtly, poetic, 'magical' image was created of immense psychological power. Edward was particularly good at creating that image, at sharing it with comrades and with his people at large, combining it nevertheless with a suitable awe. Men will do as much, or probably more, for fear as for love. A judicious combination of both makes a king men will die for.

The highwater mark of Edward's domination of France was in the late 1350s, to be confirmed, as he hoped, by coronation in Rheims. For this purpose the great campaign of 1359–60, in which as we have seen Chaucer took part, was undertaken. In the event we see that it marked the turn of the tide. The French were recovering, Edward's vast army set out a year too late to press home his advantage, and too late in the year anyway. The Treaty of Brétigny which concluded the war in May 1360 was favourable to the English more in appearance than reality, as some chroniclers realized, though it seemed to bring great gains to England. Chaucer thus as a youth came into national life and into the ambit of the king at the period of their highest success. The long following period of national and political decline and economic constriction that marked his mature lifetime may have contributed to his inner detachment and pessimistic conservatism, traditional and rational though these were.

Though no medieval king could be exactly a family man in the modern sense of the term Edward remained on sufficiently good terms with his paragon of a queen, Philippa, to give her seven sons and five daughters, of which only three died in childhood. He provided rich marriages for his children and achieved the even greater and rarer distinction for kings and fathers of all ages of remaining on excellent terms with all of them. They too remained on good terms with each other, and though this family harmony doubtless owed much to Philippa, great credit must go to Edward's geniality, sense and foresight. How valuable such a solid nucleus was to the kingdom can be seen at a glance from the distress caused by the unstabilized preferences of Edward II and Richard II.

'But all too little, waylaway the while, lasteth such joy, ythanked be Fortune, that seemeth truest when she will beguile.' So Chaucer, evoking the great commonplace of human life in contemplating the short-lived joys of Troilus. Though Edward had a long run of fifty years, the last decade and a half showed a sad decline that caused further troubles in the rest of the century. After the Treaty of Brétigny the English gains were whittled away, Edward himself, though only in his fifties, did not lead an army again, and the last half dozen years of his reign in particular were marked by hostility to the court and quite serious unrest.

A wooden effigy of Edward III made from his death mask, showing the left side of his mouth distorted, probably by a stroke

Edward's own death, however, brought forth a last expression of national unity and mourning, like that of Churchill in 1966. Froissart records how his body with great processions, lamentations and weepings, his sons behind it with all the nobles and prelates of England, was taken through the City of London 'with open visage' to Westminster Abbey, and was there buried beside the queen his wife. His tomb with the fine sculpture that with only a little stylization recreates him in the very image of a medieval king, is still to be seen. As soon as the French king heard of his death, says Froissart, he said how right nobly and valiantly he had reigned, and well he ought to be put newly in remembrance among the number of the worthies (that is, as an addition to the Nine). The king then held a service for him in the Sainte Chapelle in Paris with a great number of the nobles and prelates of France. The views of peasants and burgesses in Normandy are not recorded. Nor are Chaucer's, who was abroad at the time. But in the solemn pomp of the funeral of Arcite in The Knight's Tale we get a slightly surprising sense of how seriously he would have taken it and the proper moralizing over death, as well as a touch or two of flippancy.

Edward's character fully expressed the main traits of the characteristic courtly English culture of his time. He was not at odds with society, and in this sense he was completely conventional, and thus successful. Edward was particularly characteristic of the earlier part of the fourteenth century, before new currents of intellectual inquiry, new doubts and questions, had permeated by education into the court. One cannot imagine Edward questioning himself nor the nature of the universe, though in the latter part of the century Chaucer's own poems show that such questioning could be sympathetically received in the royal court. Edward can never have 'put himself into someone else's place' to see how it felt, can hardly have internalized any values. If he had psychological conflicts they were seen as completely external events, as in the drama he created with the Countess of Salisbury and her garter at a personal level, or, on the public stage, the whole Order of the Garter, with its externalized conflicts in the jousting he loved and excelled in, in the dramatic robes and the feasts. All this may be called conventional, if we do not assume that the convention was dull. He and the nation found it exciting and profitable. His court was full of colourful characters whom Chaucer knew at least by sight, and who affected his notions of what men might be and were.

Ladies figured much at court and intensities of feeling were surely fostered by their bright presence. They adorned feastings and dances.

> Heere (was) the revel and the jolitee
> That is nat able a dul man to devyse...
> Who koude telle yow the forme of daunces,
> So unkouthe, and swiche fresshe contenaunces,
> Swich subtil lookyng and dissymulynges
> For drede of jalouse mennes aperceyvynges?
> *Squire's Tale* C T V(F), ll. 278...86

Not only at feasts and dances, to the merry sound of the minstrels, but also at tournaments the ladies were there to admire and be admired.

Courtly amusements, to which must be added frequent hunting and hawking, in which ladies also took part, as did Queen Hypolita in *The Knight's Tale*, were themselves highly elaborate and enjoyable ceremonies, governed by strict laws of etiquette and protocol. At the same time they provided, as Chaucer's poetry shows, plenty of 'gaps' in the rigid forms, into which might slip that subtle looking and those dissimulations that provided the occasions for the often illicit joys of spontaneous sparkles of love and merriment, evasion of everyday burdens, which gave the necessary escape into a more poetic realm of personal communication, of equal love, 'when each person fully experiences the being of another'. It is this 'unofficial' element in the joys of the court that particularly interested Chaucer. The framework of courtly ceremony is always there in his courtly poems, but almost always as the background to the more individual, spontaneous, secret and intermittent life of inner feelings. Something of the complexity of the court has already been suggested, and it was becoming steadily more specialized in Chaucer's lifetime. Yet it was still very personal, 'archaic', still far from the nature of the central organization that governs a modern state.

Government was less concerned with national welfare than it is today and more with the glorifications of the king. Medieval men ... did not think a king was without duties to his subjects – they had a concept of political cooperation and no doubt many of them benefited by the more impartial justice administered by the king's judges – but neither did they think of government as being primarily utilitarian. Royal magnificence, exhibited in a splendid court, in the wearing of jewels, the maintenance of a large retinue, the building of lavish castles such as Edward III's at Windsor, and the waging of expensive wars in support of the claim to France, might sometimes be resented by those who were squeezed to pay for it, but it was generally accepted as a proper object of policy.

Nevertheless, the court must eat, receive and send money and messengers, and just as the higher element was organized, so was the lower. The higher merged into the lower, and the court had that human advantage therefore of a sense of unity and connectedness which so many medieval institutions possessed even because they were so crowded and inconvenient.

Some lists of courtiers in which Chaucer appears are very much determined by function, often quite menial. Others, for example the list of esquires given in 1369, partly abandon the functional order for a division into esquires of greater and less degree, indicating rank in the household, which was partly determined by function, partly by length of service, and partly by other factors not now to be discovered. We may consider the great career of Sir Walter Manny as an example

of how a man might rise from a relatively menial position (in this case in the queen's less important retinue) to great riches and influence. Some prelates, like William of Wykeham, who became immensely rich and powerful, show what prospects of promotion might also lie before churchmen. But most esquires remained obscure, and this was the case with Chaucer, who appears in 1369 among the esquires of less degree. Some of them held special offices. John Herlyng was the senior. He and William Walsh were ushers of the king's chamber, responsible for general organization. Herlyng might be thought of as the chamberlain. Some of the esquires managed the practical necessities. Some of them, and among these were Chaucer, were so to say King's Messengers, who travelled about, carrying letters, money, giving certain instructions, for example commandeering shipping at ports when needed, carrying out special inquiries, escorting other people. During war they served in the army about the king, as *aides-de-camp*. They also frequently travelled abroad on the king's business, often on

A squire dresses his lord by the fire

secret business as Chaucer did, on questions of money or of Richard's marriage. The recreational or occasional activities of this group of highly intelligent, well-educated men, in a court so much dedicated to 'magnificence' are suggested by the Household Book of Edward IV, written a century later, but deriving from the time of Edward III. The forty or so esquires are carefully organized. We are told of their rations, duties, pay ($7\frac{1}{2}d$. a day), clothing; how many candles, how much firewood, how much wine, etc., they are allowed. In afternoons and evenings the esquires shall 'keep honest company', 'to help occupy the court', 'in talking of chronicles of kings and of others' policies, or in piping or harping, singing, or else 'in martial acts'. Poems are not mentioned and they occupied a far less prominent place than tournaments.

The esquires who were Chaucer's companions were gentlemen, not poets, and like Chaucer often away from court. Like Chaucer, too, they received a good deal more than their daily wages, sometimes very considerable sums. The normal way of paying the esquires was by annuities, grants of land, grants of office, custody of lands belonging to heirs under age, grants allowing them to 'sell' the marriage of an heir, and corrodies, that is, rights to live free at a monastery, or be paid for not doing so. Chaucer received benefit from all these, except lands (as far as the records show) and corrodies. He received much less than some esquires, such as John Herlyng (who at various stages was given the collectorship of the petty customs of London and controllerships of customs at various ports), but more than others. Chaucer clearly occupied no post of special importance, nor was he especially cherished or favoured in the court as far as these records can show.

His colleagues were of much the same type. They were never from great families, and were usually younger sons of knights or such substantial men as merchants. John Legge, Thomas Hauteyn and Thomas Frowyk were merchants' sons. They usually had some previous appointment in the household of one of the king's children, or indeed, like Chaucer, had both.

Many of the ladies about the court, like Alice Perrers, at least in some respects, were also working courtiers and colleagues, sometimes wives, of the esquires. The lists of esquires in 1368 and 1369 are paralleled on the same page by lists of *damoiselles* of the queen, as well as of her esquires and clerks. In one case it is recorded as a meritorious action that the esquire, Edmund Rose, Keeper of the King's Horses, had married the lady, for his annuity is always marked as given for good service and because he has married Agnes Archer, formerly one of the queen's *damoiselles*. Sometimes such ladies retired on marriage from service, sometimes not. Sometimes the ladies moved from one royal household to another, like the esquires, while retaining links with the former household, as did Philippa Chaucer. One of Philippa's colleagues in the list of 1369 was Alice Perrers herself, *damoiselle* to the queen. Alice's husband, Sir William Windsor, was one of the knights of the king's chamber in 1368. Alice's greed and wealth were notorious in the 1370s, but her husband also received considerable profits for his troubles. Chaucer and his wife must have known these people reasonably well, and as already noted, Philippa Chaucer's sister Katharine Swynford, who appears in the list of 1369 as one of the *damoiselles* of the daughters of John of

John of Lancaster

Gaunt, soon became, if she was not already, his mistress. Chaucer makes no explicit comment on this society, but its presence and his response to its glamour and its vices can be felt indirectly throughout his poems. He was far from repudiating it, except perhaps at certain moments, but equally far from being totally committed to it. His rewards from it were adequate and undoubtedly much greater than the records reveal. At the same time he obviously did not seek, or at any rate did not obtain, the riches other men did. Even in the question of marriage, a number of colleagues married heiresses and became men of consequence in the country by possession of their wives' property. An esquire was a very eligible match for a moderately wealthy heiress. A woman needed a husband to protect her both legally and practically, while marriage and family are the objects of natural desire and social necessity. But though Chaucer married with social and no doubt economic profit his was not the marriage of a socially or economically ambitious man. Why should it not have been a marriage of love?

This, then, was the court, in which Chaucer was a small cog and the king the great driving wheel. Chaucer's *Knight's Tale*, remote as is the setting and fantastic as are one or two of the events, gives us the feeling of it, in the end, better than any other record. We see Theseus, another Edward, conceiving of war and love in terms of personal honour, though the poem does not neglect the horror and devastation of war. But conflict is represented rather through the clash of feeling and the stylized splendour of the tournament than in actual war. The jealousies of courtly life and festival are noted in *The Squire's Tale*, but it is in *The Knight's Tale* that the ruthless Arcite expresses the all-too-common view that

> at the kynges court, my brother,
> Ech man for hymself, ther is noon oother.
> *CT I*, ll. 1181–2

The horror of Arcite's physical suffering leading to painful death vividly recreates the undisguised brutality of death, in court as in town, village or field of battle, that was commonplace in the fourteenth century; and we share the human poignancy of grief at loss of the beloved. The philosophizings of Theseus about the inevitability of death, the acceptance of suffering, the need to make a virtue of necessity, are a high poetical rendering of the resolute sober commonplaces with which all sensible people encounter the sorrows and disasters of life and continue to live. They express how John of Gaunt must have borne the death of his beloved wife Blanche, or Joan of Kent the death of Edward the Black Prince. In the ceremoniousness of the funeral of Arcite, for all the exotic trappings of the funeral pyre so remote from English burial, we hear an echo, as the corpse is carried openly with bare face, splendid clothing, hands in white gloves, of the magnificent sorrow of England at the funerals of Edward III and the Black Prince. The marriage of the hero Palamon to Emily in the story is the fruit of love, but is also based on dynastic and utilitarian considerations, as was John of Gaunt's marriage to the great heiress Blanche of Lancaster. The career of the disguised Arcite at the court of Theseus recalls that of Sir Walter Manny and Chaucer himself, though he did not begin so low.

Beginning as a humble hewer of wood and drawer of water employed by Emily's chamberlain, Arcite's good manners, his deeds, his 'good tongue', cause Theseus to promote him to an esquire of his chamber, and to give him 'gold to maintain his degree', i.e. an annuity and other grants. This latter is exactly what some annuities were given for in ordinary life. In the court of John of Gaunt, second only to the king's in size and magnificence, a squire and his wife were given annuities that were specially noted as being *pur le mielx leur estat maintenir* — 'the better to maintain their degree'. Arcite was also helped by having a secret private income which he spent so discreetly that no one knew he had it. Theseus took to him greatly, 'no man was dearer to him'. Edward III must similarly have been friendly with one or more squires of his chamber, precisely because they were not politically or otherwise powerful, and because they minis- tered to him constantly in domestic circumstances. Chaucer's close colleague, John de Beverley, who witnessed Edward III's will, may have been such a man. But not Chaucer. Approachable, even to the point of being condescended to by high and low, in a deep sense he kept himself to himself. He was no king's favourite, nor, for all his polite deference, in the pocket of any great man, not even Gaunt. There is no evidence that anyone was his patron or patroness, with the possible exception of whatever lady, if any, is referred to in the person of Queen Alcestis in *The Legend of Good Women*. Froissart records with pride a long list of patrons, and Lydgate and Thomas Hoccleve similarly have numbers of poems addressed to named great persons. Even Gower claims that Richard II commissioned him to write *Confessio Amantis*. This absence of patronage shows paradoxically, what *The Knight's Tale* also shows, that Chaucer was completely 'inside' the court. If Romantic poets are 'outsiders' Chaucer is the supreme example of the poet as 'insider'. Chaucer earned his living within the court and he did not need to use his poetry to attach himself to it, or as a lever for reward. His poetry, especially *The Knight's Tale*, can afford to express the court's feeling about itself. It is neither flattering nor self-satirical.

Nor, as *The Canterbury Tales* reminds us, is the court the whole of life; it may be the ever-moving imaginative and social centre of the kingdom over which Chaucer so constantly travelled, but it is not the whole of the kingdom. London and the English countryside were also a part of him, he a part of them; so too Oxford, and the wider range of France and Italy. The court was not all, any more than any of the other regions of the world or of the mind was all to Chaucer. That same inner detachment that kept him independent within the court kept him independent, perhaps in the end even lonely, within the whole populous world. As he says in the poem 'Truth' about this world,

> Her is non hoom, her nis but wildernesse.

At the same time, like the fat Monk in The General Prologue, who did not allow himself to be cooped up in the cloister he belonged to but was a business man, hunter, bon viveur, anti-traditionalist, and whose opinion that 'the world must be served' is apparently approved by the poet, Chaucer himself was ready to serve and hold after the brave new world his course.

A walking-stick handle derisively shaped like a monk's head

THE UNKNOWN YEARS

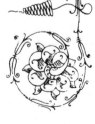

HAUCER's APPOINTMENT TO THE KING's HOUSEHOLD on 20 June 1367 committed him to serving the world pretty vigorously. Apart from the constant moving of the court itself he was sent on several journeys. On 17 July 1368 he was issued with a warrant to receive a licence to cross the sea from Dover (so old is the tedious business of passports) and he is not known to have returned before 31 October, so he might have gone as far as Italy, where Prince Lionel now was, or no further than Calais. In the following year between July and November, he was for part of the time with Gaunt on another military expedition which saw the opening of a new phase of the war, brutally raiding and burning again through the wretched regions of Artois and Picardy, like his spruce Squire of *The Canterbury Tales*.

In the summer of 1369 plague, the 'Third Pestilence' as chronicles called it, struck again and carried off Queen Philippa on 14 August. On 1 September, her sons resident in England, including Gaunt, their wives (but not including Blanche, the Duchess of Lancaster), and many members of the household, including Geoffrey and Philippa Chaucer, were issued with mourning robes for the queen. It was for her a fortunate time to die, after a decade of national success. After her death Edward himself deteriorated, and many troubles came to England. It used to be thought that Gaunt's wife Blanche the duchess, mother of his five children, including Henry Bolingbroke the future King Henry IV, died on the following 12 September. But it now appears from the discovery by Dr J. J. N. Palmer of a diplomatic letter that Blanche died on 12 September 1368. The letter is from Louis de Mâle, Count of Flanders, to Queen Philippa, and is a polite putting off of Philippa's suggestion that her son the Duke of Lancaster should marry Louis's daughter Margaret. Obviously Gaunt is now a widower. Since Margaret was married to Philip of Burgundy on 19 June 1369, Blanche's death must have occurred in the preceding September. This now explains the absence of Blanche's name, when Gaunt's and those of the wives of other sons of the king are present in the list of issues of Christmas robes to the court in December 1368 and of mourning robes on 1 September 1369, and confirms Dr Palmer's other arguments.

This diplomatic letter throws sharp light – and dark shadow – on public events, private feelings, and a poet's writing. The shadow is darker for the light. Clearly illuminated is the royal plan to marry Gaunt to Margaret. This was a

OPPOSITE *Geoffrey Chaucer – a portrait of the poet which may be seen in the National Portrait Gallery, London*

political attempt of the first importance. Louis, Count of Flanders, was lord of many fiefs, including the county of Burgundy, stretching into the very heart of French territory. His daughter Margaret would succeed to this great inheritance, not only the richest in Europe, but strategically vital to France. Edward III had already made one attempt at it, by trying to marry his son Edmund of Langley to Margaret in 1364. Gaunt had headed the diplomatic mission that had confirmed that arrangement. But Margaret was cousin to Edmund and so within the forbidden degrees of marriage. Papal dispensation was necessary. Pope Urban V, whose seat was now at Avignon, was a Frenchman, and the French king did not want an English prince as Lord of Flanders and of the county of Burgundy. So the pope had refused the dispensation and no marriage had taken place. Now, in 1368, Louis of Flanders was negotiating to marry his daughter to Philip the Bold to whom the French king had granted the duchy of Burgundy and who was therefore a vassal of the French king. Louis's letter to Philippa reveals that the English were making a desperate last-minute bid for Margaret with the only recently marriageable Gaunt. Since Louis's letter was brought to England by Sir Richard Sturry who went to Flanders on 1 December, and returned 25 December 1368, it is clear that the English bid was made in November 1368, at the latest two months after the death of Blanche. Private sentiment could not weigh against public policy; and there was anyway a hardboiled acceptance of death in the fourteenth century, even when there was an immediate wildness of grief. Gaunt's genuine love for Blanche and his grief at her death are not to be questioned. A gulf exists between public event and private feelings in all ages, but we notice it particularly in the fourteenth century because we lack the connections and filling in between the two provided by informal letters, diaries, records, gossip.

Gaunt's inner feelings are testified to by the expression of them by proxy, as it were, in Chaucer's first major poem, *The Book of the Duchess*, which is both a commemoration of the dead and a consolation offered to the living. It is an extraordinary and great poem, which has not always had the appreciation it deserves, perhaps because of its strange mixture of solemnity and flippancy, of learning and informality, sharpness and occasional longwindedness. It tells us so much about Chaucer's own inner life and general circumstances, it is so unusu-ally personal for Chaucer, that it is worth dwelling on at length. It tells us more about Chaucer than many of the later, more popular poems. What immediately strikes one is the speed with which he must have written it. The plan to marry Gaunt to Margaret of Flanders must have been discussed, even if confidentially, by mid-November. As soon as thoughts of a second marriage got about it would have been very difficult to offer Gaunt a poem expressing his undying grief for his first wife. In any case, as already noted, it was characteristic for people's passions to be violent but short-lived, and ordinary prudence would suggest writing such a poem promptly or not at all. One part of the poem tells the sad story of Ceyx and Alcyone from Ovid, and this could well have been already written because the subject of the poem, death and loss of the beloved, was one that touched Chaucer deeply. But nevertheless, the poem must have been composed as a whole and offered to Gaunt between news of Blanche's death, which Chaucer might not have had till late in September, and late in October. The poem must have been written at tremendous speed, even if the Ceyx and Alcyone section already existed. It is a different kind of poetry from modern, post-Romantic poetry, with claims to originality and obscurity. Chaucer's poetry has deep roots in the ancient world of storytelling, of poetry spoken and heard to express and vivify the great commonplaces of human experience. Poetry was used as part of courtly life (itself archaic), a recognized convention of communication, familiar as pop songs (its true descendants). Poetry was not inspirational, waiting for the spark from heaven to fall. In style Chaucer's poem draws, on the one hand, from the naïve, informal, racy style of the English romances, with its easy English provinciality; and on the other from the most up-to-date fashionable French courtly poetry of Froissart and, especially, Machaut. Chaucer was undoubtedly disturbed by the death of a beautiful and beloved young woman. But he was also prepared with a whole repertoire of phrases and motifs with which to cobble a poem together. His dependence on Machaut is so close that he may even have been modifying while at times copying from a book. Wordsworth composed his very different kind of poem, 'Tintern Abbey', 159 lines long, entirely in his head during a four or five days' ramble through the countryside. At the same speed the 1334 lines of The *Book of the Duchess* would have needed about five weeks. But so different a style and concept of poetry, along with the need for haste and the genius of the poet, with so much of phrase and framework given, might have allowed it to be composed in a fortnight, say, in late September and early October of 1368.

Why did Chaucer write it? Why does any poet write? The possible answers are many, and not mutually exclusive. The death stirred Chaucer perhaps to write, and perhaps Gaunt heard of this and wished to know the poem. The genuine sympathy for the bereaved lover in the poem may represent a genuine offer of consolation from the poet. The poem, to judge from style and content, and the historical context of the new marriage negotiations, can hardly have been commissioned. We may allow ourselves to imagine the first reading of the poem, while Gaunt was still dejected.

Gaunt himself, the great men of his council, the esquires, perhaps some ladies, would gather in the large dark room with the great fire, and the poet would enter, darkly dressed, holding the small pamphlet in which the poem was written. Only three manuscripts survive, though there must have been more, and none is Chaucer's original or written in his lifetime. He would read, or declaim, from the manuscript, by the light of a window or candle. It is a delicate consolation, indirect, courteous, discreet and flattering. Yet it is also an extraordinary poem, because for example, of the touches of humour in it, apparently irrepressible, though Chaucer knows well they are inappropriate —

> And in my game I sayde anoon —
> And yet me lyst ryght evel to pleye.
>   II. 238—9

A poet presents his work to the king — here, Charles V of France

To summarize very briefly, the poem begins by the poet remarking on his sleeplessness because of an eight-year sickness, in a passage translated from Froissart. To while away the night he reads the story of Ceyx and Alcyone, telling how King Alcyone was drowned on a voyage and Ceyx his wife died of grief. The poet then sleeps and dreams he wakes up to join a king's hunting. But he strays away from the hunt in the forest and comes across a Man in Black lamenting his sorrows. The poet questions him about his grief, and is told the story of his love, which was eventually successful – but alas, the lady died. The poem ends abruptly with a series of punning names which make it clear that the Man in Black represents Gaunt. The poet awakes.

The manners are formal, but the tone is informal. Whatever the occasion on which it was delivered it seems a curiously private, or at any rate socially intimate sort of poem. And although the subject is another man's grief it touches a personal chord. Whether or not the conventional beginning represents a real-life unsatisfied love in this recently married poet, the general subject of loss affects him. Sorrow may even account to some extent for the uncertainty of tone, the sometimes tasteless mixture of comedy and pathos. Certain temperaments are always prone to this. One thinks of Lamb, Dickens, Charlie Chaplin as similar to Chaucer in this respect – all capable of even mawkish sentimentality and pathos, yet often incapable of keeping comedy out of the portrayal of grief.

The first word of the poem is 'I' that dominating little word of egotistical lyric which arose in medieval literature to express individual aspiration. The most natural verb to follow 'I', is 'want'; and the most natural object of desire is 'you'; and here is the pattern of love lyric, which is the largest single set of secular lyrics in the Middle Ages. The *Book of the Duchess* has a lyrical expressiveness. Yet though the poem expresses the egotistical lyric 'I', it does so indirectly through the stories told by or elicited by the narrating poet. This duality of 'I' and 'not-I' is very conspicuous throughout Chaucer's poetry, though it is also a characteristic of fourteenth-century European poetry in general, a witness to the emerging individuality of the age. In Chaucer's case the constant desire to present himself in his poetry yet also to conceal himself leads to the device of as it were acting himself. This device is rich in ambiguity and comedy. It creates a curious uncertainty of tone, more noticeable in Chaucer than in any other English poet. It allows him also to represent many facets of a story, even when they seem inconsistent with each other, as the flippancy and seriousness found in *The Book of the Duchess* seem to modern taste either indecorous or inconsistent. Yet there is also an unexpected richness in this strangely mixed poetry.

It is a courtly poem. Courtly life and convention are everywhere taken as the norm. Although the framework is fantasy, we get the very texture of courtly life in its personal aspects (not administrative or political, of course). When the goddess Juno addresses her messenger we can hear the Countess Elizabeth sending her page off on a message. In the poet's courteous and tentative style of address to the Man in Black, though he speaks with a certain freedom of inquiry as from one gentleman to another, we also hear the recognition of social distance between an esquire and one of the princes of the blood. Freedom and courtesy of interchange are strictly channelled by an appropriate style of speech and a clear sense of rank. The poet-esquire uses the formal, polite second-person plural pronoun *ye, you*; the Man in Black regularly uses the intimate, condescending singular thou, thee to his questioner, though he himself uses the inferior's plural to his own lady. The poem takes the conventional literary view, derived from French poetry, that court life centres on love, and that love is the driving force of a man's proper ambition. In one way at least this is true of courts, that personal relationships were at their centre.

Death is the great challenge to personal relationships, to courtly, indeed to all purely worldly values. If they are so easily, frequently and inevitably negated by death, what kind of values can they be? This question was a constant theme of religious instruction and meditation, reinforced by a horror-stricken fear of the loss of personal consciousness and an awareness which medieval life all too readily offered of the body's physical corruption. Yet though the suffering of profound loss is a theme of so much of Chaucer's poetry before *The Canterbury Tales*, and is no doubt part of the reason that the death of Blanche disturbed him, there is in the poem no evocation of the horror of death, nor any personal fear of death, such as animates so many religious lyrics. The Man in Black actually desires death in his sorrow, but cannot die, like the Old Man in *The Pardoner's Tale*, another poem about death that Chaucer wrote many years later. The problem in *The Book of the Duchess* is how to live with loss. Both the poet in his own person and the Man in Black have suffered loss. First of all the poet, deprived of love, is a solitary reader of the tale of Ceyx and Alcyone, unredeemed loss. Then in his own dream he leaves the hunt, and is drawn into the depths of the forest, symbolically into the inner self, where there is a mourning at the very centre. Yet in the speech of the Man in Black which tells us, at the literal level, of his (as we realize immediately) lost love, there is a delib- erate re-creation of the image of the beauty whose loss the poem, and we, mourn. There is a dual movement of loss and discovery in the poem. The discovery, the consolation, is by memory.

In a curious way the poem is like a romance. In romances the hero is often represented, psychologically speaking, by several actors in the story, as two brothers, for example. So in this poem the ultimate pain and seeking of the poet is represented by both himself in the poem and the Man in Black. In romance the hero, to remedy his lack, must leave society, be tested in solitude in various ways, find his beloved, and return to be re-integrated into society, usually a more joyful and wiser man. The same general pattern is found here. A withdrawal from courtly society into the solitary forest, traditional place of adventure and testing, a 'finding' of the beloved, in terms of the re-evocation of her beauty and lovableness, and a return to society, with that possession. But in a romance there is an advance. Romance is a rite of passage, usually from adolescence to maturity, and there is a positive gain, represented in the happy ending. This typical romance movement is shown in the Man of Black's retrospective narra- tive as he tells how he loved the lady and by implication honourably won her. The poem contains though it does not realistically represent, the actual event in life. John of Gaunt did indeed love and honourably marry Blanche of Lancaster. The narrative is not so much an idealized account of life as the ideal truth to which life was so fortunate as to approximate (and history has borne out this superiority of literary imagination over actual event in that the poem survives). But the narrative, like life, continues to death. The survival of the narrative, through the act of memory, contains even death itself and is itself a triumph over death, as memory of good fair Blanche is a triumph over her extinction. That is clearly the consolation, the sympathy, that is implicitly offered. A memory. Better to have loved and lost than never to have loved at all. A bitter commonplace. Its bleakness is remarkably honest.

The poet goes to the limit of life, to the very edge, and almost looks into the abyss. The sense of edge, gap, of almost-transition is strong. Equally strong in this poem is the resolute refusal to go over. The last rite of passage, that into death, is refused: refused in an age when the enormously dominant ecclesiastical culture was continually forcing men, in constantly reiterated sermon, meditation and lyric, to look over the edge, to shudder with horror at physical dissolution, with apprehension at the just pains of hell eternally retributive of sin, and with hope for an eternity of joy. Chaucer will have none of it. He turns back through memory, and without apology, to the carnal joy of the court. He will seek no sense of resurrection. He will not even speculate about death, which appears as a refuge, though an unavailable one, from the pain of living. In this respect the poem is very modern in feeling, though Chaucer shows no realization of the dissipating, truly nihilistic effect of our modern belief in the nothingness of death which turns life to nothingness also.

Another aspect of the modernity of feeling in the poem is the literalism attrib-uted to the person of the poet in the poem. He represents himself as incapable of understanding the simplest metaphor. Literalism is one of the greatest, if not the greatest, tools of modernity. It is that concrete precision of verbal expression, that verbal truth to physical reality, singleness of meaning and absence of ambiguity (for to be double-tongued is confusing and hypocritical or lying) upon which the huge technological advances that are modern civilization depend. Ambiguity, proverbial sententiousness, hyperbole, pun, word play, the whole apparatus of rhetoric, now a dirty word, all interfere with that clarity of meaning that is the great aim of modern culture since the seventeenth century, only very recently and by minorities to be questioned as the proper total aim of human communication. Literalism is at first frustrated by the Man in Black's tradi-tional hyperbole, ambiguity and rhetoric, but the end of the poem is a literalistic acceptance of death. The rhetorical creation of the memory of Blanche is indeed allowed, but to the literal mind 'She is dead', and that is the supreme truth. Literalism is realistic; is modern.

This 'modernity', if such it may be called, has paradoxically reinforced the traditional, archaistic, conservative aspect of the courtly life whose principal value is the pride of life, which in the end can only exist in memory. Heaven and Hell are by definition (whether they exist or not) the only true present because they are eternal. All else must flow into the past. For this reason Christianity,

with its eyes on something after death, must always have something of a progressive, innovatory quality, hostile to the past, abandoning it for the true present of
eternity. Chaucer shows no profound religious sense in *The Book of the Duchess*.
Though there are the phrases of traditional piety, Chaucer disregards religion
entirely and considers only the court as 'real' life. In the end the poem is an anti-
romance. Yes, it says, you may love, and even win your love, and be loved in
turn, but you will lose your beloved. Your consolation is that what has been has
been. There is something stoical, yet at the same time frustrated, helpless, even a
hard, accepting shoulder-shrugging casualness in the abrupt ending of the poem:

Man in Black	'She ys ded!'
Poet	'Nay!'
Man in Black	'Yis, be my trouthe!'
Poet	'Is that youre los? Be God, hyt ys routhe!',
	And with that word ryght anoon
	They gan to strake forth; al was doon. . . [sound the return]
	ll. 1309–12

What a pity! Still, life must go on. There is a deliberate trailing away, a deliberate anti-climactic triviality, at the end of the poem. So it is with soldiers about
the casualties in their own ranks. The fourteenth-century court was a hard as
well as splendid world.

Of course there is still a surrounding deliberate ambiguity which frames the
literalism. Chaucer keeps many of his options open in *The Book of the Duchess*,
which makes no claim to be a complete statement, a complete image of life and
death. It is part of a larger court culture and we may put beside it, as probably
composed about the same time, *An ABC*, a fine translation of an ingenious and
pious French poem of devotion to the Virgin Mary, clear evidence of that
genuine piety that is part of Chaucer's mind and culture all his lifetime. It
hardly conflicts with the worldly values of the court life, except by implications
that few noticed, for it activates the same emotions of reverence for a woman,
acceptance of her moral superiority, desire to be taken under her wing, as does
the secular love poetry. In the secular poetry a sweetheart, in the religious poetry
a mother-image, is invoked, but each is tender, feminine, superior and
comforting. In most secular love poetry the fierce possessiveness of male sexual
desire is subdued, as in the devotion to the Virgin is excluded the fear, resentment and desire to escape which is part of the totality of attitude to the mother-
image (as we see in *Sir Gawain and the Green Knight*). The religious poetry is more
sentimentalized than the secular because some elements of both fear and fierce
desire enter the more complex secular love poetry.

The devotion to the Virgin in *An ABC* is rather a part of cultural than
personal religion, in that it had singularly little effect in mitigating the cruelties
practised by those who professed it. But it had seeds of grace, and was not
hypocritical. The seeds were ready to sprout, however, in a new domestic
tenderness, a new power of internal imagination, under the influence of certain
Italian developments in prose rather than verse. They were spreading through
Europe and Chaucer was soon to make direct contact with them.

CHAPTER SEVEN

CHAUCER AND ITALY

OR THREE YEARS AFTER THE COMPLETION OF *The Book of the Duchess* Chaucer and his wife followed the busy varied duties of courtiership, regularly collecting in person or by deputy half-yearly payments of their salaries. In August 1372 Philippa was for the first time paid also as lady-in-waiting to Gaunt's second wife Constance, when Constance, and presumably Philippa too, was at Hertford Castle. Gaunt himself was at Sandwich. Chaucer was presumably with the king somewhere else. But a further, longer separation was at hand, for in November Chaucer was commissioned to make a journey to Italy to negotiate with the doge and commonalty of Genoa, which was at that time one of the many separate small Italian states. Small as they were they were rich and powerful enough to be worth negotiating with for international trade and credit, then as now vital English concerns. A commercial treaty had recently been agreed between Genoa and England. There was now the question of arranging a special commercial port in England for the Genoese. No statement survives about the negotiations, though for the credit of our poet as political envoy we may note that at least trade flourished in the following years. The Genoese continued to use Southampton extensively and there was a group of Genoese in London, along with men from the other great Italian cities, Milan, Venice, Lucca, Florence, Siena. The Genoese also provided ships and crossbowmen, at a price, for the English king. However, Chaucer was not the principal emissary in this affair. Jacopo di Provano, a native of Carignano, and John de Mari, a Genoese, were his two companions, who had both negotiated for King Edward before. Of these two, Mari was the higher paid and more important. Chaucer himself was, however, entrusted with a further secret mission to Florence, which possibly concerned yet another international loan from one of the great Italian banking houses. Though both the Italians must have spoken English, one of Chaucer's uses may have been that he could already speak and read Italian moderately well. He might help to convey general English policy and keep an eye on the principal negotiators without himself having any particular authority. Yet Chaucer had enough individual responsibility and good enough Italian (and French) to go on to Florence on his own to convey messages and instructions.

Mari and Provano were, in the eyes of the world, the notable men on this Italian journey. Diplomacy, trade and finance help to keep us alive, and modify

OPPOSITE *'Strong was the wyn, and wel to drynke us leste': a sketch of an Italian wine shop by Pisanello*

our sensibilities. Chaucer could not have been the poet he was if he had not recognized and largely accepted the world's values, but he would have appreciated the irony that it was the fat little Englishman, with his love of private reading and writing, who turned out to be far the most significant of the three. And with all the important diplomatic and trade issues of the mission, what made it really important was that the Englishman bought two or three quite well-known books of poetry at a Florence bookstall.

Chaucer's personal allowance was 13s. 4d. a day. He left London on 1 December 1372 and arrived in Genoa between 1 and 10 January 1373 – roughly a thousand miles, averaging around thirty miles a day. At some time he left Genoa for Florence, and he probably spent some weeks in each city. At the latest he left Genoa early in April, and Florence about mid-April, arriving back in England by 23 May. The Italian journey took five to six weeks each way. His route can now be followed on the great motor roads of Europe in fewer days than he took weeks. How differently we hurtle along from his trotting slowly on horseback through some of the harshest, and gentlest, in each case some of the most beautiful, scenery in Europe. There was no forgetting the cold winter weather then, nor the fatigue of thirty miles a day on horseback.

Between the great Gothic churches of Westminster and Canterbury some of the loveliest countryside in England lay under old December's bareness everywhere, and the cold sword of winter gave some preliminary prods, gentle to what the three men would later endure. They had with them a couple of Genoese crossbowmen, perhaps one or two more men-at-arms, as escort, and some servants, all on horseback, and with packhorses too. A little cavalcade of a familiar kind. Then to Dover, to await a fair wind for France, and to cross in a bouncing round boat, taking perhaps eight hours, to land, like so many million tourists later, at Calais, then in English hands. Up till now all was familiar. Then eastwards along the flat and dreary coast with its sand dunes towards the rich merchant towns of Bruges and Ghent (whence John of Lancaster drew his name, John of Gaunt, for he was born there). These were rich and lovely towns with stone houses and fine churches. Bruges was also remarkable for its great canals. They went this way because war with France during 1372 and 1373 made travel through France dangerous if not impossible for an Englishman. This was a well-known merchant route over well-marked roads, with inns, which took them through Brussels, Maastricht, Aachen (or Aix-la-Chapelle), the ancient capital of Charlemagne. All this was flattish, well-wooded country, some of the most prosperous in Europe, with independent and rather turbulent towns, and familiar to Chaucer not only from English diplomatic relationships and military associations but because his wife's family came from Hainault in the same region, and Flemings were well known in London.

Continuing eastwards they came to the Rhine either at Cologne or Bonn. At Cologne they could have seen the colossal cathedral, still standing today though most of the centre of Cologne was destroyed in 1944. Cologne was an ancient Roman city, but more significant for medieval men because the three kings, the Magi of the Christmas story, were reputed to have finished their journeyings and

OPPOSITE *Embroidery was one of the great English arts in the thirteenth and fourteenth centuries. This sumptuous example in gold, silver and silk thread on velvet illustrates the rich culture of the period. It shows the three Magi, whose shrine was the great Cathedral of Cologne, visited by the Wife of Bath and probably by Chaucer himself.*

OVERLEAF *Lorenzetti's fresco in the Town Hall, Siena (see p. 126), showing the effects of good government on the town (above) and countryside (below)*

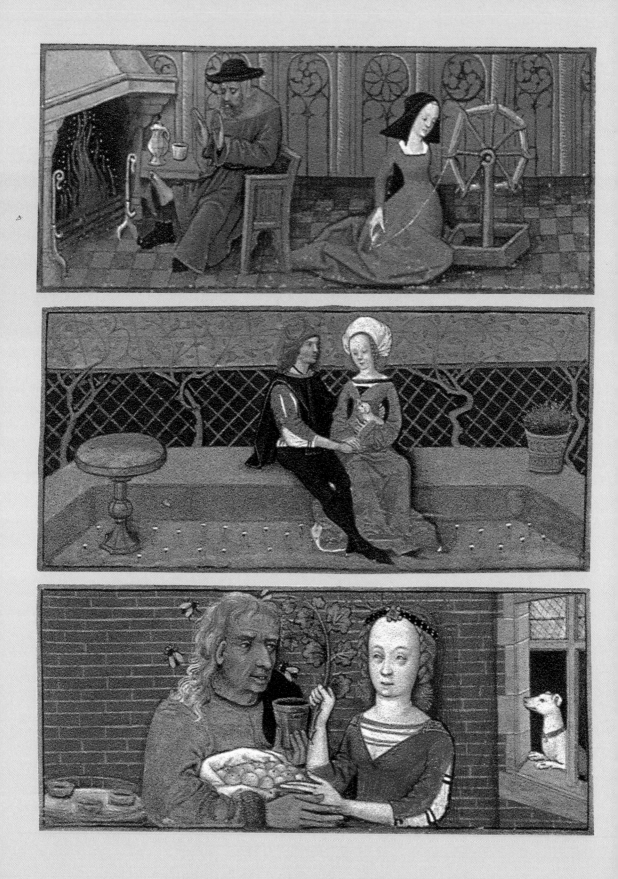

lives there. Even in Chaucer's day it was an industrial centre and some of the best armour in Europe was made there, such as was bought by the Black Prince. It was also known to the English as on the way to the Prussian border where constant warfare was carried on against the heathen Lithuanians, in which atrocious cruelty was dignified by the name of crusade. Great soldiers passed there, like Henry of Grosmont and later his grandson Henry (then of Derby, son of John of Gaunt and in the end Henry IV of England). Like them, Chaucer's own ideal Knight in the *General Prologue* had often been guest of honour in Prussia, and no man of his rank had fought so often in Lithuania and Russia. Chaucer would have imagined him as so far on the same route.

At Cologne or Bonn they took a boat and sailed or were rowed up the broad, smooth-flowing Rhine, through some of the most romantic country in Europe, edged by steep vineyards, wooded mountains, and picturesque castles then inhabited by a savage soldiery. There were great abbeys and fine churches to be seen, as well as riverside hovels of peasants and little wooden towns. The brilliantly realistic yet highly artistic painted sculpture of the churches must surely have pleased Chaucer. In the cold weather the jagged shores, whirlpools and rocks of the Loreley area might allow the formation of ice, and cause delay, but probably the journey upstream to Basle was uneventful. This is a land of legend, of Rhine maidens and the Nibelungen story, ancient in origin, and the subject of a great twelfth-century German romance; but Chaucer shows no sign of knowing German, nor of being interested in primitive, mythical or psychological folk tales, any more than he was interested in the striking barrenness of mountain scenery. He was too much a rationalistic, 'southern' man, not one for northern mistiness and mysticism, and wild nature was too close for most medieval men to have our aesthetic feeling for it. He passed under the fine bridge by noble Heidelberg and the great cathedral of Strasbourg, and no doubt felt relief that he had not to ride through the Black Forest. At Basle the three envoys had to take to horseback again and follow one of the most ancient routes to Italy, by continuing south to the severe beauty of the Lake of Geneva (Léman) at Lausanne, with the snow-covered mountains around. The most testing part was now to come, for the high Alps lay ahead. They had passed the road over rich and rolling if snowy countryside. They now turned east to Vévey, where several main routes met, and passed the lakeside château of Chillon. The huge motor road and vast spread of the modern town almost entirely prevent us from imagining the lonely chill of these parts even though this was one of the most frequented routes to Italy. They had to pass round the east of the lake to St Maurice, and then, rising all the time, to bleak little Martigny, and finally the

Domestic scenes, February (top), May, September, reflect the activities of the turning year and the cycle of life. (From the fifteenth-century calendar of Charles d'Angoulême)

long zig-zag narrow road, clinging to the mountainside, of the Great St Bernard Pass, with the hospice, founded in the eleventh century by St Bernard of Menthon, set at the top of the pass among heart-chilling snowy desolation. It can be cold and snowy there in August; in late December it must have been fearsome. However, it could be crossed. A few years later Adam Usk was carried over in December in an oxcart, half dead with cold and his eyes shut for fear of the precipices. From now on it was downhill all the way, the road still very narrow, winding and steep, but on southern slopes, past tiny hamlets, with well-established inns down to Aosta. From Basle to Aosta took ten days. This was still the territory of the Duke of Savoy, with which England had close relationships, but there was a war between Savoy and Milan, and Chaucer's party would have needed to avoid the fighting area north of Milan. So they probably made for the handsome city of Turin, and once there may have travelled a dozen miles further south to Jacopo di Provano's home town of Carignano for a brief rest. Just south of Carignano lay the rich delightful plain full of towers and cities where the scene of *The Clerk's Tale* is set, but it would have been out of Chaucer's way even if he at that time knew the story, and it is not unusual northern Italian scenery. From Carignano to the coast just west of Genoa, the ravishing Italian Riviera, and Genoa itself, with its mild climate, even in January, was easy going. Then the real work of negotiation began.

Genoa was a great commercial centre and port, and notable for the skill and aggressiveness of its sailors. At this date it governed a great colonial empire, extending as far as the Crimea, Syria and North Africa, though war was coming with Venice from the consequent collision of interests, which would lead to defeat in 1380; and the anarchic internal strife that is the curse of Italy was already leading to Genoa's fifteenth-century submission to a succession of foreign masters. Chaucer saw what is now the Old Town, with narrow streets but fine houses, and the cathedral with its characteristic bands of parti-coloured marble which so strike a northern eye, though we must remember that medieval buildings in England itself were much brighter than they are now.

It took about a week to go from Genoa to Florence, first along the coast road south, to Pisa, through that countryside which used to be the most beautiful in the world. Pisa itself is on a flat plain and was a splendid city which had reached its peak of greatness in the twelfth and thirteenth centuries, and with the surrounding countryside constituted one of the small Italian city-states. Its archi-tecture is ornate yet sober, and the early twelfth-century cathedral is magnificent, with an early fourteenth-century pulpit of great elaboration whose Gothic realism Chaucer would have enjoyed. Of course he saw the Leaning Tower, not quite so dramatically tilted as today, and only finished twenty years before, but still well out of true. There were magnificent palaces and churches among which was (and is) the church of Santa Maria della Spina with the famous relic of a thorn from Christ's crown. The Gothic sculptures of Pisa and other towns remind one of the descriptions of the temple in *The House of Fame*.

From Pisa he turned east along the general line of the valley of the Arno, a fertile well-tilled plain, with lovely towns, Lucca and Pistoia most notably, though alas so often at war with each other. And so to Florence, 'flower of cities all', with all due apologies to medieval London, for more business.

Florence was a great and beautiful city, with fine bridges over the river, including the Ponte Vecchio, which must have reminded Chaucer of London Bridge, being very like it with its shops and houses. But whereas London was built of wood, apart from churches, Florence was of stone. We can still see the narrow fourteenth-century streets, with their tall houses, which he saw, especially

FLORENTIA

The spacious and beautiful city of Florence as Chaucer saw it

to the east of the Palazzo Vecchio, and among which is the house where Dante was born, now the Via Dante Alighieri. Chaucer saw the square, or piazza, of the Signoria and the Palazzo della Signoria with its great halls and extraordinary tower, so striking a demonstration of civic lay power even to a Londoner. The Uffizi Galleries and many another great Renaissance palace were not there but the sturdy Bargello, another civic building, had been built, with its noble court-yard, though not yet enlarged and sterilized into a museum. Many of the fine buildings of the Borgo degli Albizi were there, if not quite so high, and also such buildings, more than half fortresses, as the Palazzo Castellani, a nobleman's palace, not far from the river Arno. Most of the great churches which house so many works of art were already there. The cathedral itself and the Campanile, said to have been designed by Giotto, with their red, white and green marble and fine sculpture, shone in pristine splendour, though the cathedral was still unfinished and an earlier dome was in the place of Brunelleschi's cupola. Santa Croce lacked its modern white façade and the clutter of selfimportant late Renaissance tombs, but was none the worse for that, and had many fine frescoes in their first brilliance. Most striking to Chaucer, since only just finished, must have been the remarkably rich adornment inside Or San Michele, near the great central Piazza della Signoria, for which the artist Orcagna was paid huge sums; and the great church of Santa Maria Novella. Most notable in Santa Maria Novella were the Strozzi Chapel with its then recent altarpiece by Orcagna, and the vastly elaborate frescoes of the Spanish Chapel, finished about 1355 by Andrea da Firenze.

The population of Florence at the time of Chaucer's visit was about 60,000 and increasing rapidly. It was a much bigger and more magnificent city than London, with a tremendous artistic interest, several large bookshops, and already a cult of the poet Dante, widespread not only among the educated but all classes. Chaucer unquestionably improved his knowledge of Italian. Perhaps he had heard of Dante from Italian friends in England, but here, I suspect, he actually bought his own copy of *The Divine Comedy*. He also came across Boccaccio's poems probably for the first time, and bought copies of *Il Filostrato*, basis of his *Troilus and Criseyde*, and *Teseida*, basis of *The Knight's Tale*. Some copies of Boccaccio's works were superbly illustrated and surely Chaucer looked at those and other pictures with interest, just as he must have dwelled on the pictures in churches and noted not only their beauty but many of the technical details. For example the quality and intensity of colours, especially blue, were an index of the power and emotional effects of the picture. There is a lot of documentary evidence from fifteenth century Florence about both the artistic and financial consideration given to this matter, because the best colours were naturally the most expensive. Chaucer in *The Knight's Tale* makes what is perhaps the earliest reference to the question, earlier even than the rich Italian evidence. He always had a real interest in cost – he refers to Theseus's expenses elsewhere (CT I, l. 1882). In describing a picture in the temple of Diana he writes

> Wel koude he peynten lifly that it wroghte;
> With many a floryn he the hewes boghte   [colours]
> *I*, ll. 2087–8

Chaucer may well have associated florins with Florence, for Florentine coins were sometimes called Florences in English and confused with the different coins called florins because of their flower design, a lily.

Chaucer responded both consciously and unconsciously to the stimulus of Italy. It was exactly what he needed to reinforce his own characteristic attitudes and interests. The conscious effect can be traced in the poems by Dante and Boccaccio that he used. The unconscious can be deduced. Italy has always had a vividness and splendour for certain types of Englishmen. The milder air and

bluer sky warm and loosen their responses and clarify their minds. The splen
dour of Italian cities and art, the liveliness of ordinary life, vivify more northern
temperaments. In the fourteenth century Italy led European culture. The most
highly organized cities, the biggest industries, the richest merchants and
bankers, the best doctors, the best cloakmakers, the most ingenious technicians,
the best painters and sculptors, the best Latinists, the best vernacular poets, the
most learned scholars in mid
fourteenth
century Europe, were Italian. In Italy
the old feudal system had never quite taken hold, thanks to the continuation of
cities. Hard work, rational enterprise and fair dealing were highly valued and
were the expected stairway to success. Commercial calculation, civic organiza
tion, education dedicated to the acquisition of knowledge and method, were
notably in advance. There was a conscious ideal of literally civilized existence;
of public responsibility spread and fostered by secular elective government, and
private life based on personal responsibility and the cultivation of affectionate
family domesticity. Both public and private were integrated and celebrated by
communal civic and religious ceremony and worship. There were, as always, in
Italy as elsewhere, the bad luck, the horrors and inconsistencies, cruelty and
folly, vice and crime, common to men (and women), but being common
contributed less to the experience of being in Italy.

Italy had a peculiar mixture of the religious and secular. Although Rome was
the Eternal City and the normal city of the Pope, the Pope was in fact at
Avignon, and soon the Great Schism would begin, in 1378, when there were two
rival popes, each claiming uniquely to represent God. Chaucer reveals no interest
in this world of international politics, though it must have fed some aspects of his
scepticism and anti
clericalism. More important as corresponding to his own
attitudes were the powerful new movements of secularism, which included new
feelings about religion. The new lay individualism of the fourteenth century in
Europe was particularly noticeable in Italy. There were many gilds and confrater
nities for laymen, often with religious purposes, which he would have recognized
as similar to, but more developed than, those in England. If Chaucer could have
seen Siena he would have seen the splendid frescoes of Ambrogio Lorenzetti in
the Town Hall which so remarkably represent medieval secular painting and the
spirit of lay government as to deserve a brief digression.

The reclining figure of Peace from Lorenzetti's fresco in the Town Hall, Siena

They represent Good and Bad Government. With poetic justice Bad
Government has largely perished. Good Government is represented by an old
but strong and authoritative man enthroned, probably representing well
governed republican Siena itself, but an adequate image for a kingdom as well
as a republic. Almost equal with him on a long bench are his counsellors, the
civic virtues; justice with a sword, holding reward and punishment in her lap in
the characteristic either/or fourteenth
century form of a crown (in a republic!)
and a cut
off head. Beneath her are soldiers and criminals. Then Temperance
with an hourglass as a symbol of patience; Magnanimity with a bowl from
which she hands out gold money; Prudence, inviting thought about past,
present, future; Fortitude, armed as defender of the State; and last, the famous
Peace, a girl in a beautifully relaxed posture. Above are the Theological Virtues

of Faith, Hope and Charity. This is a civic not a feudal representation, and the civic virtues are larger and felt to be more important, than the theological. Chaucer might well feel that all this represented his own ideals. There is a regal figure to the right of Good Government, and a little lower, who is clearly Queen to his King. She is Justice, again, raising her eyes to Wisdom. Her angels deal out rewards and punishments, and beneath her sits Concord. One might fancy here a representation of Edward's Queen Philippa herself, though Mercy would have been more fitting than Justice as her name. At the foot of the picture are the substantial citizens of Siena. Below, the education required for Good Government is represented by images of the three Liberal Arts of the Trivium, Grammar, Dialectic and Rhetoric. Alongside is an extensive panorama of the effects of Good Government in city and countryside. The city is clearly Siena. The countryside can be recognized, even today, as that most delightful one surrounding Siena. The panorama is full of enchanting local detail: dancing, buying and selling, a university lecture, building, travelling, reaping, threshing, hunting. Granted a certain idealization this fresco gives an almost photographically realistic and vivid impression of what 'life was like', of how it appeared to Chaucer, in fourteenth-century Italy. We see too something of the underlying structures; the rich and poor; the close relationship of town and country, but also the clear-cut distinction between the two; the either/or of reward and punishment; growing individualism; the lay spirit (not anti-Christian); the delight in detail, and in the world around us. Here is a European specimen of the background of *The Canterbury Tales*.

Lorenzetti's frescoes give us a vivid practical picture, but they derive from a greater master, Giotto, whose work Chaucer certainly saw. If you stand between the Baptistery and Duomo in Florence you surely stand where Chaucer once stood, at the foot of Giotto's tower, that great multicoloured campanile soaring up to the blue sky. Giotto who died in 1337 was acknowledged in Italy as the great master of the art of his age, and the great influence. His work would appeal to Chaucer particularly for its new lifelike realism – 'wel koude he peynten lifly'. In the work of Giotto and his followers is seen a new feeling in the history of art for 'natural' space and solidity in pictures. His work places the figures of Holy Scripture in realizable, even identifiable, environments. He values the natural world, as did, from one point of view, St Francis of Assisi, 'the jester of God' who preached most famously to the birds. In the church of St Francis at Assisi the life of the saint was portrayed in Giottesque style. St Francis's metaphorical marriage with the Lady poverty is represented in the Lower Church of Assisi with vividly natural literalism. Following Giotto and the general spirit of the age, fourteenth-century Italian painters show an increasing literalism in portraying the concrete metaphors with which preachers expressed spiritual truths. This literalism, or realism of appearances, particularly appealed to Chaucer, I imagine, since he practises it so much in his poetry, though there is often something other than realism as well.

Though Giotto's realism was still there for all to see, in the 1370s it had been complicated, and more recent painters displayed a different quality, or used realism in a different way, which Chaucer also responded to. After Giotto's death the 1340s had been a bad time in Italy and the confidence that the earlier part of the century had developed in the way of the world was badly shaken. Economic depression came, to a large extent caused by the bankruptcy of two great Florentine banks, the Bardi and Peruzzi, itself due in great part to Edward III's failure to pay his debts to them. (One wonders why ever anyone lent him money again.) There were bad harvests, and then the Black Death, which probably killed half the 90,000 inhabitants of the close-packed city of Florence in 1348. Many people took the series of disasters as the judgments of God on a worldly generation and there was a wave of bequests to churches sufficient to switch the main power of the patronage of art away from civic authorities to religious orders and institutions, in other words, to intensify the religious functions of artistic endeavour. Some of these pictures were very grim, like the violently disturbing fresco, *The Triumph of Death*, by Francesco Traini, painted about 1350, which Chaucer surely looked at in the Campo Santo of Pisa when he passed through. The immense sums given by the pious to Or San Michele allowed the church to commission Orcagna's solemn and elaborate masterpiece that we can still wonder at. It was the bequest of a merchant whose wife had died in the plague that allowed the Dominicans to pay for the rich frescoes of the Spanish Chapel in Santa Maria Novella by Andrea da Firenze in the 1350s, which Chaucer surely saw in their primal freshness.

The frescoes in the Spanish Chapel heavily emphasize the importance of orthodox doctrine, with the visual dominance of the great encyclopedic theologian, St Thomas Aquinas, and the schematic coverage of the frescoes themselves. There is a renewed emphasis on guilt, penance and the authority of the Church. I do not imagine that Chaucer, with his sceptical anti-clericalism and mockery of the friars (of whom the Dominicans were the first and one of the greatest orders), cared for these frescoes any more than have Renaissance and later art lovers, and they remain relatively little known and less loved. Still, they express the spirit of the age, and a similar spirit was to be found, a little later in Chaucer's life, in the English church. In some respects these frescoes, and other work like them (Orcagna's altarpiece in the Strozzi Chapel in the same church, his masterpiece in the Or San Michele), returned to the past, to traditional, non-naturalistic presentation and imagery, emphasizing the transcendence of God and the saints, their splendid, commanding, demanding, priestlike authority.

Yet they could not altogether deny the modern developments in realistic presentation discovered by Giotto and his followers. So they have in abundance what thirteenth-century art lacked, a vivid local realistic detail in feature, clothing, gesture, just as Chaucer's poetry has. So forms sometimes seem shown in depth, with a 'natural' perspective, and at other times, in the same picture, seem to be shown as if all on the same plane, without naturalistic depth and proportion. The general pattern of the picture is both asserted and concealed. The result is an effect of ambiguity and tension very characteristic of late Gothic art. The transcendent thought-world behind the picture is presented in vivid but sometimes inconsistently realistic images. Many people dislike the curious tensions of this kind of art and prefer the idealized realism of the greater painters of the Renaissance who would appear in Florence a century later. Even these have some suppressed ambiguities, but I think that Chaucer too would have preferred them. Yet this later fourteenth-century tense ambiguity represents something of the nature of Chaucer's own poetic art. He too has curious incon-sistencies of character and a tension sometimes between local natural detail and the general thought-world. We must also remember how at the end of his life, in the Retractation of *The Canterbury Tales*, he condemns all his secular poetry, even *The Book of the Duchess*, which seems innocent enough to us. But it is secular. The Retractations represent in Chaucer's life what the frescoes in the Spanish Chapel represent – the triumph of ecclesiasticism.

That is to look ahead. Florence, and the nearby Siena, offered in the early 1370s something that appealed much more to Chaucer, and was much more part of his present world. The response to the crisis of the mid-century was not only a reassertion of orthodoxy. The paradoxical and ironical nature of Christ's teaching, and of Christianity, ensure that for every firm assertion of authority, tradition, formal structure, there is a counter-assertion of new individualism, of the need to destroy formality and achieve an instant communion with God, an instant equality with and love for one's fellow human beings. Hermits, monks, friars, Lollards, Protestants, Evangelicals, and in modern times Pentecostalists – even hippies and drop-outs in their way – have all expressed this human neces-sity. It was very strong in Italy in the 1360s and 1370s, and in Chaucer's life and poetry. Italy did not cause it in him, but must have encouraged it.

The counter-assertion of Christianity often depends on taking literally the words of Christ. Literalism is both method and part inspiration. In Italy there was a widespread movement among the Franciscans to take literally the Gospel injunctions of absolute poverty, and Florence in the 1370s was one of the headquarters of these Fraticelli, Little Brothers (of St Francis). One of them was indeed burned at the stake in Florence in 1389, just as the partly comparable Lollards were in fifteenth-century England, for the Church and State Establish-ment are threatened by such spiritual and economic radicalism. What is even more significant is that lay people took up the movement. In Italy (the English were more cautious) they were liable to give away all their goods to the poor, advocate democracy, and reject all ritual, books and intellectual effort. For these they substituted prayer and singing together for long hours with like-minded unorganized groups 'burning with the love of the Holy Spirit'.

A most interesting and outstanding example, whom Chaucer must have heard of in his visit to Florence, was St Catherine of Siena. She was born in 1347, and was creating a considerable stir in the early 1370s. Her father was a dyer in Siena, and she the youngest of his twenty-five children. From a very early age she developed a rich spiritual life and soon began to incur the condemnation of religious authority. She wished to live outside regular ecclesiastical rule and she became the centre of a lay group whose rule, she said, came straight from God. Like others she proclaimed the love of God and the sinfulness of man, but love was for her more important than penitence. An illiterate until in adult life

St Francis renounces his earthly father to seek a life of poverty

she learned to read, she believed that assiduous introspection, bringing knowl-edge of one's own self, would lead to love of others. This confident, inner-directed religion, with warm emotionalism, was more characteristic of Siena than of Florence, perhaps of women than of men, but Chaucer's poem, An ABC, directed to the Blessed Virgin, though a translation, shows its attraction for him. St Catherine also had an English disciple whom Chaucer could have heard of, William Flete. He was an Austin Friar who was at Cambridge in 1352 and became Bachelor of Theology by 1359, when he might have been about thirty. He left England in the same year to pursue his vocation as a hermit and was admitted by the Convent of Lecceto, two miles from Siena. He made a cell for himself in a cave nearby and retreated there every day with his books. Clearly he was both very like, and very unlike, Chaucer. The convent is in a beautifully hilly, wooded spot, still relatively unfrequented, although alas a good motor road is now being built nearby. William acquired a high local reputation for learning and judgment and by the time of Chaucer's visit to Florence was one of the most prominent of St Catherine's friends and devotees. His presence shows from a different side the international network of communication over Europe.

This communication of people, ideas and feelings is illustrated by another connection between the English court and Italian piety which has not so far been noticed. Around 1300 an Italian, Giovanni de San Gimignano, wrote a book that became immensely popular all over Europe, called *Meditationes Vitae Christi*, 'Meditations on the Life of Christ'. At its core is a brief domestic biography of Christ, emphasizing the personal tragedy and pain, omitting emphasis on God's grand plan of redemption. The supernatural is suppressed and new domestic-realistic-pathetic material supplied. The Virgin Mary took up sewing when the family was in Egypt to help make ends meet, like any good lower-class house-wife. Monologues by major figures in the story and conversation between them, expressing their passionate feelings, emphasize the significance of the narrative. It is easy to see how this intensifies feeling for the story, promotes a personal, private response. This book was eventually turned into English by a Carmelite Friar, Nicholas Love, with the title *A Mirror of the Life of Christ*. *A Mirror* is usually dated as written about 1410, but it seems likely that the work was known in some version earlier in England. It corresponds with parts of what we may guess about the piety of the English court in Chaucer's day.

The Virgin weaves while Jesus practises in his walking frame

The similarities of feeling and attitude go deeper than the obvious pious subject matter. The style of feeling, the methods of evoking it, extend to Chaucer's secular poetry. The expansion in the *Meditationes*, and its English translation, of the original Biblical stories of the childhood of Christ with extra realism in fourteenth-century terms, the expansion of the narrative and creation of emotion by means of monologue and dialogue, the additional weight of pathos and pity, are exactly comparable (though on a different scale) with the expansions and additional feeling that Chaucer creates in his own retelling of the story of *Troilus and Criseyde* from Boccaccio's original. The secular sexual love story is rather surprisingly in the same general vein of sentiment as the retold life of Christ. Different as the stories are to the point of opposition in the question of sex, each has the same interest in domestic realism and personal suffering. Chaucer's version has also a moral, supernatural ending which might be thought of as a kind of serious parody of Christ's Resurrection. Chaucer would have been surprised to hear his poem, which he repudiated at the end of his life, so described, but it is indeed the case that *Troilus and Criseyde*, with its Italian base, its warm Italianate feeling and detail, is the great English secular counterpart of this characteristically Italian mixture of personal domestic realism, internalized pathos and pity. The tension between the novel-like presentation in many parts of *Troilus* and the ultimately non-naturalistic structure has the characteristic ambiguity of late Gothic painting.

Chaucer did not exactly learn such qualities from Italy: they were in the air, and corresponded with tendencies in himself, in the English court and in London. Italian influence does seem to have brought out these tendencies more richly. There seems to be nothing comparable in French life and literature, nor in that of Germany, which could have given anything like the same encourage-ment. The religious and civic life of the Low Countries, commercially prosperous, with the affective personal piety of the Modern Devotion which was eventually realized with such wide appeal by Thomas à Kempis's *Imitation of Christ*, offered something similar, but there were no great literary figures like

Dante and Boccaccio who could give such feelings literary form and body.

Boccaccio was alive and famous, though not in Florence, when Chaucer was there; Petrarch, the most famous of all literary men in Europe, was also an Italian, living in Italy, during Chaucer's visit, and it is natural to wonder if he met them, or what he heard from his acquaintances about them. We cannot reconstruct any literary discussions that Chaucer may have had with his Italian acquaintances. It is hard to believe that such civilized men had none in the eighty to a hundred days that he spent in Italy. He must surely have heard the names of Dante, Petrarch and Boccaccio mentioned. The first two he mentions in his poetry, though his knowledge could have come from his books. Boccaccio's name he never mentions even when translating his *Il Filostrato* quite closely and making much use of his *Teseida*. There is no evidence to suggest he met either Boccaccio or Petrarch. Petrarch's voluminous correspondence makes no mention of meeting the English envoy, as it surely would have done if he had made the necessary special journey to Arquà where the elderly Petrarch was living. I cannot imagine Chaucer going out of his way to meet any celebrity. Nor was he interested, as the Italians were, in rare manuscripts, or in discovering lost ancient classics. He tells us in *The Parliament of Fowls* that his copy of Macro-bius — an old-fashioned encyclopedic commentary — was an old torn book, while Petrarch's manuscripts are all things of beauty. I do not suppose that Chaucer cherished books as physical objects any more than he sought out celeb-rities. He was an informal man, who went quietly about his own business.

I imagine he loved Italy. But he was not there for pleasure, and in early or mid-April, the beautiful perfumed springtime, he had to leave. Probably he went back to Genoa to pick up his companions, and they returned the same way, over Alps hardly less snowy, through to an English spring in May. He could alternatively have crossed the Apennines to Bologna, another grand city, continued to Verona and up another well-known route to Bolzano, Merano, the Reschen-Seideck pass through the mighty Dolomites, and so through Germany.

And so back home, though it is hard to know even where that would be. From April, Constance of Castile, the wife of Gaunt, had been at Tutbury Castle in Staffordshire, so presumably Philippa Chaucer was there too. So were Gaunt's children, and their governess, Philippa's sister Katharine Swynford, the mistress of Gaunt. It was quite a family party, though the duke himself was absent, preparing for another campaign in France.

The business details of the Italian journey fizzled slowly on. In August Chaucer was sent to Dartmouth to deliver a release of a Genoese vessel from arrest in that port, and there heard of a well-known ship's captain who later became the model of the Shipman in *The Canterbury Tales* — odd fruit of the Italian visit and an example of the long storing up of impressions in that fertile mind. Even the more important literary fruits of his Italian visit took time to mature, probably because Chaucer was unable to get a job that gave him leisure enough to read and write. His next poem, *The House of Fame*, shows his discon-tent with his situation, and with a job that was out of the frying pan of constant travel into the fire of constant office work.

CHAPTER EIGHT

LONDON, FLOWER OF CITIES ALL

AFTER THE ITALIAN JOURNEY CHAUCER IN HIS middle thirties, with a wife, perhaps a child or two, with a lot of books he wanted to read and a lot of poems in his head, having written much but not satisfied himself, might well have felt it was time to be more settled and to be paid more handsomely. His petitions were not extravagant or at least not extravagantly fulfilled. On the day of the Feast of the Garter, St George's day, 23 April 1374, he was made the not very usual, nor very generous, grant of a pitcher of wine (about a gallon) a day. Something better turned up on 8 June, when he was given the office of Controller of the Wool Custom and Subsidy and of the petty Customs with the obligation to keep accounts in his own hand. He thereby became the first and so far the only English poet who was a customs officer and accountant. On 13 June he was awarded an annuity of £10 by John of Gaunt in consideration of his services to Gaunt, and of Philippa's services to Gaunt's wife Constance and earlier Queen Philippa. Although it may have been the result of a personal petition this does not make Gaunt a patron of Chaucer's poetry. The grant is formal and quite usual in linking husband and wife. It was mainly for Philippa who remained lady-in-waiting to Constance. The richest lord in the kingdom with a huge income fee'd many a person on the fringe of his vast retinue. In May, no doubt in anticipation of these benefits, Chaucer had taken out a lease of the dwelling above the gate of Aldgate on the eastern side of the City. The Controllership of the Wool Custom was technically distinct from that of the petty Custom and what was known as the Petty Subsidy, while all involved dealings not only with accounts but also with the 'troner and peser' (who did, or was responsible for, the weighing), and with searchers, packers and porters; but the technical details must be left aside, especially as the degree of Chaucer's personal involvement is uncertain.

The uncertainty is partly because, although the wool custom in particular was an important source of revenue to the Crown, and was relatively efficiently collected by what has been called the most efficient (for its time) civil service in Christendom, the significant officials were the collectors, not the controller. The collectors, of whom two were appointed, or re-appointed, each year, were great merchant-financiers like Nicholas Brembre, William Walworth, John Philipot, who were rich enough to lend money to the Crown. They did not spend time hanging about the quays, which was done by their employees; they managed the

OPPOSITE *London, although a smaller and less impressive city than Florence in Chaucer's time, was nevertheless a bustling commercial centre*

accounts. Some £24,600 a year revenue was accounted for as going through their hands, the equivalent of several million pounds sterling in modern currency. The collectors' salary was £20 a year each, but none of the men concerned would have done the job for such a trivial sum. They paid themselves out of unrecorded fees. This was not bribery and corruption in the modern sense, it was the way things worked. In operating the system, goods entering or leaving the kingdom were weighed, checked, and when the duty was paid were stamped with a 'cocket' seal. The controller was supposed to retain one-half of the cocket seal so that he could check the weight and duty paid and only join his half of the seal to the collectors' half when satisfied; then the goods could be properly stamped. The controller was also supposed to return his own independent accounts to the Exchequer. Thus in theory he supervised the collectors in the king's interest. But since the controller was a much less important person to the government than the collectors, who actually paid his salary from their revenues, his superiority was merely notional. Moreover, his half of the cocket seal was sometimes surrendered by the government to the king's creditors to enable them to claim revenues to settle debts. In 1379 it was surrendered to the City of London, and held by the mayor. The mayor was John Philipot, who also happened to be a collector. So he held both halves. Philipot also happened to be a friend of Chaucer's, one of his witnesses to Cecily Champain's release to Chaucer in the peculiar case of her raptus. So on the whole we may assume that our official earned his official £10 a year plus bonus of £6. 13s. 4d. without too great a strain. Being a member of the king's household he had probably not had to pay for his office, and he must also have received from it, or in it, substantial unrecorded fees, though the controller had to take an oath not to accept any gifts. Even the requirement that the controller should write his accounts in his own hand was not always insisted on. In other words, when one adds to the salary some additional fees (probably regulated by ancient custom as a third of what the collectors received), and such windfalls as the grant of £71. 4s. 6d. in July 1376 from the fine levied on a would-be customs dodger, Chaucer's office was reasonably well paid. It was the sort of thing naturally given to a king's esquire, who after all still had other jobs to do. Chaucer himself was sent away with Sir John Burley in late 1376 on the king's secret affairs – the secret has been very well kept. He was sent away again on journeys with Sir Thomas Percy and others to Flanders and France in the first half of 1377 to negotiate peace, and also discuss the possible marriage of the king's grandson Richard with a daughter of 'his adversary of France'. He also went to Italy again from May to September 1378 on more diplomatic business in Lombardy, though on this occasion he appointed a deputy at the customs to act in his absence. This was his last major journey, and Chaucer did not appoint another temporary deputy till 1383. He obtained a licence for a regular deputy in February 1385, when he was beginning to pull out from London.

The job was, therefore, not exactly the modern regular nine-to-five civil servant's employment throughout the year, though to hear Chaucer's humorous complaint one might think it was. In that extraordinary poem *The House of Fame* in which he represents himself, fat as he is, as carried off into the sky by a talkative eagle, he refers to himself as having no tidings of 'Love's folk', of hearing no news either from far country or from his very next-door neighbours, because when he has done his work and made all his reckonings for the day, he goes straight home and 'dumb as any stone' sits at another book until his eyes are dazed. And thus he lives like a hermit, though his abstinence is small (perhaps that pitcher of wine had to be finished). The reference is clearly to his labours in the customs house and his home in Aldgate. 'Love's folk' may be courtiers, and Chaucer may have regretted his relative absence from the fountainhead of benefits, while at the same time he was glad to indulge in the imaginative and intellectual delights of reading at night. The poem shows that his job was not a complete sinecure, as does the absence of a deputy for most of the time. He must have had to put in some time on accounts even if he could at a pinch get secre-tarial assistance. *The Parliament of Fowls* was probably also written during his customs-house period and shows something of the same deep inner dissatisfac-tion and seeking, but in it he also claims to have read in his old torn book for a whole long day which seemed short to him. Considerable leisure could be avail-able. The poem also implies a courtly situation, possibly a courtly festival of St Valentine's Day, 14 February. So things were not too bad. It was more worth his while to use his arithmetical expertise in doing his own accounting than to pay a permanent deputy. Perhaps he also enjoyed the arithmetic, since as I have argued, it deeply affected his attitude to the world. In *The House of Fame* he comments on his own metre, and remarks that it often lacks a syllable (l. 1098). This is a numerical self-consciousness about English metre that is quite new. The House of Fame is written in the same short 'octosyllabic' line as *The Book of the Duchess*, but seems more regular. Under both lies the regular tick-tock of the repetitive beat that native English verse historically lacked, but which the new fourteenth-century feeling for mechanical repetition was beginning to develop. (Chaucer incidentally knew a clockmaker from Germany, John of Cologne, in 1388.) *The Parliament of Fowls* shows a modulated regularity of metre perhaps for the first time in English. These poems also show the influence of his new Italian reading.

A fourteenth-century glazed jug in the British Museum

For a parallel to Chaucer's situation we can again refer to that other, greater accountant, also a literary genius though not a poet, the diarist, Samuel Pepys. Pepys shows us the life of an important official in the Navy Office on the fringe of Charles II's court in a situation not dissimilar to Chaucer's. We see from his Diary how jobs go by status, connections and influence, and fees and gifts are more significant than salaries. Most of the really great men get huge sums for doing little or nothing directly, but they head large groups of followers and spend or give away as much or indeed, like medieval kings, more, than they receive. Lesser men, of varying degrees of conscientiousness, receive varying rewards, but if they are prudent they build up comfortable fortunes, like Pepys and in all probability Chaucer. By the end of his customs-house period Chaucer was probably able to buy, or had by then accumulated, a nice little estate in Kent.

No one kept a personal diary in fourteenth-century England. That particular kind of self-consciousness and introspection had not yet developed historically, though the religious teaching of confession, and the cultural advances in Italy, where diaries were beginning to be kept, had set it well on the way. If anyone in England could have kept a diary it was surely Chaucer, as *The House of Fame*'s autobiographical passage suggests. If we had Chaucer's daily diary we should find that he, like Pepys, walked to and fro about the City of London, meeting an extraordinary variety of citizens. His daily work, his family, and his court connections, which he certainly did not relinquish, provided a cross-section of much of English society, though he had to walk almost three miles to the court at Westminster. From Aldgate to the Wool Quay, which was near Billingsgate, where Walworth and Mawfield lived, between the Tower and London Bridge, was half a mile. He had to cross Thames Street at its eastern end, but it was only another ten minutes' walk along Thames Street to the west to his father's house in the Vintry Ward. Many other substantial merchants lived and worked around here. Three very notable such merchants, whose names frequently occur together, were all collectors in Chaucer's time at the Wool Customs – Brembre, Walworth and Philipot. These three, with a few others, lent the king £10,000 in September 1377, taking the crown jewels as pledge of repayment, which was made in May 1378. All three were knighted by the king in 1381 as it were on the field of battle, for their brave and resolute behaviour in the Peasants' Revolt, which had so contrasted with the feebleness of the nobles surrounding the young Richard. It is notable that all were of the victualling gilds, which were generally dominant in London's highly factional trade politics, and much opposed to John of Gaunt. Brembre alone lent the king £2000 in 1382. He was a member of the Grocers' Company and Mayor of London in 1377 and 1383–4–5. Walworth was Mayor of London in 1381. He personally killed Wat Tyler, leader of the peasants. When he died in 1385 he left a number of books (above, p. 38). Philipot was about the same age as Walworth, a man of remarkable ability and resolution, and a closer acquaintance, if not friend, of Chaucer's, than the other two, though no less an enemy of Gaunt. Philipot was particularly notable for equipping a fleet at his own expense and capturing a notorious Scottish pirate called John the Mercer. He did this in 1378, when Gaunt had been defeated at sea at St Malo. The merchant Philipot had put the professional chivalry to shame and won a great reputation in London. The Commons in Parliament insisted that Walworth and Philipot should be treasurers of the war funds – a tribute of trust in them and distrust of the late king's and new king's advisers, especially Gaunt. Such hostilities should not be assumed to have been very systematic. These men were by no means hostile to the court or nobility generally. They needed the king for their success as much as he needed them and Brembre finally met a miserable end by being accused in the Merciless Parlia-ment of 1388 of too much influence with the king. The king himself tried to defend him, and it was only by making use of the notorious enmities that existed between certain of the city companies that Brembre's enemies were able to get him condemned to die a traitor's death at Tyburn.

Another friend of Chaucer's hardly less rich and eminent was the draper John Hende. The drapers being non-victuallers were generally at odds with the victualling gilds, such as the Grocers (Brembre) and Fishmongers (Walworth

The lady and her couturier. Notice the scissors; Chaucer is the first person recorded as using the word in English — earlier, people used shears which were not pivoted

and Philipot), but it is characteristic of Chaucer to have had friends in opposing camps. Hende had some very stormy passages in his career. He was a brave or at least an obstinate man, who clashed in a lawsuit with the court, so that Chaucer's mainprising of him in 1381 shows the poet no coward in standing by his friends. Mainprising was guaranteeing a form of bail, and that a person would appear at the proper time before the judge. Another mainpernor of Hende was Ralph Strode, whom Chaucer refers to at the end of his poem Troilus and Criseyde. Hende was thus part of an interestingly literary and legal group, since Strode was probably a lawyer. Hende, who was frequently an alderman, married first the widow of a Suffolk landowner, and second the daughter of Sir John Norbury. When he died in 1418 his widow married the future Baron Sudeley. His younger son became first, like Chaucer, an esquire of the king, and later marshal of the hall. This is a family like Chaucer's own, of property and wealth, trade and gentry, with close relationships to the court and learned professions. Another acquaintance was Gilbert Mawfield (Maufeld, Maghfeld), a Collector of Customs after Chaucer's time, and comparable in wealth and status with Philipot and his friends. He was a moneylender and Chaucer borrowed from him, as did John Gower, and many courtiers and other acquaintances. Professor

Manly thought he was the original of the Merchant in The General Prologue. He seems to have died bankrupt.

At the other end of the social scale comes Matilda Nemeg, or Nemeghen, whose name suggests that she came from Nijmegen in the Netherlands, and who was a servant woman. She left her mistress in 1388 before the end of her contract and was allegedly abducted by John the Clockmaker of Cologne. Chaucer with three other men, none of note, mainprised her appearance before the court, when her mistress brought an action against her. As usual, we know no more; the incident, trivial in Chaucer's life, shows him in touch with the lower levels of social class, and with the variety of nationalities in medieval London. He could be acquainted with the margins of society without losing touch with the centre.

During the period at the customs house, which extended to 1385, he built up a literary circle. The poet John Gower was given power of attorney by Chaucer when he went to Lombardy in 1378. Power of attorney gave the right for a substitute to appear in a court of law, or perform certain legal responsibilities. Gower, together with Richard Forester, another king's esquire, was given this power by Chaucer so that Chaucer would not lose any lawsuits that might be brought against him in his absence through not appearing in court to answer the case. In so litigious a society it was a valuable precaution and one is surprised that more such records do not exist, but maybe they are lost, or Chaucer on this occasion had reason to expect that a case might be brought. At any rate it shows him on good terms with Gower, a learned man, poet in French, Latin, and later, following Chaucer's own example, in English, landowner in Kent and elsewhere. Gower is addressed at the end of Troilus together with 'philosophical Strode'. The latter leased the dwelling over another city gate, Aldersgate, about the same period that Chaucer leased his over Aldgate. He was probably the London lawyer of the name, and may have been the Oxford philosopher of the same name who argued against Wyclif, and who seems to have been a fellow of Merton College, Oxford, 1359–60. He died in 1387. This London friend points us in the direction of Chaucer's Oxford, specifically Merton, contacts, but those must be left till later. We may allow ourselves to imagine meetings of Gower, Strode and Chaucer in one or other of their houses in London, for a cheerful drink, a discussion of literature, of scientific and scholarly matters in which they were all interested, and of the bad state of the nation.

Chaucer's reputation as a poet in the latter part of his customs-house period certainly extended beyond the court and into the City. Another Londoner, who was a great admirer of Chaucer's, was Thomas Usk. He wrote the long prose Testament of Love of which no manuscript survives but which was printed by Thynne in his edition of The Workes of 1532. The absence of manuscripts suggests no great popularity for this curious and rather tedious allegory which is modelled on Chaucer's Boece and borrows heavily from Chaucer's Troilus and other poems written before 1387. Whether Chaucer, who is addressed by Usk as 'the noble philosophical poet' was altogether pleased is a question. Usk illus- trates a very disagreeable aspect of London life. He was first of all secretary to John of Northampton, the draper, who had built up a following in the City among the lesser gilds and crafts. John of Northampton was a friend of Gaunt's and enemy of the victualling gilds, especially the Fishmongers. John of Northampton's plans failed, and Usk was imprisoned in 1384–5 and compelled to give testimony against his master. He switched sides and joined the party of John of Northampton's enemy, Brembre, when Brembre was prominent as an adviser to Richard II, and Usk was awarded the post of undersheriff of Middlesex by Brembre's influence. But in another drastic political change Brembre was dislodged, accused and executed, as already noted, in 1388, and the miserable Usk fell with him. On 4 March 1388 Usk was disembowelled, hanged, cut down while still alive, and beheaded – the usual punishment for treason. It took nearly thirty strokes of the sword to kill him. (In these barbarous punishments we see again, if it does not seem heartless to say so, the nonutilitarian, demonstrative nature of the age.) Usk's *Testament* shows a longstanding engagement with Chaucer's works up to that date, and they must have known each other. His fate shows the savage hostilities possible between Chaucer's acquaintances in various factions, and the fearful penalties that might be incurred for being on the wrong side in a crisis; though it must be said that 1388 was exceptional, and there was even then no question of a reign of terror. There is no reason to suppose that Chaucer went shivering in his shoes in 1388. Usk's fate, with that of Brembre, and court acquaintances like Sir Simon Burley, recalls the turbulent state of London and national politics – a sombre backcloth to Chaucer's own improving situation throughout the 1370s.

The 1370s were a disastrous decade in which the strains on society culminated in the socalled Peasants' Revolt of 1381 in which Walworth, Philipot and Brembre showed their mettle. The war in France was resumed with decreasing success in 1369, and instead of a flow of loot and a sense of success the country had to contend with a sense of failure together with high taxation to pay for it. There was an exceptionally bad harvest in 1369, plague in 1374–5. There was poor leadership. Edward III, fiftyseven years old in 1369 when Queen Philippa died, rapidly went to seed, dominated by Alice Perrers. The Black Prince was a sick man. He was admired throughout Europe as a knight, but with his impatience, arrogance, love of gambling and battle, was no statesman. Gaunt, though he had some force of character and immense riches and prestige, was as conventional as Edward without his flair for action: he was a mediocre man, when all is said and done. In the 1370s he became more and more interested in the crown of Castile which he claimed through his wife, and was often abroad. His military expeditions were obvious failures, but even negotiations for peace, culminating in the truce of Bruges in 1375, were mishandled, so that the truce deprived some lords of the fruits of an unaccustomed victory at Quimperlé. No other prince or great lord offered hope. In 1371 the discontented lords in Parliament expelled the bishops who were the great officers of the Crown, but the laymen did no better, and there was actually fear of revolt by merchants in London and other towns. Ireland was as usual a source of trouble.

In so dangerous a situation the government was reluctant to call a Parliament but was forced by pressure of business and need for taxes to summon one in

April 1376, which came to be known as the Good Parliament. The Commons, that is, the knights of the shires and the burgesses of the towns, in all some one hundred and thirty strong, met in the Chapter House of Westminster Abbey, where a lectern was set up from which the speakers addressed the meeting, and the members sat on the seats around the wall and on benches. It is easy when there now to imagine an animated scene, for some fourteenth-century frescoes give us a glimpse of interested faces. The Commons had many complaints and for the first time elected a spokesman, or Speaker, to present their arguments to the Lords. He was a brave man, Sir Peter de la Mare, later imprisoned for a while for his bold actions. Many people were accused of financial corruption, among others Alice Perrers and Richard Lyons. All these accusations were made in the name of the king, but of course attacked his household and administration. Gaunt was in effect the main target and extremely unpopular. Scandalous rumours were circulated, some absurd, as that he was no true son of the king's but a Flemish changeling, others true, as that he lived in open sin with his daughters' governess, Chaucer's sister-in-law, Katharine Swynford.

Parliament proposed reforms, changes were made, though it is not clear that all accusations, even of Richard Lyons, were true. Amid all this the Black Prince died, to universal and genuine sorrow. It was thought, with no evidence, that he supported the Commons' causes. The publicity of his deathbed, the elaborate organization of his funeral cortège from London to Canterbury, the

Chaucer must have seen this exquisitely painted retable which hung above the altar in Westminster Abbey during his lifetime

richness of his tomb in Canterbury Cathedral, still to be seen with its magnificent effigy, all demonstrate the splendour and quality of the age quite as
significantly as the details of hard political bargaining. There is an extraordinary
mixture of pride and humility; bravery as one dies yet morbid dwelling on
corruption, spirituality and materialism, all natural in the death of a great person
at any time, but here with a Gothic exaggeration and sharpness of contrast. The
Good Parliament confirmed his son Richard as the heir-apparent.

In the following year another parliament was called that undid much of the
work of the Good Parliament. It had a somewhat different membership (for
members of the Commons were often called only to one parliament, and the
membership was fluid), while the lords, who did not appreciate the Commons'
new activity, were a permanent body. The Commons were soothed by a general
pardon and were disposed to grant taxes. But a tremendous row broke out
between Gaunt and Courtenay, the Bishop of London, over the government's
exclusion from pardon of William of Wykeham, Bishop of Winchester, who
had been sentenced to loss of his revenues for supposed delinquencies when
chancellor ten years before. Courtenay was a strong character of noble family,
and he would not stand for this slight to the Church.

The clash between Courtenay and Gaunt was focused on John Wyclif. He
was a combative theologian from Yorkshire who had been an Oxford don for
many years, and had steadily argued himself into a position in which he denied
the Church's rights to endowments and her power of excommunication. The
arguments were complex, with very important ramifications and implications
even up to the sixteenth-century Reformation. I cannot, as Chaucer said of other
theological problems, 'bolt it to the bran', sieve out its components. In general
Wyclif's hostility to the Church and its wealth, and to the eucharistic doctrine
that Christ's body is really present in the consecrated bread of the Mass, was part
of the developing literalism and hostility to structure and tradition that marked
the age, and of which one of the results was Lollardy. More superficially it was
politically useful to Gaunt and the English government in their hostility to the
French-dominated Pope, and in their readiness to take over the Church's
wealth. It was part of the steady emergence of lay, as opposed to clerical power.
Wyclif was thus at this period Gaunt's protégé and known to be so. Courtenay
attacked Gaunt indirectly by summoning Wyclif to appear before convocation
in February 1377 to answer charges against his teaching. Gaunt engaged four
doctors of divinity to help Wyclif in his defence, and, more to the point, himself
attended the trial, held in Old St Paul's, with Henry Percy, Earl of Northumberland, and an armed following. The trial was thus prevented and broke up in
uproar. Afterwards a mob of Londoners surged along the Strand to Gaunt's
house, the Savoy, chased men wearing his livery from the streets, and hung his
arms reversed – as a sign of treason – in Cheapside. Gaunt and Percy were
dining at the house of the rich Flemish wool merchant, John of Ipres. When
warned that the mob was out to get them the great lords had to escape from the
back door, Gaunt badly barking his shin as he sprang up from the table. They
had to take refuge with the Princess Joan at nearby Kennington and get her to

act as mediator between them and the irate Londoners. In the end the Londoners had to climb down, the mayor was deposed, Parliament had to send a deputation to the old king to receive his pardon, and on 23 February Parliament was dissolved. Chaucer himself was in Flanders and France on a diplomatic mission, so he missed these excitements, but his senior on the mission was Sir Thomas Percy, Northumberland's brother, so he must sooner or later have heard about them, and no doubt sympathized with the court side.

Edward was dying, and it was also to the Princess Joan that Chaucer's friends Walworth and Philipot went to ask for Richard's favour and protection against Gaunt. So no doubt Chaucer also heard the other side too, and like Joan, hoped for reconciliation. On the whole Gaunt came off best and had made the government's position firmer, at the cost of great personal unpopularity, especially in London. He was doing his best for Richard; when Edward died on 21 June 1377, from a stroke, of which the effects can still be seen in the very realistic effigy of him in Westminster Abbey Cloister Museum, he firmly supported the new boy-king, though many a person must have quoted, like Langland, 'Woe to the land where a child is king!' (Ecclesiastes 10:16).

Chaucer, being still abroad, missed being issued with mourning robes for Edward's death, though he was back for the splendid pageantry of the coronation on 16 July. No doubt he enjoyed it in his rather detached way. He certainly supported the royal prerogative as firmly as did Gaunt, to judge from the way in which in a later poem he called on Richard to 'show forth his sword of castigation' ('Lak of Stedfastnesse') even while giving him polite advice to behave better. Everybody felt the need for stability, which could only be realized by the king's firm government, though the same people were also behaving in a way that threatened stability – such is the nature of deep social crisis. For the moment everybody pulled together. It had been Bishop Courtenay, Gaunt's opponent, who had calmed the London mob when it was out for Gaunt's blood. Gaunt himself now worked hard for reconciliation. The London merchants needed internal calm and successful defence of the coast and the trade routes of the seas, which could only be continuously provided by effective government. The Commons in Parliament obviously needed peace at home and successful war abroad to justify at least, if not reduce, heavy taxation. The tragedy of the situation was that the contending parties' own short-term interests were pursued to the detriment of their long-term interests, and mutual distrust, all too often justified, in the end prevented the necessary consensus.

A new Parliament met in October and Walworth, Philipot and two other rich merchants made a loan of £10,000. Lancaster made a dramatic public declaration of loyalty that so to say brought tears to everyone's eyes; he proclaimed the need for unity, and that he would forgive all insults and injuries offered to him. Even the Commons were deeply touched and made a generous grant of taxation, though accompanied by the demand that Philipot and Walworth should be made treasurers and that the funds should be used only for war.

A less conciliatory note was struck when the Commons demanded trial of Alice Perrers, who had fled from the court as Edward died, not neglecting, according to report, to take the rings from the dying king's fingers before she departed. Among the Commons' petitions were fourteen items taken almost verbatim from petitions presented in 1311 to Edward II; someone wished to remind the court that kings who behaved badly had been dealt with severely in the not-too-distant past. Tensions continued to develop and in 1378, with Lancaster's military failures and Philipot's success against the Scottish pirate, cracks were appearing again. A terrible violation of a prisoner's right of sanctuary in Westminster Abbey, with his murder on the steps of the altar itself, shook the government. Courtenay and Gaunt clashed over this, and Wyclif was again brought into the fray. A Parliament held at Gloucester in the chapter house of the great abbey there (now the cathedral) seemed to go Gaunt's way and against the London merchants. Philipot and Walworth were not appointed as treasurers. But financial affairs were still very bad, and only a few months later still, in 1379, another Parliament had to be called which rebuffed Lancaster and secured the return of Walworth and Philipot to a committee to survey, in effect to censure, the conduct of the national finances. It also granted a poll tax.

Within this national to-and-fro of conflicting sectional interest there was in London also the series of conflicts already referred to, between the powerful victualling gilds, represented by Philipot, Walworth and Brembre, and some of the non-victualling and other minor gilds, led by the draper John of Northampton and favoured by Gaunt. Chaucer was certainly in a position to know the ins-and-outs of these; it is highly likely that he took sides with neither. When he describes five gildsmen from London in *The General Prologue* to *The Canterbury Tales* he makes them a Haberdasher, Carpenter, Weaver, Dyer and Tapicer (weaver of tapestries and blankets) – non-victualling crafts indeed, but ones that had stood neutral in the conflict between John of Northampton and the victuallers. Since his gildsmen are in fact all from one gild it must have been a non-trade fraternity based on a parish – a kind of local mutual-benefit society, which often supported a priest to say masses for the dead on behalf of the whole group, and undertook other charitable and benevolent works. (These community associations and structures need to be remembered and set against the story of conflict and contest.) There was such a gild in London dedicated to St Thomas of Canterbury, based on the chapel on London Bridge and the parish of St Magnus Martyr not far off. The gildsmen, who are not individualized, may be thought of as belonging to this gild, or one like it. Chaucer described them with his frequent leg-pulling, punning ambivalence:

> Everich, for the wisdom that he kan [knew]
> Was shaply for to been an alderman.
> CT I, II 371–2

An alderman was the highest office in the self-government of London, under the mayor, who was chosen from the aldermen. *Shaply* means capable, likely to be; it also implies 'shaped like' i.e. fat. The gildsmen's wives have an innocent snobbery of social climbing which the courtier and the male in Chaucer gently deride. The gildsmen's cook, Hodge of Ware, was a rascal probably known as a petty criminal as well as a cook and local restaurant owner to Chaucer and his primary audience. He, and the bawdy tale he only begins to tell, show that Chaucer was well aware of the low life of London, as indeed his walks, duties and acquaintances, together with his interest in the unofficial, improper and marginal, would lead one to expect.

With Hodge of Ware we have truly come to the margins of Chaucer's social life and knowledge, the remoter context of his life at this period. His central concerns kept him personally remote, as may be suggested by the fact that the scabrous city anecdote, a salesman's dirty story, which was no doubt intended to be *The Cook's Tale*, was not more than started on, and we shall perhaps fortu-nately never know what it was to be. The nearest equivalent is *The Canon's Yeoman's Tale*, which is a city story about trickery in London, but it is fuelled by Chaucer's passionate interest in, and rejection of, the pseudo-science of alchemy.

While national and London politics were in turmoil, Chaucer when he was not abroad on duty got on with his work and his reading and writing. What else could such a man do? His poetry reflects his own interests, not public events.

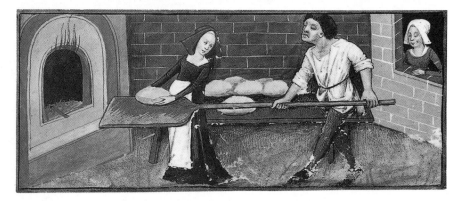

A customer waits for a fresh-baked loaf

The House of Fame, like *The Book of the Duchess*, is rich in literary allusion, to which now Italian references and more scientific knowledge are added. Its tone is light and humorous, yet it also reveals something of personal dissatisfaction and something of the deeper stresses of the age.

The poem begins with a scientific as well as personal problem – what causes dreams? But he had a wonderful dream, he says, last 10 December (though he does not tell us, and no one knows, what is the significance of so precise a date). He dreamed he was in a temple of glass, saw first a portrait of Venus 'naked, floating in a sea' and then the whole story of Virgil's *Aeneid* written on a plate of brass but which he actually tells largely in terms of pictures, and with great emphasis on the sorrows of Queen Dido, whom Aeneas loved and left. A list of similarly betrayed ladies is included. The betrayed lady is a frequent image with him of what Wordsworth (who also sometimes associated it with dreams) refers to as 'a sense/Death-like, of treacherous desertion' (*Prelude X*, ll. 413–14). At the conclusion of this disproportionate summary of the *Aeneid* the poet tells how he rambled outside the temple and found himself in a sandy desert. Then a golden eagle approached from the sky, and the first 'book' of the poem concludes. The second opens with a light-hearted plea to every man who can understand English to listen to his dream, and an invocation, borrowed from Dante, but less solemn than his work, to Venus and his own Thought. Then we 'hear' (perhaps the first audience – say Gower and Strode in the house above the city gate – literally heard) how the fat poet was snatched up by the eagle and endured a comical pseudo-lecture on the properties of sound to explain why all the stories and rumours of the world land up at the House of Fame (or Rumour). The eagle seemed to know him well, for he called him Geoffrey and prefaced his lecture with the remarks that make the autobiographical passage about accounts and evening reading and isolation which has already been mentioned. The poet's nervous, reluctant, terse replies, as the eagle soars higher and higher, are a masterpiece of understated self-mocking comedy. Then he is landed and the second 'book' finishes. The third begins with another invocation and the poet tells how first he climbed a hill of ice, carved with partly obliterated names, then came to a wonderfully Gothic castle, with minstrels and storytellers on the towers and all sorts of musicians and courtly entertainers. Inside was another crowd of people, including heralds who praise 'rich folk'. This was the Hall of Worldly Fame, and on pillars throughout the hall were statues of great poets and historians. And this hall was dominated by a noble queen, though at times she seemed very small and at others reached from earth to heaven – the very Goddess of Renown or Fame. The poet saw bands of people come for her approval, some good men, some bad, some having done much, some nothing, and the Goddess rewarded them totally arbitrarily without any justice. Such is fame in this world. Someone asked the poet, had he come there for fame?

> 'Nay, forsothe, frend,' quod y;
> 'I cam noght hyder, graunt mercy,   [thank you very much]
> For no such cause, by my hed!
> Sufficeth me, as I were ded,   [I should be satisfied, if I were dead]
> That no wight have my name in honde.
> I wot myself best how y stonde;
> For what I drye, or what I thynke,   [As to what I endure or think]
> I wil myselven al hyt drynke,   [I will contain it all within myself]
> Certeyn, for the more part,   [greater part]
> As fer forth as I kan myn art.'   [In so far as I have any skill]
> ll. 1873–82

This is a notable expression of Chaucer's fundamental independence of other people's opinion, remarkable in many ways, but particularly in a poet who sought to be, and succeeds admirably in being, a public entertainer. But why then was he there? Because, the poet replied, he was anxious to learn some new tidings, some new things, he doesn't know what,

> Of love, or suche thynges glade.
> l. 1889

(Once again, one is reminded of Pepys, who describes himself, early in his *Diary*, so eager as to be 'with child' to see a certain sight.) So the poet was taken out of the castle to a wonderful, vast, multicoloured wickerwork house, sixty miles long, in the valley, that spun round on its axis, and gave out a tremendous roar, like the roar of a stone hurled from a siege engine (a rare personal reminiscence from Chaucer's soldiering days). The noise came from all the 'tidings', the news gathered in the house. The poet remarked, with an astonishment that does not astonish us, that he had never before seen such a place. Luckily his eagle was perched nearby on a stone, and on hearing how eager the poet was to see the house, that he might learn something good, or that would please him, he repeated how Jove had taken pity on the poet's forlorn state, hopeless of any job, with his heart ready to break, and took him up and flew into a window and set him down on the floor, full of all sorts of people exchanging news and lies, and sailors and pilgrims, pardoners, couriers, messengers. Then, with a greater noise, and the rush of a crowd, the poet saw a man come forth, who seemed to be a man of great authority . . . and there the poem breaks off.

I have told the story of the poem so fully because as with *The Book of the Duchess* there seems something more personal in it than is revealed by the more assured and greater art of the later poems. Again like *The Book of the Duchess* only three manuscripts survive, though Caxton printed it in 1483 from another manuscript. Chaucer acknowledged the poem as his, but must have left it unfinished. He had a less unified notion of a work of art than we have, less of a sense that a poem is a separate self-enclosed thing. He must also have felt that it was too good to throw away, and that it expressed something valuable to him. Yet it could never have been widely circulated and must have both entertained and puzzled its first readers and hearers. He probably wrote it in the middle 1370s. He is trying to absorb the new Italian material, but still writing in what will soon be, by his own standards, the old-fashioned style of octosyllabic verse, and in the manner of the French love visions of the previous hundred years. There were plenty of these, and the poem takes something of its general structure, things like the hill of ice, and many details, from them. But what astonishing originality it has within the conventions.

For all its humour and lightness of touch the poem surely expresses an inner discontent and an inner seeking. We cannot tie it to any external occasion. Some have thought that it might be a prelude to an actual great man's actual announcement of some important matter at a courtly occasion. If so, what a strange rambling introduction. What announcement could follow? The poem must have been abandoned because Chaucer could not think how to end it, not surprisingly. The interest of this is that Chaucer, probably unconsciously, simply cannot bring himself to be a mouthpiece for authority. In this respect the poem expresses the general social unrest, the seeking of new ways, of that troubled time. The flight into the skies is an ancient literary motif well known to Chaucer from earlier famous Latin poems which he jestingly refers to, and corresponds with something of Dante's exploration of Hell, Purgatory and Heaven, but Chaucer's flight is told in a very flippant way. It expresses the ambivalence found elsewhere in the poem, because besides the deliberately trivializing flippancy there is a real aspiration for wider, 'higher' experience that could also be rediscovery of something felt to be lost, a recovery from the Fall. The archaic mythic imagery of the mountain, of being carried up to heaven by a bird, expresses, as Mircea Eliade has shown, in many cultures, the desire to reach out to the true living origin of creation, out of time, in paradise. In paradise, says Eliade, men are immortal, spontaneous, free (just like the rumours in the wickerwork house). They express that sense of human community and exaltation which sometimes comes at conversion, at moments of transition, the crossing of boundaries, breaking of structures, changes of one's way of life; moments of community and exaltation which were found, in their various ways, by those Italians who rejected the Church and worldly possessions, by the followers of Wyclif, by the Lollards – and by the murderous London mob. The House of Fame is a revolutionary, anti-formal poem in all sorts of ways. Unlike most expressions of spontaneous action it never hardens into a new structure – it was never finished. It remains always as it were fluid; certainly questioning and questionable. One feels that it was written in a mood like that of a contemporary religious poet:

> In a valey of this restles minde
> I soughte in mounteine and in mede
> Trustinge a trewe love for to finde.

Chaucer too gives at least conventional hints about the lack of a true love, as well as invoking his not – to us – very powerful image of deserted loving ladies. But he seeks at this stage no religious solution, and finds no other. He is as resolutely a layman as those who expelled the clerical officers of the Crown in 1371. He turns to Italy, in its guise of classical Roman poets, for help, and cannot yet break out of the French convention, or make best use of it.

His attitude to Fame is partly traditional contempt, but also in part deeply personal in a way that suggests an internal struggle with an interesting outcome. The first Temple of Fame is the ordinary idea of renown, and this must surely have tempted him, a great poet. Like all of the best people he perceives its arbitrariness and rejects it, but that he was there at all shows the earlier temptation. His own declaration of independence shows a powerful internalization of values which again shows a rejection of the external value structures of the world at a personal psychological level. Though secular in expression it again reminds us of the Italian Fraticelli and the English Lollards, as well as the other-worldly elements in mainstream religious feeling that caused men to become monks or hermits, women to become recluses.

Though he rejects the first Temple of Fame he is characteristically fascinated by the House of Rumour, grotesque as the invention is. Here all is unstructured, spontaneous, free, away from the ordinary world, but closely related to it, with a strong personal human interest, and a highly questionable relationship, dangerous, but creative, to actual truth. What can authority and form do here? We are free. Yet in the end we cannot complete anything without accepting some kind of authority and form.

CHAPTER NINE

RAPE AND RAPINE

ON 1 MAY 1380 A YEAR OR TWO AFTER THE NON-completion of *The House of Fame*, a most curious legal document in the Latin of the Court of Chancery appears in which Cecily Champain (a delightfully fizzy name) releases Geoffrey Chaucer of all actions concerning her *raptus* and of all other matters. This is witnessed by William Beauchamp the king's chamberlain, Sir John Clanvowe, Sir William Neville, John Philipot and Richard Morel. On 4 May, the document continues, the aforesaid Cecily came to the King's Chancery at Westminster and acknowledged the said document and all its contents in the said form. The same lady, if she was a lady, signed a somewhat similar release, though without reference to any *raptus*, on 28 June, to two prominent citizens, Richard Goodchild, a cutler, and John Grove, armourer, though there are no witnesses mentioned. On the same day Goodchild and Grove signed another similar release to Chaucer himself, also without witnesses. To add to the mystery, though the story remains for ever incomplete, a few days later on 2 July, not withstanding the release he had received from Cecily, Grove gave a recognizance before the mayor and aldermen that he owed Cecily Champain £10, which he later paid.

This baffling series of records has puzzled scholars and is open to various interpretations, from the most scabrous to the simply technical. The technical explanation is the one most favourable to Chaucer. It has been devised and cogently argued by Professor D. W. Robertson. He argues that the explanation of the whole series must be assumed to lie in some financial transaction, as is implied in the Grove-Goodchild documents. Robertson cites a case where a man was falsely accused of rape so that when he was in prison his wife could be brought to court on the accusation of her opponents and caused to pay a fine, because of a quarrel over property. In Cecily's case Chaucer might have been forestalling such a trick, and the sexual element would be purely notional. It must be confessed that there is no evidence quoted of such a defensive legal device in unquestioned use. Robertson argues that Cecily was an agent of Grove and Goodchild (both very respectable citizens), to whom the Customs owed some money, and that Chaucer insisted that Cecily sign the quitclaim to forestall any action on the part of the claimants to embarrass him or put force upon him. If so, though the device seems to have worked in his lifetime, it has singularly failed with his reputation in the twentieth century. If we discard the notion of legal

OPPOSITE *'When Adam delved and Eve span, | Who was then the gentleman? A stained-glass panel in Mulbarton Church, Norfolk*

fictions we are forced back on to the peculiar situation that Chaucer demanded (presumably) Cecily's quitclaim of *raptus*, and got his friends to witness it as publicly as possible. We should have to assume either a further act of bullying on his part, after the 'rape', or a substantial payment to Cecily. But either seems improbable. Why should the bullying succeed, or why should he not get a simple receipt for his money? Fear of further blackmail could not be the reason for being content with a mere receipt, since he had already gone to some trouble to enlist his friends to make the quitclaim decidedly public. Its publicity is notable compared with the unwitnessed signatures of the other quitclaims. Nevertheless, Chaucer does not seem to dispute the accusation of *raptus*: he apparently merely acquires immunity from its consequences, and from 'all other matters'.

There is a considerable problem with the meaning of *raptus*. It could mean either rape or abduction. Chaucer's father as a boy had been subjected to *raptus* in this sense of abduction. If Chaucer was guilty (and we have nothing more than the release — no legal accusation tested in a court of law) was he guilty of rape or abduction in some family quarrel? The legal historian Professor Plucknett states that there is really no evidence for the charge of rape. Essentially he takes the usual modern male lawyer's view that the lady was probably seduced and after regretted it. K. B. McFarlane states quite bluntly that Chaucer had been guilty of the rape of Cecily, and that the release by Cecily was given 'in return for a fairly liberal gift of money'. There is simply no evidence for this. The only money mentioned is Grove's debt which he repaid to Cecily. It is possible that Chaucer paid Grove who paid Cecily, but that is only speculation, and how the cutler and armourer could become involved in the rape is beyond speculation. Rape was a serious crime in fourteenth-century London, and could be punished with sentences varying from heavy fines to imprisonment and personal maiming. It could hardly be shrugged off, or paid off with £10. When all is so baffling and the evidence so incomplete, it is better to do what a court of law would have done and find Chaucer not guilty. Whatever the tensions, inconsistencies and violence in his poetry and life there is nothing in them that would lead us to imagine he could commit rape. One would like to know what it was all about, but we never shall. He was soon to witness a much more horrifying explosion of violence, the Peasants' Revolt, which swept through the very gate over which he lived.

As with all great events it had many causes. It was actually sparked off by discontent with taxation, but there were naturally deeper forces at work. However, the obvious causes for discontent were bad enough. To the longstanding attempt to hold down wages and prevent movement of labour when prices were rising; to deep resentment against serfdom; to political and military malaise and failure; to financial corruption; to plague; was added a series of novel taxes, the galling poll taxes in 1377, 1379 and 1380. A poll tax was a levy on each adult person, and it was collected by collectors with royal letters patent coming round village by village, with lists of names, asking for cash. In 1377 a poll tax of 4d. a head had caused much discontent. The poll tax of 1379 was graduated, but for various reasons had not yielded enough revenue. Incidentally, it gives yet another list of gradations in society recognized in terms of hard cash. The Dukes

ABOVE *A medieval spade with iron edge found at Walthamstow, Essex — exactly like the tool with which Adam is 'delving' in the stained-glass panel on page 148*

ABOVE RIGHT *Peasants at work — ploughing, sowing, hoeing, carding wool, pruning and spinning*

of Lancaster and Brittany come highest at £6. 13s. 4d. Chaucer would have paid 6s. 8d, his aldermen friends 40s., like serjeants-at-law, and a simple ploughman 4d. But in November 1380 a tax of 1s. a head was imposed, without gradation. The money was urgently needed to pay English troops in France before there was large-scale desertion. This was very unjust. A ploughman earning 12s. a year would have to pay 2s. for himself and his wife — as much as Chaucer, who probably earned one way and another, with his wife, perhaps a hundred times the ploughman's wage. The rich were adjured to help the poor, but general exhortations of that kind are of little use, and in many villages there was no resident rich man to have the opportunity to be generous. There was tremendous evasion, and the collectors' lists appeared to show that the population had declined by a third in the past eighteen months. So the government in March 1381 and later sent out commissions to re-assess and enforce payment of tax. These were efficient and consequently disastrous. One commission was sent to John de Bampton, a lord's steward in the area of Brentwood in southern Essex, who was the great man of those parts. He displayed the commission (a formal letter) and on 1 June 1381 he summoned the men from local villages to come and pay properly. The men of Fobbing (prophetically named) refused, on the ground that they had already paid. John had two royal serjeants-at-arms (presumably with a handful of troops) with him and he threatened the villagers. They asked for help from two other villages, and the men of all three to the number of more than a hundred (but note how small the villages were) went to John and told him that they would not pay. John tried to get the serjeants-at-arms to arrest the men, but the men resisted and were ready to kill all three, at which confrontation John fled to London and the villagers to the woods, where they hid for a few hours and then began to go about to incite other people to rebel. The Chief Justice of the Common Bench, Sir Robert Bealknap, was sent down from London to discover and arrest the rebels, and many people were terrified. But the rebels boldly confronted him and he lost his nerve. They made him swear on the Bible that he would never again hold such sessions of inquiry, and he was also made to tell the names of those who were prepared to swear to the identity of the rebels. The rebels beheaded the informers and destroyed their houses. Sir Robert rushed back home, having by his failure to stamp out the spark of a few men's defiance allowed the whole countryside to be set ablaze. At first men hunted out the local instruments of their oppressions, hated tax collectors and informers, but these soon became generalized to lawyers, to the king's chief ministers, particularly Archbishop Sudbury and the Treasurer, Sir Robert Hales, and of course to Gaunt, the richest, most influential man in the kingdom. This hatred they combined with a sincere, even passionate, devotion to the boy king himself, the symbol of justice, and in person too young to be blamed for the disasters of the previous decade. The revolt spread around southern and eastern counties in much the same way, provoked by commissions put into effect by the local sheriffs or other notables and by the news of refusal deliberately spread by those who had refused. All manner of grievances added fuel to the flames, including the desire to pay off old scores. Other factors, idealism, hooliganism, hatred of foreigners, variously helped.

Two men fighting with heavy swords — though the carver's playful ingenuity ensures that they will never be in a position to harm each other

Although the rebellion started in Essex it was most vigorous in Chaucer's county of Kent, where he may already have been a minor landowner. A large number of the disaffected gathered together at Dartford on 5 June and made the notable arrangement that everyone living within twelve leagues of the coast should stay where he was in order to guard against invasion – eloquent testimony to the responsibility and capacity for organization of the rebels, and of the government's failure, for all its taxes, to provide adequate defences. A league, according to Trevisa's contemporary translation of Bartholomaeus, was 1500 paces, and a mile 1000 paces. The Kentish men on 6 June clashed with Sir Simon Burley, the king's tutor, at Rochester and set free from prison a man whom he had claimed as a runaway serf. Burley, though a simple knight and not one of Chaucer's friends, was very much a power behind the throne, and as a chamber knight must have been well known to Chaucer. On Friday 7 June, the Kentish men advanced to Maidstone, joined up with a large crowd from Essex, and elected Wat Tyler as their leader. Who he really was is unknown. He may have been a tiler, as his name suggests. Froissart describes him as a disbanded soldier; he may have been a younger member, with a bad record, of the well-known family of Kentish gentry, the Culpepers. None of these possibilities excludes the others. He was a man of high ability. Dr Dobson sees the revolt as one of discontented artisans rather more than of peasants, and Tyler may represent that. There was some organizing ability among the rebels too that may have derived from former soldiers. And some gentry took part, though for discreditable reasons.

The element not so far described in the revolt was supplied when the Kentish and Essex men reached Canterbury on 10 June, and invaded the cathedral at High Mass, telling the monks to elect one of themselves as archbishop, for the present Archbishop Sudbury was a traitor and they would behead him. The rebels released a certain priest, John Ball, from the archbishop's prison and he added the religious idealism needed for enthusiastic rebellion telling them to get rid of all lords, archbishops and other ecclesiastical ranks, save one archbishop only, who would be himself. Church property should be divided among the laity (an early form of privatisation). Ball was expressing, if in parodic form, the characteristic 'anti-structuralism' of the period, the desire for equality, liberty and fraternity, for pure, free, spontaneous, human community and mutuality, that was expressed in Italy by the Fraticelli and others and in the Rhineland and Netherlands by the Brethren of the Common Life. It is not surprising that this predominantly social and political expression by the rebels of the need for community in England was regarded by the chroniclers, who being monks were hostile to it, as associated with Lollardy.

Then, 'with Ball as their prophet and Tyler as their captain', the rebels turned to London and accomplished the seventy-mile march in two days, gathering at Blackheath. Meanwhile, a large contingent moved up from Essex and camped at Mile End in the fields just outside Aldgate and Chaucer's house. He could have heard the menacing murmur from his windows, if he risked staying there. He certainly recognized what most sensible people felt about the mob, as he shows in a stanza of his own invention, independent of the source, in *The Clerk's Tale*.

'O stormy peple! unsad and evere untrewe!   [unstable]
Ay undiscreet and chaungynge as a fane!   [weathercock]
Delitynge evere in rumbul that is newe,
For lyk the moone ay wexe ye and wane!
Ay ful of clappyng, deere ynogh a jane!   [chatter; too dear at a farthing]
Youre doom is fals, youre constance yvele   [judgment; constancy shows up
    preeveth   badly when tested]
A ful greet fool is he that on yow leeveth.'   [believes you]
        CT. IV, ll. 995–1001

That, he goes on to say, is what serious people said,

Thus seyden sadde folk in that citee.
            ll. 1002

He does not go so far as to take the view of 'serious people' entirely to himself.

The rude peple, as it no wonder is,
Wenden ful wel that it hadde be right so.
                ll. 750–1

Rude means 'rough, simple' and is not contemptuous. It was natural, he says, that simple people, without inside information, should think that the document cunningly forged by their lord to deceive them, was perfectly correct. Chaucer seems remarkably tolerant. Although he shows no great respect for their stability or good sense, he does not seem to have had the arrogance or hostility towards the common people shown by his secular contemporaries. This is the more remarkable in that the people are often represented in his poetry as noisy and agitated, as they must usually have been in England. Chaucer's fundamental radicalism, or anti-structuralism, shows in his sympathy for the people, independent of its Christian and clerical basis. So I do not envisage him sharing Gower's excited apprehension or hostility to the rebels, nor Sir Simon Burley's arrogance, nor the panic that seems to have struck the higher nobility. Although he could never have been on the side of the mob he may have shared some of the same sympathy for them that was felt by, or at least attributed to, some prominent citizens.

When the rebels assembled to the east and southeast of London Richard hurriedly moved from Windsor to the Tower, itself on the southeast corner of the City, where many members of court and council were already assembled. At least he and his advisers were moving to the centre of the trouble, even if the Tower was also attractive as an apparently impregnable fortress. We do not know if Chaucer was there, but he was in the City during this period and if he was at home on Wednesday night, 12 June, he had a nasty experience. The resolute mayor, William Walworth, had ordered all the gates of the City to be closed against the rebels, and particularly Aldgate, above which Chaucer lived. But one William Tonge, an alderman, was later accused of opening the gate and letting the mob from Essex camped at Mile End enter. The truth of the accusation is doubtful, but somebody let them in – one hopes it was not Chaucer. What that section of the mob did that night is not at all clear. Perhaps some of the looting and arson around the northern suburbs and Highgate attrib- uted to other moments in those few fraught days took place then. But even rebels must sleep. The main attack came from the south next day, but probably the presence of the Essex men already in the City encouraged disaffected Londoners to gather and riot within the walls. This would explain the rapidity with which trouble spread in the morning of Thursday 13 June.

Thursday, Friday and Saturday, 13–15 June, was the key period of the revolt and centred on London. Apart from Mayor Walworth's order to secure the gates nothing seems to have been done in the preceding days to make any prepa- ration for attack. Some of the chroniclers consider that the leaders were stricken with panic. Modern historians have thought that perhaps the king's advisers, realizing that there was widespread sympathy for the rebels in the City, would not risk a hard line. It is equally likely that information was slow and uncertain, while the unprecedented nature of the crisis would also make action difficult. On Thursday morning, which was the feast of Corpus Christi, when there were normally feasts and processions and miracle plays, there was great tension. Several grand houses on the outskirts of London had already been burned. The king went by water from the Tower with some of his council to Greenwich, but the crowd seemed so frantic that though the king himself, the fourteen-year-old boy with memories of a famously brave father and grandfather was willing to venture, the chancellor and treasurer would not let him land. The crowd had already demanded the heads of Gaunt and of the chancellor and treasurer.

Since the rebels under Wat Tyler were frustrated of their meeting with the king they swarmed up to Southwark, the suburb south of the river which was the starting point of the road to Canterbury, broke open the Marshalsea prison and released the prisoners, destroyed the house of the marshal and several other houses, then went on to Lambeth to burn the chancery records. Documentation of any kind, but especially records, is naturally the target of such rebellion. Records both preserve and symbolize the intellectually re-alized structure and judgments of society. Wat Tyler then led his men to London Bridge, where they broke down a brothel occupied by Flemish women, who, says the author of the *Anonimalle Chronicle*, 'farmed' it from the Mayor of London. It is likely that the rebels destroyed the brothel not from outraged morality but from hostility to the foreigners, specifically the Flemish. But one of the aldermen, Walter Sybyle, later accused of treacherously admitting the mob over London Bridge, is reported to have said that the building (presumably the brothel) had deserved destruction for the last twenty years. Whether or not spoken by Sybyle the sentiment was no doubt truly felt by those whose idealism might respond to certain chords among the many struck by the revolt. The chain and drawbridge of London Bridge had been raised by Walworth's orders so that the rebels should not pass. But the keepers then let down the bridge and the mob rushed across. Several London aldermen, John Horn, Walter Sybyle, John Fresch, William Tonge, Adam Carlyll, were later accused of treachery by opening the gates to allow the mob in.

This accusation in itself may have been yet one more skirmish in a different battle, between John of Northampton, who succeeded Walworth as mayor in October 1381, and the victualling gilds. The accused aldermen were victuallers, and when they were eventually brought to trial in January 1384 Nicholas Brembre, the grocer and opponent of John of Northampton, had succeeded as mayor, and they were found not guilty, probably quite rightly. The fact that the mob was able to frighten the gatekeepers into letting them cross the bridge may be due to the presence of the Essex men and London rioters already inside and equally threatening. Nevertheless, it seems quite probable that some prominent citizens, perhaps the ones named, did share some of the sympathy felt more obviously by the lower classes with the rebels. To feel some sympathy would not mean completely throwing in one's lot with the rebels, any more than the Lollard knights, for all their sympathy with somewhat similar tendencies, actually threw in their lot with poor itinerant heretical preachers. Most people contain complex sets of partly incompatible values and interests, and in times of crisis like the last quarter of the fourteenth century this complexity seems particularly noticeable because the crises highlight the inconsistencies. Chaucer himself knew one or two of the accused aldermen. Walter Sybyle was one of his customs collectors from March 1381 to December 1382 and he, therefore, had constant dealings with him. Chaucer would have known the truth, presumably, of what happened on London Bridge. John Fresch was one of the sheriffs of London in 1385 who dealt with the customs audit.

Once the mob had burst in over London Bridge on Thursday morning they swarmed up the hill to Ludgate and Fleet Street, doing no damage on the way, and broke open the Fleet prison, releasing the prisoners, attacked the Temple, one of the lawyers' Inns, to destroy more records, and destroyed the great houses of a number of court officials. Either the same mob, or another composed mainly of Londoners who started earlier, rushed along Fleet Street to the Strand and the Savoy (where the Savoy Hotel now stands), the richest and most beautifully furnished house in England, belonging to Gaunt, and destroyed it utterly, burning with great deliberation all the fine napery and hangings and beautifully decorated headboards, burning the hall and rooms, and finishing the job off, whether deliberately or not, by blowing up the whole with three barrels of gunpowder thrown on to the fire. Such hostility and destruction to Gaunt must surely have frightened and distressed Chaucer, whatever his detachment.

The king from a turret of the Tower of London saw the Savoy and a number of other houses in the City in flames. The writer of the *Anonimalle Chronicle* says that he called his lords around him in a room below and asked their advice, but they completely failed him. So the young king himself said that he would get the mayor to issue a proclamation that all Londoners should go on the following morning to Mile End to meet him there at seven o'clock. Some modern historians reject this attribution to a boy of fourteen and doubt whether the mayor was in a position to command all Londoners to go to Mile End, but at any rate the event took place, the Essex men being mainly concerned, and thousands of

God's blessing is on the poor, while devils preside over the rich man's feast. The mob that destroyed the Savoy palace had some reason to feel that their anger was righteous

people passing through Aldgate underneath Chaucer's living quarters early that day. The king and a number of councillors with him met the rebels, who honoured him as king, and asked for traitors to be handed over to them, a request which Richard turned adroitly. They then petitioned for the abolition of villeinage (by which men were restricted at birth by law to a certain place and to oppressive services to their lord), for labour services by free contract (and consequent absence of wage restraint), and for the right to rent land at 4*d*. an acre.

Meanwhile, however, various mobs continued on the rampage throughout the City, and it is clear that a large hooligan element now entered in, looting, burning and killing. Richard Lyons, among a number of unpopular men, was beheaded in Cheapside. In the Vintry, where Chaucer had grown up, around the western end of Thames Street, there was a particularly savage pursuit and slaughter of Flemings, and the City of London Letter Book Account states that in one heap in the Vintry there were lying forty headless bodies. Thirty-five Flemings were said to have been dragged out of St Martin's in the Vintry and beheaded. Decapitation was much favoured as a method of killing by the rebels – simple stabbing to the heart was not enough. One of the most notable leaders of these mobs was Jack Straw, about whom nothing is known. Chaucer heard the wild shouts of Jack Straw's men as they hunted for Flemings in the loud turmoil of the streets, as would appear from his one reference to the revolt, which would take any prize ever offered in a newspaper competition for the most

dismissive comment ever made on a great national tragedy. The comment
occurs as a comic climax to the glorious account of the pursuit of the fox who
has seized the cock in *The Nun's Priest's Tale*:

> So hydous was the noyse, a, benedicitee![bless us]
> Certes, he Jakke Straw and his meynee [company]
> Ne made nevere shoutes half so shrill
> Whan that they wolden any Flemyng kille,
> As thilke day was maad upon the fox.
> *CT VII*, ll. 3393–7

A typical hyperbole accompanies the touch of realism, and both convey a heartless detachment that removes Chaucer far from modern humanitarianism. He
shows the same readiness to use the screams of misery to point a joke when he
describes the old man January's reaction to seeing his wife grossly embraced by
his squire in a tree (as Chaucer says, she is so treated as I may not express it,
unless I would speak uncourteously);

> And up he yaf a roryng and a cry[gave]
> As dooth the mooder whan the child shal dye.[mother]
> *CT IV*, ll. 2364–5

Both similes have a Gothic and Chaucerian indecorum that is highly amusing;
they show that Chaucer's occasional indifference to the accepted 'official' values
of his society is more profound and extensive than would be the case if he adhered
to any cause or wished to promote any reform. Any sympathy with the rebels was
not a modern humanitarian liberalism or Marxism born before its time.

While part of the mob was thus disporting itself in the City, another part
entered the Tower itself, clearly by treachery from within, since it had a garrison
of 1200 men. Joan of Kent was treated insolently and not one of her knights
ventured to interfere. Archbishop Sudbury, the treasurer Hales, a notorious
royal serjeant-at-arms and the tax collector John Legge, and Gaunt's doctor,
friar William Appleton, who were all at prayer in the twelfth-century Tower
chapel (still to be seen), were hustled with blows out to Tower Hill and
immediately beheaded. Their heads were placed on wooden poles and then set
up on spikes at London Bridge where traitors' heads were usually placed pour
encourager les autres. The rebels proclaimed that whoever could catch a
Fleming or any other foreigner might cut off his head. Besides the Flemings
slaughtered, the Italians in Lombard Street also suffered plundering of their
houses. All this must have alarmed and repelled the poet of pity.

On the next day, Saturday, the revolt continued and more people were
beheaded. At three o'clock in the afternoon the king came to Westminster
Abbey, met half-way by the abbot, monks and canons, said his prayers
devoutly, and had an interview with the resident recluse, a walled-in anchorite
of holy life. Then a proclamation was made that all should go to Smithfield, on
the northwest of the City; so back they all went again to the open place by the
church of St Bartholomew. Here the boy-king faced the huge rebel company of
the Kentish men led by the redoubtable Wat Tyler.

Wat Tyler had real command over the rebels and some general practical grasp of grievances. It also seems clear that his great success so far had given him overweening self-confidence, and something of the arrogance of those he opposed. The events of the Smithfield meeting are variously recounted by chroniclers whose distance from them also varies, but who are uniform in their hostility. Tyler seems to have treated the king with a jovial, insolent familiarity, and all the accounts agree that the king's knights did nothing. The demands that Tyler presented were in part similar to those of the Essex men, abolition of villeinage, abolition of the process of outlawing for crime, and return to 'the law of Winchester' – perhaps meaning the old system of laws without newfangled taxation and wage restraint. At the same time he repeated John Ball's demands that there should be no more lordship save that of the king, that the Church should be disendowed, and all bishops save one abolished, which we have already noted. The king agreed, or appeared to agree, to these demands, and behaved with remarkable coolness and composure. As the talks proceeded, however, tempers arose from remarks made on either side, and whether or not Tyler, as the *Anonimalle Chronicle* alleges, first struck Walworth with a dagger, which was turned by the armour Walworth was prudently wearing, perhaps under his robes, it seems certain that Walworth then struck Tyler, who was run through by the swords of others in the king's retinue, who then found enough courage to kill a wounded man. There was a roar of anger and indeed anguish from the crowd, who prepared to shoot their arrows at the group; but Richard in his greatest moment spurred his horse forward to meet them and shouted 'Sirs, will you shoot your king? I am your captain, follow me!' And he ordered them all to go to Clerkenwell Fields, a few hundred yards to the north, while the dying Tyler was hastily carried to the hospital for the poor near St Bartholomew's. Walworth, who matched Tyler in his formidable decisiveness, had him out again and beheaded, and also gathered a mixed force of Londoners and troops who surrounded what the chronicler now calls 'the sheep-like multi-tude'. Richard prevented more fighting, sent the peasants home, and contented himself with replacing Sudbury's head on London Bridge with Tyler's. Walworth he knighted on the spot, as already mentioned, along with Brembre and Philipot, and one Richard Lunde. The revolt, as far as London was concerned, was over as suddenly as it began.

There were a number of revolts in other towns, and the abbeys at Bury and at St Albans were particularly severely attacked. The University of Cambridge had a bonfire made of its records on the Market Place in a riot led by the mayor and bailiffs, expressing the hostility of town to gown by the practical and symbolic destruction of files.

Such anti-structural general upheavals must find a structure of their own in order to continue or must fade away. The less violent religious movements in Italy which expressed some of the same fundamental feelings soon organized themselves and were associated with the mainstream religion. Even Lollardy, though perse-cuted in the fifteenth century, persisted underground through the positive nature of its intellectual demands. The Peasants' Revolt had neither the will nor the means to do so. The tired and hungry men had lost their one outstanding leader; a good part of their aims must have seemed to have been achieved; the hay harvest was calling; they obeyed the king's command to go home.

They were not grossly mistaken. The poll tax was immediately abandoned. Villeinage continued to decay. The vague and grandiose millenarian demands of John Ball must always have seemed impractical when the excitement died down, and they and the equally vague promises to meet them that were offered by the king were easily forgotten on both sides. The government when it recovered its nerve was sensibly restrained. Though most of the principal leaders were caught and after legal trial suffered the horrible death of traitors, a number were pardoned and there was no reign of terror.

A few short poems arose out of the revolt as well as the couplet made famous by John Ball which so well expressed his millenarian levelling ideal:

When Adam delved and Eve span
Who was then the gentleman?

Probably more poems circulated orally; but none by Chaucer. Yet we can hear an echo of social and deeper unrest in his next important poem *The Parliament of Fowls*, though the poem itself demonstrates his increasing power of integrating, or at least holding together, not dispersing, the multiple conflicting elements in his mind and culture. He succeeds, as he had not in *The House of Fame*, in reaching out to include discordant elements, almost as the goddess Nature herself, the viceroy of the Almighty, combines the discordant elements of creation 'in even numbers of accord'. Chaucer now binds together his interest in general philosophy and in the details of ordinary vulgar behaviour, his love of beauty and acceptance of coarseness. He uses his Italian and Latin reading to build on the basis offered by the old-fashioned French love visions and *Le Roman de la Rose*. He uses the theme of love still as prime instance and symbol of the puzzling nature of life and its mixture of joy and pain, but includes by implication much more. The penalty he must pay for this inclusiveness, or the deep image of his own lack, is that he must himself be spectator not participant. From now on he represents himself in his poetry not merely as unsuccessful in love, but as for ever excluded from it, though for ever fascinated by it. I earlier called Chaucer 'the poet as "inside" ' because of his fundamental sympathy with the courtly values of his secular poetry, and he recognizes this sympathy with worldly values implicitly himself when he 'revokes' all such poems in the Retractation at the end of his career. But in that very Retractation he placed himself outside the secular courtly culture in one way; and by resolutely keeping to the role of spectator in his self-presentation in the courtly poems he keeps himself outside, marginal, in another. In this respect he is unlike contemporary courtier-poets or such later examples as Sir Thomas Wyatt, or even Shakespeare in his Sonnets, all of whom are using poems as part of the action in which they are engaged, for pleading, sorrowing, rejecting or rejoicing – counters to be used in the game of love. If Chaucer ever wrote such poems they are lost. He chooses the way of contemplation, transposing it from the religious to the secular sphere,

'The swerd of wynter, keene and coold' – the hardships of winter accentuated the plight of the poor

identifying himself with what interests him, but not directly participating in it.

In the *Parliament* he once again uses the image of the flight to heaven, though this time it is in the *Dream of Scipio* which he describes, and he himself does not take it. In his own dream he is, however, thrust into the ambivalent beautiful park of everlasting spring. It is a garden of love genuinely paradisal in itself, though it contains both the good and bad of love's adventures, neither of which, he is told, is for him. Here is another set of archetypal images, of the park itself, of Cupid, of the all-but-naked Venus in her warm and spicy temple – Italian imagery – and the goddess Nature on her hill of flowers, with all the birds in the world gathered before her to choose their mates, for it is St Valentine's Day.

Within these lovely images is set a conflict and a quarrel, among the birds, arising from love that is transcending yet frustrated, of higher satisfactions destroyed by their own nobility, of lower satisfactions comically coarse and selfish but successfully achieved, with contempt for the higher. Three noble birds, the birds of prey, compete for one beautiful eagle in the best traditions of *fine amour*. They are humble to her, though fierce to everyone else, are willing to die if convicted of any vice, will love her and only her for ever. Each one's love, he feels, constitutes an absolute claim on her, though all each asks of her is her 'mercy', 'grace'. The models of such feelings are the feudal obligations to one's lord, the Christian's adoration of God, 'vertical', not 'lateral' personal relation-ships. Marriage is the desired crown of this refined love, but the 'lady' cannot marry all of them. Most of the lower birds give this high-falutin' sentiment short shrift. If she will not love him, says the goose, let him love another. Others speak to much the same coarse effect, untrue both to the psychology of love and to moral refinement, but admirable working common sense. The mutual hostility and incomprehension between the classes come out strongly, except for the turtle dove, a lower-class bird who believes in love faithful even beyond death. In the end Nature refers to the beautiful object of all this commotion herself. But she, like Emily in *The Knight's Tale* and many women in actual life in the fourteenth century, with very good reason, does not want to serve love at all. Since the essence of love is that choice must be free on both sides Nature postpones the decision for a year; the lower birds easily choose their mates, sing a beautiful song of welcome to summer, and fly away. The poet is wakened by the noise and takes himself to other books in hope to fare the better. He had begun the poem by reading avidly in a learned, but torn old book, 'a certain thing to learn'. But the poem expresses, though indirectly and lightly, the usual sense of deprivation, of seeking and failing to find, that drives his earlier poems.

The inner personal quality does not deny the public, social interest of the poem. There are a number of St Valentine's Day poems in French and English in the fourteenth century (Chaucer's *Complaint of Mars* is another) and there must have been some courtly game or cult, some sort of literary 'club' where Valentine poems were read, and where there were probably courtly 'love games' in which ladies and gentlemen chose their 'valentines' for the coming year. There were two associations, one of the Flower and one of the Leaf, complementing each other, in Richard's court in the 1380s, as we know from *The Prologue* to *The Legend of Good*

'On huntyng be they riden roially.' All classes loved hunting, though the poor could not enjoy the sumptuous day-long sport of the nobility, and Chaucer hardly idealizes it as he does virtuous poverty

Women. A rather elaborate *Cour Amoureuse* complete with charter and 'king' was set up in the French court to meet on St Valentine's Day, 1400, and subsequently. There had been a literary society in London itself in the late thirteenth century called a Pui (after the French) which held a festival once a year to choose its prince and to hold a competition of songs in honour of virtuous ladies. In later centuries the cult of St Valentine's Day spread from its origins in the English court further into society. Pepys mentions it; Sam Weller sends a Valentine in *The Pickwick Papers*; it is a children's game in the twentieth century in the United States. In the fourteenth century it was one of the adult (more truly, adolescent) 'games of love', part of the general game of love, that sociable public convention which formalized, made to some extent more superficial and manageable, the deeper sexual passion. The game could be played and indulged in various degrees of seriousness, using poems and music as its counters.

The *Parliament* is no plea for love, no counter in the game, and it has surprising depths beneath the sparkling surface. But it could surely entertain an audience variously interested in the subject of love, and few people are not. We may imagine Chaucer as one of a group of courtiers, perhaps including the young king and queen themselves who had been married on 20 January 1382, aged fifteen. It would have been a varied group, with young knights and esquires, the queen's ladies of various ages, hard-bitten middle-aged warriors and administrators, the occasional lawyer like Strode, grocer like Brembre, bishop like Arundel. They would have met in some large painted chamber with fire and candlelight, to enjoy the wine and spicy cakes, music, dancing, jests and games. Then a pause for the well-known poet, the little plump man, less often about the court these last years since he was given the customs job, and whose remarks one sometimes hardly knew how to take; he stood up and delivered his poem with dramatic expression and gesture, musically spoken in the descriptions, vigorous in noble speech, inimitably comic in its witty mimicry of vulgar rustic accents. After the applause several listeners surely asked for copies of the poem which they themselves might copy, or have copied, to read over at leisure.

It is not an overt political allegory, though it arouses social echoes of the marriage of great ones, and of unrest and questioning in society. These are not at its heart, but there is a real attempt to link more general moral and imaginative compulsions with the empirical difficulties of the hurly-burly of ordinary life and its common concerns. The ancient motif of a flight into the heavens to find truth and the use of dream to enter a free, spontaneous, ambivalent 'space' where personal relationships are explored, are linked, loosely, with a sense of everyday actuality. The Parliament is only 699 lines but includes almost the whole range of Chaucer's mature interests in a style as rich and varied as the subject matter.

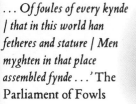

... Of foules of every kynde | that in this world han fetheres and stature | Men myghten in that place assembled fynde ...' The Parliament of Fowls

CHAPTER TEN

TOWARDS THE INNER LIFE

A TREMENDOUS PRESSURE OF ACCUMULATED EXPERI-
ence and thought had built up in Chaucer by the early 1380s. The middle of
the decade saw a major effort and a great breakthrough to inner security and
freedom, to an even wider range unhindered by the tugging sense of loss. In
his translation of Boece and the great poem Troilus Chaucer confronted both
intellectually and imaginatively the greatest joy and the greatest sorrow of life. In
modern times the usual image for penetrating the inner life is to go inwards and
downwards, into depth and darkness. In earlier cultures, and for Chaucer, it
was to go upwards and outwards, preferably as a resurrection after a death of
sorrow, of the ordinary self. In his last and greatest use of the image of the flight
into the sky at the end of the Troilus Chaucer at last broke through to an acceptance of worldly loss and spiritual gain. From remoteness he found freedom and
new energy to explore this very present world of people and knowledge.

Personal, individualized, even solitary, as such self-abandonment and
discovery must be, requiring immense nerve and persistence, it is a journey we
must all attempt, and which many people in the later fourteenth century were
attempting in new ways. The milling social unrest, the turmoil of external political events, were interrelated with deep inner stirrings and confusions, the
painful birth of new feelings about the individual and his relation to the world.
A developing interest in the outer world accompanied a developing need for
inner experience, as inner and outer became more clearly separated, and the
apparently divergent drives towards outer and inner experience needed ordering
and reconciliation. Hence an outcry of pain and complaint as inner and outer
strove, new and old, reason and faith. At almost every level was an alarmed
sense of crisis. 'What an increasing number of men wanted to discover afresh
was the inner reality to which the concepts embodied in the institution of the
Church and in Christian practice corresponded.'

There were many apparently contradictory ways that people followed in their
anxious search. Lollardy was one, and the most obvious since it had strong
political connections, but many who might better be described as orthodox
evangelical Christians shared the Lollards' general concerns without their
extremism. Wyclif's own written works gave an intellectual backbone and to
some extent even a political programme to the Lollards, but Wyclif himself
opposed in intellectual terms that main tendency of fourteenth-century thought

OPPOSITE *St Edward the Confessor, King of England, and John the Baptist present a youthful
Richard II to the Virgin; a panel from the Wilton Diptych (the Virgin in on another panel)*

which also promoted the interiorization of values which Lollardy represented. This main tendency of thought is certainly reflected in Chaucer who equally certainly shares certain Lollard interests and had some Lollard friends. As usual he overlaps with several different circles and is completely identified with none.

The main stream of thought in the fourteenth century may be said, by a simplification, to derive from the early fourteenth-century Oxford Franciscans, Duns Scotus and William Ockham. There is no evidence that Chaucer read their treatises or those of any of the university theologians, but their influence gradually pervaded the thought and attitudes of the century. The effect of their work was to emphasize the inadequacy of human thought to plumb the mysteries of God. God's purpose was expressed in terms of the divine will, which could function unpredictably. Human reason could operate only upon human experience. Faith, though necessary, was cut off from rational justification. The harmonization of salvation with rationality that had been achieved in the thirteenth century by Thomas Aquinas was shattered. The notion of universal governing ideas which is called (rather confusingly) Realism, was destroyed by Ockham's emphasis on empirical experience, which came to be known as Nominalism (as it were, one word for one thing). Nominalism encouraged exactly that mixture of scepticism and empirical 'realism' (in our modern sense of representing physical appearances) which we find in Chaucer.

It also made the problem of salvation unintelligible and raised almost to the level of an obsession the questions of free will, foreknowledge and divine grace as they affected the individual's fate. Thus Troilus meditates on the nature of causality and freedom, at the very heart of his loss, though, as Chaucer says of himself more flippantly of scholastic discussions of the same problem in *The Nun's Priest Tale*, he cannot 'bolt it to the bran'. It was a real and pressing problem, affecting both behaviour and faith.

Since the human condition cannot avoid taking some things as given, and even atheists must base themselves on non-rational value judgements, an act of faith is implicit in any continuation of human life at all. In the fourteenth century as at any other period there was plenty of faith, and some of it, as at any other period, the more fervent for the lack of rationalization. We can distinguish three broadly different kinds of response, which nevertheless might merge: that of mystical religion; that of conventional piety; and that of various scholastics which culminates in the work of Wyclif, and extends to Lollardy.

The fourteenth century is the great period of English mysticism. There were a number of writers, but the three greatest, during Chaucer's lifetime, were Walter Hilton, then the unknown author of *The Cloud of Unknowing* and other treatises, and finally that remarkable woman, Julian of Norwich. These three differ greatly between themselves, but they all reveal a direct experience of God which is the result of a profound and moving religious faith quite consonant with the absence of rationalization. They deny the power of reason in the most significant human experience, and though the author of *The Cloud of Unknowing* is admirably sane, sensible, cool and logical, the title of his work is exact. It is remarkable that these mystics had much in common with Catherine of Siena, yet retreated into their cells and themselves. Whereas Chaucer must have known something about Catherine he seems to have known nothing about the English mystics, though in a curious way his secular attitudes and quietism corresponds to their religious one without being connected with it. The strict intellectual counterpart of mysticism is some version of a theory of illumination, of direct contact with the mind of God, which may support scientific inquiry, or prophecy, or poetry. There are traces of this theory in Chaucer's poetry, particularly in *The House of Fame*, but it is much more relevant to Langland's poetry than Chaucer's. Fond as Chaucer is of both presenting and masking himself, he never takes upon himself the mantle of prophet or inspired poet. His response took other turns.

One of these was another aspect of religious faith that could be undisturbed by sceptical Nominalism, and which flourished in the fourteenth century. This was the pleasure in sympathetic piety and pity that we have already seen in *An ABC*. The same pleasure at a rather more severe level is effectively evoked in the saint's life that Chaucer wrote, some time in the 1370s or early 1380s, that of St Cecilia, which he eventually put in *The Canterbury Tales* for *The Second Nun's Tale*. It is most beautifully presented in the charm and pathos of the beautiful *Prioress's Tale* about the little boy murdered by the Jews, which he must have written quite late in life. This sincere religious affection for the images of holy and gentle women and children is expressed in much beautiful and moving Gothic religious art in Europe in the late fourteenth century, in what is sometimes called the International Gothic Style, delicate, refined, rich with blue and red and gold. Beauty is intrinsic to it. It is part of that luxurious cultural religion which is so evident in the royal court, for example in Edward III's devotions. In English art of the time its loveliest expression is in the remarkable Wilton Diptych, which shows an idealized Richard II, with St John the Baptist, and the Anglo-Saxon royal saints Edmund and Edward standing behind him, kneeling to the Virgin and Child with angels. This is the same religious sentiment expressed in thousands of manuscript illuminations, pictures and frescoes all over Europe in the medieval centuries, which honours the carpenter's son with his artisan-class mother and earthly father, with his poverty and criminal's death, by representing him and his mother in the most luxurious royal wealth and splendour.

Although these pictures have an idealized beauty of person and setting that deliberately moves them far from the ordinary world into one that is rich and strange, they convey the spirit of the times with their vividly realistic, often domestic detail, which has a fascinating delicacy and charm, both in the main picture and those small pictures that so often border the large, either in manuscript borders, or in Italy the *predella* at the foot of the main picture. This is the same type of realism that is found in the domestic details of the *Mirror of the Life of Christ*, accompanying the expressive sentiments of monologues of complaint and pity equally realistic in their way. We find them in the religious *Prioress's Tale* and transposed to the secular sphere in *Troilus*. This cultural religion includes gently comic or grotesque elements, even to an occasional touch of amusing impropriety such as we find in the extraordinary mixture on the borders of the Beatus page (first page of the Psalms) of the Ormesby Psalter.

BELOW *Man terrified by a snail – a marginal joke in the Ormesby Psalter*

The impulse so to honour divinity (or even a good story) by dressing it up in the greatest conceivable earthly glory is natural enough. It did not prevent the apparently opposite impulse to conceive of poverty as the truly human, and as with some mystics and many ascetics (though not Chaucer), actually to seek pain, deprivation and desolation as the truest way to God. Chaucer does indeed represent something of this in the stories of Constance and Griselda. But the honouring of divinity as royalty, though it has biblical precedent, does at times seem to be at best a kind of capturing of Christianity by the rich and powerful, at worst a strange perversion of Christ's way and truth and life. This may be so even when the delicacy of the picture conveys an unexpected harshness of meaning if, as some have thought, the Wilton Diptych was painted for some political purpose to recommend Richard's policies. The luxury of the medium, and its implicit contrast with the humility of the message, was quite as much churchy as courtly. It could be seen in Florence in Or San Michele and Santa Croce, or in England in St Stephen's Chapel at Westminster Abbey which rivalled the Sainte-Chapelle in Paris, and in Becket's tomb, and the proud riches of the Black Prince's tomb (for all its self-mortifying verses) at Canterbury Cathedral.

At the same time as Chaucer would occasionally match these ambiguous splendours in his verse he could also, like many others, see the implicit contrast. A sense of the contrast prompted another opposite response, hostile to the worldly splendour of religion, in himself and in many contemporaries. Some of these, like William Flete, chose a traditionally ascetic eremitical life, or entered a severely disciplined monastic order, but it was now rather more characteristic of the times to take a newer, less clerical, version of the strait way to heaven, found in its more extreme form in the Lollard doctrines. We may take them as they derive from Wyclif, a priest and university theologian, though it is very important to remember how strong was the lay element in Lollardy. Wyclif himself took up an old-fashioned view of the problems of free will and predestination which enabled him to assert both God's foreknowledge and a humanly uncertain future. But since this technical theology was not specially significant to Lollardy and Chaucer shows no knowledge of it we may leave it aside. More available was Wyclif's assertion of the unassailable truth and hence authority of the Bible. This could and did lead to literalistic interpretations of biblical language, if not in Wyclif himself, at least in some of his followers. Since most ecclesiastical ceremonies and images are not mentioned in the Bible, and are in many cases even condemned in it, they were suspect if not positively wrong. Transubstantiation, whereby the priest changed bread and wine into the body and blood of Christ as God, was questioned. In Wyclif's view the lay power might in certain circumstances be superior to the Church, and it was questionable whether the Church should be richly endowed. All such points were simplified, emphasized and extended by Lollards in a series of English tracts in the last twenty years of the fourteenth century and in the fifteenth. An early form of these doctrines, or rather, a set of attitudes sympathetic to them, had penetrated the household of Joan of Kent, the king's mother and widow of the Black Prince, and the court itself, and are particularly associated with an interesting

Knights conversing

group called the Lollard knights, though just what they believed and how far they can be rightly called Lollards is still hard to know. Chaucer was not one of them but he was closely associated with some. Their lives and attitudes illustrate some of the Gothic contrasts of the age, and of Chaucer himself.

A total of ten knights were accused by two chroniclers of Lollardy but six are particularly important, Sir Richard Sturry, Sir Lewis Clifford, Sir Thomas Latimer, Sir William Neville, Sir John Clanvowe, Sir John Montagu. Although they came from different parts of the country they were associated together for many years in many documents, as witnesses, trustees, mainpernors, executors, and it is clear that they were friends with many financial and other interests in common. Four of them, Sturry, Clifford, Clanvowe and Neville, were knights of the king's chamber. Of the twenty-odd knights who held that position during the whole reign of Richard these four set themselves apart as a distinct group plus two other chamber knights, not accused by the chroniclers of Lollardy, Sir William Beauchamp and Sir Philip de la Vache (born 1346), who was Sir Lewis Clifford's son-in-law and heir. Of all these, Sturry, the eldest, born in the late 1320s, was a frequent associate of Chaucer in court business, notably the embassy of 1377, and was also a friend of Froissart. Clifford, born in 1336 or earlier, carried a poem by the French poet Eustache Deschamps in praise of Chaucer to him. Neville and Clanvowe, born about 1341 along with Sir William Beauchamp, were witnesses to the release that Chaucer made Cecily Champain give him concerning her *raptus*, and were thus important friends; Clanvowe was also author of the poem *The Book of Cupide* which is much influenced by *The Parliament of Fowls*. Latimer, the most extreme Lollard of them all, and Montagu, son of a peer and at least ten years younger than Chaucer, were not associated with him.

Chaucer's particular friends were thus the four chamber knights, Sturry, Clifford, Neville and Clanvowe, and in addition the rather older Sir William Beauchamp, and the slightly younger Sir Philip de la Vache. The focus of all, including Chaucer, is the court and household of Richard II, though most of them had some service with the Black Prince, which in the case of Clifford, Clanvowe and Vache continued with his widow until her death. But while they were certainly friends, even close friends, Chaucer cannot exactly be described as of the circle. The documents do not show him so intimately and continuously connected with them as they were with each other. Once again he evades classification and bestrides boundaries.

The careers of Chaucer's friends were roughly similar. They were all gentry, but none the head of a great family. Sir William Beauchamp was younger brother of the Earl of Warwick, Neville was the younger brother of John Lord Neville of Raby and of Alexander, Archbishop of York. These were the two grandest. Vache inherited some land, Clanvowe inherited a small estate. Sturry and Clifford started out as landless knights but they made considerable fortunes and all must be accounted rich, successful and powerful men of the world.

Sturry began as a yeoman of Edward III, 1349 to 1363, probably through the influence of a relative already at court, then esquire till 1366, then knight of the chamber which he continued with Richard II. He was serving at sea in 1347 at about the age of seventeen and was captured by the French, like Chaucer, on the same campaign of 1359–60. His bravery is noted by his friend Froissart. He is last found on active service in 1378. He married a rich and noble widow in 1374. His literary interests are witnessed to not only by his friendship with Froissart but his ownership of a copy of *Le Roman de la Rose*, now in the British Library (MS. 19 B XIII). His embassy to the French court in 1377, with Chaucer as a relatively junior associate, may have been important as bringing Chaucer in touch with French literary circles, though there is no specific result that we can point to for this, since Chaucer's knowledge of French literary culture through books was already extensive long before this.

Clifford, whose family is also quite obscure, became an esquire of the Black Prince, and after moved to the service of his widow and his son. He was taken prisoner in France in 1352, fought in Spain in 1367 with the Black Prince, in France with Gaunt in 1373, and again is last known to have been on active service in 1378. He too married a rich woman, widow of one peer and daughter of another. In 1378 he was made Knight of the Garter, and about the same time a knight of the king's household. He was the only one of the group to be invited to join the international crusading order of the Chevaliers de la Passion, a project of the French Philippe de Mezières. (Gaunt and Sir Oton de Granson, the Savoyard knight whose poetry in French was admired by Chaucer, and who spent much time in England, were also invited to join.) The chronicler Thomas Walsingham says that in 1378 Clifford terrified the bishops out of their intention to prosecute Wyclif. He received grants from both Joan of Kent and Gaunt as well as many grants from the king. In 1382, 1387 and 1395, chroniclers refer to his Lollardy, but he continued high in the councils of the government. In 1390, when he was at least fifty-five, he was one of the Englishmen who attended the famous jousts at St Inglevert near Calais, during a truce in the war, and was described by Froissart as very valiant and honourable. Soon after this tournament he took part in an international crusade to Barbary along with a number of distinguished Frenchmen. In the 1390s he, like Sturry, was several times an ambassador to France. In 1402, when he was nearly eighty, he is said by Walsingham to have supplied the Archbishop of Canterbury with a list of Lollard tenets and of heretical persons. This looks like recantation or treachery, but it was under the seal of the confessional, and even if it is true may have been the result of refined bullying as well as a betrayal of confidence by the archbishop. Clifford seems not to have undergone any change of heart or loss of friends, for a couple of years later he chose prominent Lollard leaders as executors to his will in 1404, and the will has such typical Lollard traits as extreme expressions of unworthiness, contempt for the body, refusal of funeral pomp.

Clifford establishes a link between Chaucer and the contemporary French poet Deschamps. Deschamps praises Chaucer as a 'great translator', presumably referring to Chaucer's early translation of *Le Roman de la Rose*, of which only a fragment exists. Since Deschamps does not appear to have known any English he must have been relying on Chaucer's general reputation as a poet in the

French fashion, perhaps relayed to him by Clifford. From early on Clifford had paid private visits to France in the intervals of what appear to us those wantonly destructive wars. Deschamps in another poem associates Clifford with such French noblemen as he was with on the expedition to Barbary, the Comte d'Eu, the Comte d'Harcourt, and Charles d'Albret, and with others of the most brilliant French society of the day. In this poem Deschamps says that he wishes to marry, asks the advice of the Seneschal d'Eu (not the same man as the comte, but chief author of a famous collection of love poems *Livre de Cent Ballades*) and refers the seneschal, if in doubt, to a higher authority on the problems of love –

Demandez ent a l'amoureux Cliffort

– ask the amorous Clifford about it. Strange epithet for a Lollard. This poem by Deschamps, like the one to Chaucer, is probably to be dated in the first half of the 1380s, perhaps as late as 1385–6. It gives us another brief glimpse into that brilliant international culture that filled in the gaps and margins of political events. It was personal, evanescent, unofficial, disregarded by chroniclers, lawyers and account, ants, yet of equal if not greater significance than major external events in the inner lives of people living at the time, and constituted the true milieu of Chaucer's poetry. Another glimpse comes in *The Prologue* to *The Legend of Good Women*, which refers implicitly to several of Deschamps' poems and to the courtly groups of the Flower and the Leaf. It is from Deschamps' poems we learn that Gaunt's eldest daughter Philippa was the great patroness of the Flower in England.

The apparent contradictions in Clifford's life are even more sharply focused in Sir John Clanvowe's, because he gave expression to them in writing. His ancestors were Welsh and his father an esquire of Edward III's household in 1349. He inherited an estate in the southern borderland between England and Wales where other Lollard knights also had territorial connections, and where several famous Lollard preachers found refuge. Clanvowe, like Chaucer and the rest, fought in French campaigns. He fought bravely at the skirmish at Lussac Bridge in 1369 so vividly described by Froissart, where the great soldier Sir John Chandos was killed. He, like the others, must have profited consider, ably from loot and ransoms as they rose in eminence, as Chaucer did not, in successive campaigns. Clanvowe was knight bachelor to the Earl of Hereford and on his death in 1373 moved to the service of Edward III. From the earl he received a life annuity of £40 and from Edward one of £50. On Edward III's death he moved to Richard's household, and followed the usual career of lucra, tive offices at home and embassies abroad, including the crusade to Barbary in 1390. His great friend was Neville and in the 1380s they are frequently found mentioned together – most notably, from Chaucer's point of view, in Cecily Champain's release to Chaucer concerning her *raptus*. He is last heard of at his death in October 1391 near Constantinople. Neville was with him and is said to have refused food from grief at his death and to have consequently died two days later (it might well have been from the same germ).

He wrote two very interesting works. One is a poem, *The Boke of Cupide*, a purely secular love-vision containing a debate about the nature of love, of a

characteristic courtly nature. It owes something to French poems, but is essentially modelled on *The Parliament of Fowls* and it begins with a quotation from *The
Knight's Tale*. Clanvowe probably wrote it in the second half of the 1380s when he
was in his late forties; he refers to himself as 'old and unlusty', but still a lover,
shaken by love sickness every May. It is another Valentine poem, and ends with
a compliment to 'the Queen at Woodstock' (palace). Perhaps it and *The Parliament* were part of a series of festival poems.

Clanvowe's other work is almost startlingly unlike. It is a religious tract in
prose, possibly the earliest religious tract by a layman in English and very well
written. This rich, successful soldier and courtier in his prose heartily condemns
war and the luxurious life of courts. He urges us to strive against the Devil, the
Flesh and the World, despise comfort and riches and honour and the evil
company of this world, which is called 'good fellows'; 'for they that will waste
the goods that God hath sent them, in pride of the world, and in lusts of their
flesh, and go to the tavern and to the brothel, and play at the dice, wake long at
nights, and swear fast, and drink, and chatter too much, scorn, backbite, jape
(i.e. jest), glose (i.e. flatter), boast, lie, fight, and are bawds for their fellows, and
live all in sin and vanity, they are held "Good fellows".' One feels that he
knows what he is talking about. ('Good fellows' is a phrase that Chaucer also
uses sarcastically in relation to drink and sex.) The right thing to do is to keep
the ten commandments, which Clanvowe rehearses – shades of the Primer –
and to love God, and our neighbour as ourselves. He emphasizes the poverty of
Christ's birth and life, the suffering of his death. He seems to take to himself,
though indirectly, the word 'loller' (idler) often contemptuously applied to
Lollards, but he does not expound any specific Lollard doctrines. He does not
demand the disendowment of the Church; he neglects it entirely and preaches a

*A carved panel from a ches.
illustrating all the events of
The Pardoner's Tale*

simple, literal, New Testament Christianity. Yet how literally did he take all this himself in his life? We should never guess from the external facts of his career that he felt this deep religious concern. But neither should we have guessed that Henry of Grosmont, thirty or forty years before, had the same religious concern if we did not have his *Livre de Seintz Medecines* (Book of Holy Medicines).

In one respect Clanvowe continues a recognizable line of serious devotion in the court whose sincerity is unquestionable and which is too easily overlooked when dealing only with records and events. With him it moves from French into the English language and takes over a vein of authority remarkable in a layman, but characteristic of the behaviour of the Lollard knights. Clifford had outfaced the bishops. Neville, and Sir Thomas Latimer actively protected Lollard preachers. They also had the reputation of showing their contempt for the 'miracle' of the Mass by retaining their hoods on their heads in its presence. From this they were sometimes called the 'hooded knights'. Even so, it is hard to guess, especially in the light of Clanvowe's treatise, how far they identified themselves with specific aspects of the Lollard programme, partly because this programme was worked out piecemeal from Wyclif's Latin works and from many English tracts that are impossible to date with any certainty. The first obviously public Lollard statement was the famous 'Twelve Conclusions' pinned up on the doors of St Paul's and of Westminster Abbey in 1395. Maybe those of the knights still alive had something to do with them, but if so their views had become more explicit than they were in the 1380s, and thus further from Chaucer.

A brief word may be added about the two remaining friends of Chaucer in this set. Sir William Beauchamp was the younger son of Thomas Earl of Warwick, and was born in the 1320s. It was he who had the closest connection with Gaunt, for though the others served him in war and received occasional grants and gifts, Beauchamp was indentured to him in peace as well as war, a much closer relationship. He was connected with Gaunt's household as early as 1340. He followed the usual career of well-rewarded appointments, became chamberlain of Richard's household as already mentioned, and eventually Lord Bergavenny. His support of Chaucer in the case of Cecily Champain was probably the act of a friend rather than merely an instance of an official supporting one of his subordinates, for Chaucer along with John Beverley, another very well-rewarded esquire, had himself mainprised Beauchamp in 1378. This was in connection with the king's grant to Beauchamp to 'farm' some of the estates of the Earl of Pembroke, to whom he was related, and whose heir he was. The latter being a minor his revenue went to the king, who farmed the estates out to other people. They paid the king a fee (in Beauchamp's case £500 per annum, which shows what big business it was), and then got what they could out of the estate to pay themselves, with the obligation to keep it in good condi-tion. It appears that Beauchamp neglected this obligation, or at least his officials did, and he was eventually deprived of the right to farm. In 1387 he was Captain of Calais and on the side of the Lords Appellant against the king. Chaucer intended to accompany him from England to Calais on 5 July 1387, though as Chaucer was back in England on 1 August, and his wife was probably ill if not dead about this time, he may not actually have gone. Although associated with the Lollard knights Beauchamp gave grants of land to religious bodies in the 1390s. He seems not to have been very prominent as a courtier in the last decade of Richard's reign but flourished under Henry IV and died in 1412. He became a Knight of the Garter and married a rich heiress. He may have been more impor-tant to Chaucer than at first appears, because one of several of his lawyers was Thomas Pinchbeck, who dared to contradict him in his claim to Pembroke's estates while the young earl was still alive. Pinchbeck is probably the original of Chaucer's satirical portrait of the land-acquiring Man of Law in *The General Prologue*. The satirical portrait there of the rascally Reeve of Norfolk may also result from a Beauchamp connection, if, as seems likely, it is based on an official who managed some of the Pembroke estates in Norfolk. Beauchamp might very well have subscribed to Clanvowe's sentiments expressed in The Two Ways without going so far as his younger friends.

Sir Philip de la Vache, to whom Chaucer addressed his serious short poem 'Truth', was perhaps born in 1346. His father had been a soldier and courtier who had gradually acquired the estates and status of a country gentleman. Our first glimpse of Philip is the petition of his father to the Pope in 1358 on behalf of his son, aged twelve, for a benefice (i.e. position in the Church) of the value of £30 in the gift of the Bishop of Lincoln. He also asked for another, worth £40, for another son, Edward, aged eleven. Both were granted. A curate would have been put in to do the actual work of the parish at a wage of about ten marks (£6. 13s. 4d.) a year. This was the kind of thing that enraged Lollards and other serious-minded men, and an odd beginning for a Lollard sympathizer. Vache became a knight of the chamber at the end of Edward's reign and, incidentally, like Beverley, was asked to tell what he knew about Alice Perrers in the case of Richard Lyons. Like Beverley he gave a courtier's reply, to the effect that when he heard Alice discussing her business he went out of the room. He received some very large grants, and apart from a period of obscurity from 1386 to 1389 prospered exceedingly and married the daughter of Clifford, who was not poor. He too was made a Knight of the Garter. He died in 1408. It looks as if he did a good deal of struggling for the hoarded wealth of this world, which Chaucer in his poem to Vache says brings only hatred. Yet he was also at least convention-ally pious, as the charitable bequests in his will show, and Clifford had bequeathed him his mass book (prayerbook) and his breviary (a collection of psalms, readings, extracts of saints' lives). If Vache was greedy he was at least susceptible to Chaucer's serious but genial approach, perhaps reproach, in his poem with its witty puns.

To sum up, these knights were brave, competent, worldly, serious gentlemen, who were a most significant element in Chaucer's life and primary audience. Their inconsistencies were probably little greater than those in our own lives, but we lack the intimate historical knowledge that might help to resolve theirs. Their Lollardy was more general than particular, and may have been tainted by the desire to acquire, or retain, Church endowments, but it is impossible to dispute their vein of serious thought about spiritual matters and it should not be sneered at as cant. It went along with a direct knowledge of what it is to be a soldier, to kill and run the risk of being killed, to be responsible for men's lives; to help in the management of armies and of the country; to know Europe even in its further reaches to the Middle East and the borders of Russia; to be a member of the international class of European nobility; to read and perhaps write in two or three languages; to have a sophisticated interest in the most imaginative of personal worldly experience, sexual love, with all its pains and joys. It was not unreasonable for such men to be concerned with their own personal advancement and that of their families – which of us, apart from monks or recluses, is not? Even monks and recluses must rely on such men's support to enable them to pursue their own life of self-abnegation. Chaucer's Knight is described in *The General Prologue* as having a distinguished record as a soldier and Christian, loving chivalry and

BELOW *A lady arms her knight. The Bermondsey Dish, English* c. 1325

> Trouthe and honour, fredom, and curteisie. [generosity]
> CT I, l. 46

BOTTOM *A fourteenth century silver spoon with diamond-point finial*

There are soldiers like that, even in this century; and it is not hard to think of Clifford or Clanvowe in these same terms. The Knight tells a noble tale of love, as Clifford might have done, with its characteristic love problems.

The inclination to Lollardy in these knights testifies to a sympathy with the progressive interiorization of values that marks the age. We may leave aside the special Lollard doctrines since they do not appear to have concerned Chaucer. The hostility towards images, the refusal to accept the miracle of Transubstantiation of bread and wine in the Mass, the scepticism about outward ceremony of all kinds, including pilgrimage, show how the attribution of sacredness was being withdrawn from external objects and concentrated in the individual human mind. The external world and its forms were becoming more 'objective', neutral in value. Interiorization thus promoted a greater sense of the individual in himself as against the world. Social and religious structures, being general and less personal, seemed not only less valuable, they seemed a positive hindrance to free and loving communion between individuals. The interiorization of values made both inner and outer life more vivid, though more separate. It made it harder to match inner with outer, and thus promoted both sceptical realism (in our sense) and fervent faith. It raised extremely difficult problems of causality and salvation. It did not necessarily deny either the pleasures of the world, or of piety, though it made them more precarious, perhaps more superficial, more luxurious. The elaboration of prettiness might be indulged, and its possession, as with the dozens of silver spoons, cups, etc., listed in the wills of Vache and others.

Although Chaucer was more in the line of Ockham's sceptical Nominalism than Wyclif's own Realism it is easy to see how the separately derived influences might in part coincide. The emphasis on empirical objective experience might for example derive from both. The atmosphere of theological debate engendered by Lollardy could encourage the interest of laymen in the deep problems of free will and determinism. Chaucer's own scepticism may owe more to the Ockhamist influence, but a certain anti-intellectualism in Lollardy could also encourage it. A new significance was attributed to individual experience and responsibility by both lines of influence. Both encouraged literalistic interpretations of language. In one respect Lollardy might be particularly influential – in encouraging the use of the English language. Wyclif's emphasis on Scripture included impressive arguments for having the Scripture in the mother tongue, and this was avidly taken up by laymen, with powerful effects ultimately for English culture. Many other forces encouraged the development of English in the late fourteenth century, but religious need and desire were certainly not the least. Finally the lay element deserves to be emphasized again. Although the original powerhouses of thought were in the universities there is a real sense of the English people as a whole stirring with new consciousnesses.

It will not do to emphasize total novelty. Many lay people had long shown an interest in religious problems that had irritated Oxford theologians. The roots of feeling and knowledge went deep. There is a powerful force for interiorized values in the New Testament from the very beginning. What was known of classical philosophy and ethics also sowed seeds of inner spiritual strength. It was to an amalgam of these influences in the work of Boethius that Chaucer turned to work out the problems of his own spiritual interests. Even this was characteristic of layman's interest. Boethius's *Consolation of Philosophy* is an extremely eclectic work. Boethius, who died in 524, was a Christian who was well acquainted with Plato and Aristotle, and the Latin authorities Cicero and Seneca. After a distinguished career he was imprisoned and put to death. The Consolation claims to have been written in prison by Boethius to reason himself into accepting his fate. It was immensely popular and influential in the Middle Ages, and is indeed a noble and moving work. Boethius does not use Christian revelation with which to console himself, though he might have done, but the processes of rational thought distilled from Greek philosophy. As a technical work of philosophy it is open to obvious objections and had long been left behind by the clerics in the medieval universities. It is indeed a kind of poor man's Plato. But in its attempt at rationalization of faith, its struggle with the problems of free will and predestination, its quest for inner confidence and true happiness, it was very well suited for consideration by serious-minded men of the world, who longed for happiness in contemplating the world's adversities, and who were not professional theologians and philosophers. It stood at a central place in the cross-currents of thought where Chaucer stood. Its old-fashioned rationality meets a perpetual human need but in terms that could appeal to a Wycliffite Realism which ultimately derived from Plato. The long debate on free will and destiny particularly appealed to those affected by Ockhamist scepticism. The way in which Boethius presents himself as a character in his own work engaged in a debate with the Lady Philosophy was attractive to the emerging individualism of the age and Chaucer's own ambivalence towards himself. The work is written in alternate prose and verse, and the interpolated philosophical songs are of great beauty. (Chaucer incorporates one of them entire in *Troilus*.) The grand image of Fortune's wheel, so influential throughout the Middle Ages, and many of Boethius's incidental thoughts and

This fine White Hart, from the back of the Wilton Diptych, was Richard II's personal badge and thus has an heraldic significance – but it is painted with a delicately idealized naturalism. The diptych itself (see p. 167) has the same quality, though it may also have served as political propaganda

phrases, all made the work immensely attractive to Chaucer. He had known about it for many years, for it is extensively used in *Le Roman de la Rose*, but in about the early 1380s, Chaucer confronted its difficult Latin with resolution and the aid of a French crib and commentary, and began the massive task of trans‑ lating it into careful English prose. It is not too much to say that he was obsessed with it, and *Troilus* and *The Knight's Tale*, together with those short, highly personal, poems 'The Former Age', 'Fortune', 'Truth', 'Gentilesse', 'Lak of stedfastnesse', are all shot through with Boethian thought and feeling.

The essence of the *Consolation* is the assertion that mind is superior to matter. True reality is different from worldly appearances which are often positively false. Reality is good and loving, and the only true and lasting happiness is to perceive reality, which can be done not through the physical body but by the eye of the mind. Nevertheless, Chaucer's *Boece* is only a translation. The great embodiment and transformation of the values of the *Consolation* is in the *Troilus*, one of the greatest poems in the language in that majestic procession of *Beowulf*, *The Faerie Queene*, *Paradise Lost*, *The Dunciad*, *The Prelude*. Yet it differs from these in a characteristically Gothic and Chaucerian way in not having a 'great' subject. The hero is indeed a prince of Troy and the heroine a lady, but the love story is private, in fact secret, cut off from the social and public world which in the end unknowingly and impersonally destroys it. The gulf between public and private opens almost as wide in the poem as it does in our knowledge of Chaucer's own life and of what we can deduce of his contemporaries.

Chaucer took the story from Boccaccio's *Il Filostrato*, itself an expansion of older, briefer accounts of the love of Troilus and Criseyde. Chaucer expanded it again, with the sort of domestic realistic detail noticed in the *Mirror of the Life of Christ* and, by analogy, in Italian art. He enriched it with Boethian philosophy, a varied style, and a regular metre that never becomes monotonous. In itself the poem seems inexhaustible to scholars and critics. For an account of Chaucer's life and times we must restrict ourselves to the central images of Troilus's falling in love, the beauty of his life when he has won Criseyde, and the depth of his sorrow when she deserts him. Besides these two there is only one other significant character, Pandarus, of indeterminate age, friend of Troilus, uncle of Criseyde, and a most lively, delightful character. The great soldier Troilus is too shy and decent to seduce Criseyde, and it is Pandarus who by shady means brings them together in bed. From him comes our word pander, a bawd; a function regarded in the fourteenth century as deeply shameful. No parents, literally or symboli‑ cally, hinder the affair, only the modesty and inhibitions of Troilus and Criseyde. The whole story is told most realistically and we are completely in Fortune's world. When Troilus wins Criseyde they are both completely happy, and there is a daily beauty in Troilus's life: he is the very incarnation of *trouthe* and *gentilesse*, which are inspired by love.

Rush‑strewn floors were by no means universal. Beautifully inlaid tile floors, like this one from William Canynge's house in Bristol were found in rich merchant's houses and palaces alike. No doubt this is how we are to imagine the 'paved parlour' in which Criseyde and her ladies sat and 'herden a mayden reden hem the geste | Of the Sege of Thebes, whyl hem leste.'

But al to litel, weylaway the whyle,	[alas the time]
Lasteth swich joie, ythonked be Fortune,	[such]
That semeth trewest whan she wol bygyle,	
And kan to fooles so hire song entune	

That she hem hent and blent, traitour commune[catches & blinds them]
And whan a wight is from hire whiel ythrowe,
Than laugheth she, and maketh hym the mowe.[makes a face at him]
IV ll. 1–7

Criseyde is forced to go to the Greek camp, where she becomes the mistress of the unworthy Diomede. To match the period of joy we have a long, painful account of Troilus's waiting, self-deception about Criseyde's intentions, and his final bitterness, though he never ceases to love Criseyde. This is the fullest confrontation by Chaucer of that inner sense of loss and betrayal that his earlier poems all allude to. No one could have written it without having experienced it; it is the loss of love, though whether Chaucer himself experienced it as loss of a beloved woman or in some other way we shall never know. In one form or another it is a very common experience which few people escape.

Troilus is never reconciled to his loss, but is killed in battle. Then his spirit goes up to the eighth sphere and he looks down upon this little speck of earth, and laughs at the sorrow of those mourning for him. This ending has aroused great controversy, contradicting as it does the apparently novel-like realism of the telling of the story, and apparently mocking our natural sympathy for the sufferings of Troilus. Is the flight to heaven mere escape from our denial of the difficulties of life?

I do not think so. The poet in telling the poem constantly takes up different attitudes to the central subject, now serious, now flippant, and this last view, perhaps the most important, is not a cancellation of what has gone before. Chaucer's poetic insight has taken Boethius one stage further. In the Consolation Boethius has a fine poem about the bond of love by which God controls even the physical universe and men and women (*II*, m.8). Chaucer puts this whole poem into a song by Troilus (*III*, ll. 1744ff). God loves the world, even though it is flawed. But according to Boethius, man should love not the world, but God in heaven. Here is no home. Here n'is but wilderness. Troilus loves the world, in the person of Criseyde, and of course the world will always let one down – if people do not betray one, they die, as did Blanche. But Troilus's own love is not false or unstable. Stability is the crucial value for Boethius and Chaucer, signifying faith, loyalty, truth (Boece *III*, m.11), which is God himself, and which also must dwell in oneself as much as in heaven. Troilus is a virtuous man who is absolutely loyal, faithful, stable and though his love affair is not validated by marriage he always treats it as if it were (Criseyde is another matter). The poem is not a moralistic one; it is about profound human experience. Whereas Boethius seems to lean towards an otherworldly asceticism, Chaucer seems to assert that a transient joy, though transient, is nevertheless a real joy. Troilus loved an unstable object. He would have suffered less had he loved a stable one, the only stable one, God in Christ, but his suffering does not negate his joy. There is implicit here a sort of Protestant Christian materialism that may owe something to Lollard influence. In 1395 the Twelve Conclusions of the Lollards attacked vows of chastity for men and women as leading to worse vices than unchastity – not that fourteenth-century courts were hotbeds of chastity, anyway.

The world: Appearance (top) and Reality (above)

The long, painful portrayal of Troilus's desolation reminds us of the Black Knight's sorrow, implicitly consoled by the recollection of joy. Along with memory in *Troilus* is the distancing effect of the long view of human life, and the real alternative of the love of God. Balancing all these together, Chaucer by recognizing and expressing loss seems to have begun to reconcile himself to it.

Another form of reconciliation comes in *Palamon and Arcite*, now *The Knight's Tale*, written about the same time. Here we have two heroes or, symbolically, two aspects of the same protagonist, the one aggressive (*Arcite*) and the other more passive and respectful (*Palamon*), though in worth as knights they are equal. Both love the beautiful Emily. Again, the story is taken from Boccaccio, this time from his would-be epic, *Teseida*, though Chaucer transforms it into a Boethian romance. The two knights, though sworn brothers, fight over Emily, and Arcite is killed. After years of mourning Palamon marries her. It is a most splendid poem. What the story in Chaucer's hands seems to show is that you stand a fifty-fifty chance of happiness. It also states quite explicitly, in Boethian speeches put into the mouth of the noble Duke Theseus and his aged father, that you have to accept death as part of life, and 'make a virtue of necessity'. In this poem many of the themes of Chaucer's earlier poems and thought about life come together; questions of love, of necessity and free will, of courtly life, of death, are seriously considered (not without some flippant asides), and are effectively resolved, by resolution, independence and acceptance.

In these two poems, *Troilus* and *Palamon and Arcite*, Chaucer achieved a full maturity that remained unchallenged till his deathbed. The proof lies in the relative failure of his next poem, *The Legend of Good Women*. It has plenty of interest with a most delightful 'Prologue' that has an authentic autobiographical touch, and a series of poems that effectively exploit a vein of plain narrative and pathos. They are the stories of betrayed and deserted women that had always affected Chaucer. No stories told by Chaucer could be badly done, but there are signs of a lack of interest, and of some score promised, only nine are told, with the last not quite complete. It looks as if they were indeed commissioned, as the 'prologue' suggests, but the steam had gone out of the engine. Chaucer had written himself out on the subject. He used it once again, in *The Franklin's Tale*, but in a somewhat ambivalent tone. From now on he was free. Always experimental, he would turn to other stories, of great variety, with supreme artistic virtuosity, as a spokesman for many different attitudes in the culture of the time; he would be a kind of prism showing the spectrum of light of his day. Having plumbed the depths of loss he could return to the surface; with a greater sense of reality he could contemplate appearances with a detached yet loving interest; he could afford to treat this little world as if of central importance, knowing in his heart it was marginal.

CHAPTER ELEVEN

AMONG THE MUSES IN KENT

But here I ame in Kent and Christendome
Emong the muses where I rede and ryme.
Wyatt, Satires

FROM FEBRUARY 1385 CHAUCER BEGAN TO WITHDRAW from his engagement with London and Westminster. Now in his middle-to-late forties, the great plan of *The Canterbury Tales* must have been taking shape. His relatively modest financial requirements were being met. In February 1385 he was granted permission to appoint a permanent deputy controller at the wool quay. (He still had the responsibility of reporting in person at the Exchequer to witness that the collectors' accounts were accurate, without actually doing the daily work.) This permission was countersigned by the Earl of Oxford, Robert de Vere, the king's hereditary chamberlain and greatest favourite, being only five years older than Richard, and thus now twenty-three. On 10 October of the same year Chaucer was appointed a justice of the peace for the county of Kent. It is most unlikely that he received such an appointment without being a landowner in Kent. In August 1386 he was elected Knight of the Shire for Kent for the Parliament that was called for 1 October 1386, and this is another indication that he was a man of substance in Kent. He gave up his accommodation over Aldgate in September or therea-bouts, for another man took it over on 5 October 1386. In December 1386 successors were appointed to his posts in the customs, which he had held rather longer than usual. No documents survive of his landownership, but he probably lived in Greenwich 'there many a shrew is in' as he jokes in *The Canter-bury Tales* (I, l. 3907).

So he moved his desk with its sloping top and cupboards underneath full of books, his chests of clothes and silver and pewter, his two children and perhaps ailing wife out to more wholesome air by the riverside. By this time he had written, according to the first form of the *Prologue* to *The Legend of Good Women*, all the works already mentioned, including the *Life of St Cecilia* and the now lost *Origenes upon the Magdalen*, and many balades, roundels and virelayes (short poems with complicated rhyme schemes). He may also have written some of the individual legends themselves. *The Prologue* itself is a bridge between the two major works of his maturity, *Troilus* and *The Canterbury Tales*. It sums up a long period of courtly writing, but with some things in common with later works. Although it has some inconsistency it is the most successful part of the whole work. Chaucer himself must have felt both the shortcomings and the success for he revised the first version of the *Prologue* (now labelled 'F') after he had effectively abandoned the individual stories, and some time after the death of Queen Anne

OPPOSITE '... *in the joly tyme of May | When that I here smale foules syneg | And that the floures gynne for to sprynge ....' Rich and poor go into the fields to pick may*

on 7 June 1394, for in this second ('G' version) the reference in F to presenting the book when finished to the queen, at either Eltham or Sheen, is deleted.

This reference in F to the queen is one of the very few references in Chaucer's poetry to anyone who could be remotely regarded as patron or patroness. Another possible reference, also to Queen Anne, is the apparent compliment in *Troilus* (I, l. 171) to her, 'right as our first letter is now an A', though this remark was also a religious commonplace (above p. 55). In the case of the *Prologue* it seems sensible to take it at face value. Perhaps the queen herself, or others, really had complained of Chaucer's presentation in *Troilus* of an unfaithful woman; feminism has as long a history, presumably, as male chauvinism, and Chaucer's work illustrates both; but he had a deep sympathy with women. If it is agreed that there is a real difference between men and women there seems something characteristically feminine in his sympathy for others, his lack of aggression, a certain tenderness of feeling. Moreover, the relatively marginal, inferior and 'unofficial' position of women in fourteenth-century courtly society, whose official culture was dominated by masculine military and ecclesiastical values, was a position which in his poetry and as a poet Chaucer normally chose for himself. The sympathy the poet expresses for Criseyde in the course of telling the story is not cynical, even though the course of events reveals her treachery. The reference to the queen is a precious glimpse of the acceptability of Chaucer's poetry to courtly society. *The Prologue*, along with other poems like *Troilus* and *The Knight's Tale*, which specifically address an audience of knights and ladies, or an audience of 'lovers', must have been read to such groups, often by the poet himself, as the story of Thebes was read to Criseyde and her ladies in her paved parlour, and as poets have read to friends, admirers – and critics – in all ages. The Prologue also refers to the orders of the Flower and of the Leaf, as already mentioned. At this stage it comes as no surprise that Chaucer refuses to take sides with either. No poem of Chaucer brings us closer to the social circumstances of much of his work. This *Prologue* is the last of his literary love visions and perhaps another St Valentine's Day poem, which very consciously borrows heavily from Deschamps in particular, yet it also gives us a startlingly fresh sense of pleasure in nature, even granted the consciously absurd fiction of his going out into the fields in May to worship the awaking daisy. Those lines in which he relates his devotion to reading, except,

> certeynly, whan that the month of May
> Is comen, and that I here the foules synge,
> And that the floures gynnen for to sprynge,
> Farewel my bok, and my devocioun!
> Pro L G W (F) ll. 35–9

are rightly among the best known of all his work. He could easily have reached the fields from his dwelling over Aldgate, and the little garden that he describes might have been there too, for there was plenty of space around. But perhaps Kent, the Garden of England, was even in the fourteenth century a more natural setting for a vision of the God of Love and the daisy-strewn meadows. The poem wherever composed would have been part of some festival at the royal palaces, say at Richmond, just south of the river, not too far from Greenwich.

It is not likely that being a justice of the peace much interrupted Chaucer's reading. The office was not very onerous, any more than it was very welcome. It developed during the fourteenth century and was a device for linking the power of the Crown to the interests of the local gentry for the benefit of both in keeping the country under control, literally keeping the peace. The justices' job was to investigate felonies, i.e. serious crimes, like murder, as well as a variety of less important offences, like assault, infringements of food laws and of labour laws. These were dealt with at four sessions a year of three days each. Unluckily no records for the sessions in Kent during Chaucer's time remain. At times out of session justices might have to perform various duties concerning local elections, or to stamp passes for migrating labourers, act as sureties, etc. It all meant some degree of involvement in the local community. The busy and very rich financier Richard Lyons thought it worth his while, in 1380, to buy exemption for life from being made sheriff, escheator, coroner, collector of taxes, or J.P.

The significance of Chaucer's appointment from our point of view is that it shows Chaucer's relatively, but only relatively, high status, and some of his associates. A total of eighteen are named with him on the two commissions on which he served, and these were traditionally divided into three groups — magnates, lawyers and local gentry. The chief magnate was Sir Simon Burley, the tutor of Richard II, now the master of the household, and a power behind the throne, but also constable of Dover Castle, to which he owed this position. He was a career courtier like Clifford and Sturry, and Chaucer must have known him moderately well for some time. He came from a family who had held lands in Herefordshire from soon after the Conquest. His uncle, Walter Burley, had been in the earlier part of the century a don at Merton and was a renowned philosopher who had been tutor to the Black Prince. Simon and his brother John had as usual been soldiers, and connected with the Black Prince, with Edward III, and then with Richard's household. They had been richly rewarded. They were both Knights of the Garter, and frequently on embassies. Sir John was Chaucer's senior associate on a secret mission abroad in 1376–7. In 1366 he went as one of an embassy from the Black Prince in Bordeaux to Bayonne just north of Spain to meet Don Pedro the Cruel. This is the kind of journey Chaucer had made in that same year, perhaps about the same business. Sir Simon was a man of culture who left twenty-one books. They include a Bible, a book of saint's lives, Sydrak (a religious work) and other religious works, books on philosophy, history, government, and no less than eight books of romances in French, one of them at least on King Arthur. There was a book of the prophecies of Merlin (a curious kind of political work) and a multilingual dictionary. The Bible may have been in French (such vernacular translation never being forbidden to the aristocracy, only English to Englishmen), and he had at least one book (title unknown) in Latin. Simon Burley may have been arrogant; at all events he was soon to come to a very sticky end at the hands of the Lords Appellant in the Merciless Parliament. He was the senior person named in the Commission of the Peace for Kent and he alone was constituted as the quorum (i.e. the essential member) in 1386, so he is bound to have attended the sessions. We may hope that he and Chaucer, old acquaintances, were able to discuss *Le Roman de la Rose,* or problems of love, as well as problems of felony, in the intervals of cases. Another magnate was John de Cobham, from an old family in Kent and one of the most important barons of the day. He was, however, on the side of the Lords Appellant, and there can have been little love lost between him and Burley. Sir John Devereux was also associated with the Lords Appellant, though both he and Cobham seem to have been moderate men.

There were two more magnates, equally distinguished, and six lawyers, of whom five were serjeants-at-law. Since, however, at least four of them were justices in the king's court and had their names *ex officio* on very many county commissions of the peace, it is unlikely that they ever sat, though Chaucer would obviously have known them. One of them, William Rickhill, was also a landowner in Kent and may have sat. He headed another commission on which Chaucer also sat, and served on the Surrey commission that investigated the assault made on Chaucer in 1390.

There were eight members of the gentry who were rich landowners in Kent, who had been to the wars, served on various commissions, were knights of the shire in Parliament, or served as sheriff, etc. Two of them, Hugh Fastolf and William Topcliffe, were king's esquires. Fastolf had been paid money for winter and summer robes along with Chaucer in 1373, so presumably was another old acquaintance. He was also a rich citizen of London, yet another fishmonger, and became sheriff of London in 1387. He and Chaucer might have had a lot in common. Chaucer's social and financial status must have equalled that of his associates. He too served as M.P., and must have been a well-to-do local landowner like them. He ceased to be a J.P. in 1389, probably because he was at the same time appointed Clerk of the King's Works.

He served as M.P., that is, as Knight of the Shire in the parliament of October 1386, no doubt with much reluctance. There was a good deal of reluctance to become knights, except for men from great families, or those who were trying to carve out a career and a heritage with their swords. Chairborne warriors who wrote chronicles in the quiet safety of their monasteries might deplore it, but most squires and gentlemen very understandably preferred to cultivate their own farms and attend to personal business, rather than perform the usually unpaid, expensive, often unpopular and sometimes dangerous public duties that government was trying to lay upon men of a certain substance. Chaucer certainly had more interesting things to do, namely read and write. Nevertheless there must have been a certain amount of local pressure as well as pressure from government, particularly to obtain knights for parliamentary representation, and thus many of the parliamentary 'knights of the shire' who made up the bulk of the Commons, and who were necessary to government especially for the granting of taxes, were in fact local squires and gentlemen who had not been ceremonially knighted at all. There is no reason to think that Chaucer any more than Froissart, who gives a detailed account of the knighting ceremony, with its vigil, bathing, girding with sword and spur, deplored or sneered at it. Chaucer seems to have accepted such ceremonies and shared their

Roofers at work: Chaucer as Clerk of the King's Works was responsible for managing and paying men who worked on the buildings

underlying values, without wishing to take part in them himself. So I presume he undertook the duty of attending Parliament, since he could not honourably or practicably evade it, with as much efficiency as he could command, without any enthusiasm whatever. Thirty-three of the seventy-one shire representatives were not real knights and perhaps felt much like him. They were a fairly mixed lot, however, some of whom attended parliament more than once, and must have varied in the degree of interest they took.

It was not a session that would encourage a man to wish to try another, though it earned the name of the 'Wonderful Parliament'. The state of affairs in the country was extremely alarming and the king made matters worse. There was a widespread fear of French invasion, while at home bands of unpaid soldiers terrorized the suburbs of London and the counties round about. The king had quarrelled bitterly with Gaunt in 1384 and especially in 1385, when together they led a large army with lamentably feeble effect into Scotland. Richard disliked the warlike magnates, though they were the king's natural counsellors and comrades, and preferred his own more indolent, pacific, and frivolous circle of young friends, his little queen, and indulgent elders. His mother Joan, the most stabilizing and reconciling element at court, died in July 1385 (Chaucer receiving three and a half ells of black cloth for mourning, as one of the king's esquires). Richard was only a nineteen-year-old boy, highly intelligent and sensitive, brought up in circum-stances that could only make him extraordinarily conceited and wilful. It was not surprising that he preferred the company of Robert de Vere, Earl of Oxford, who seems to have been a handsome, fairly silly young man, as spoiled as Richard, to the dour violence of Thomas of Woodstock, Duke of Gloucester, Richard's youngest uncle, only twelve years older than him, who represented the general feeling of the magnates, hankering after the old ways of successful war. Whoever was close to the king made a large profit in power and possessions. So did De Vere, and another of his counsellors

Michael de la Pole, son of the great merchant, who had become chancellor in 1383. This ensured the enmity of the magnates. Pole had been made Earl of Suffolk and granted a large estate in 1385, in which year Richard also created De Vere a marquess – a title whose novelty increased its offence. Gaunt, who might have smoothed things over between his nephew and youngest brother, in 1386 went off seeking castles in Spain. Parliament, instigated by Gloucester, demanded Pole's resignation. Richard withdrew to his palace at Eltham and replied that he would not dismiss even one of his scullions at the request of Parliament. However, he made some concessions after menacing references were made to him about Edward II. Pole, who was probably least guilty, was dismissed, impeached by parliament and imprisoned, and a continual council, including Gloucester and Chaucer's two colleagues on the Commission of the Peace for Kent, Cobham and Devereux, as well as several bishops, was set up to guide the king. All this happened in a couple of months, and during this time Chaucer also made his deposition in the Scrope-Grosvenor trial through which we guess his age (above, pp. 15–16). On 28 November, he received a warrant for payment of his expenses for sixty-one days in Parliament.

Since some minor officials lost their jobs about this time it may be that Chaucer was forced out of the customs as one of the king's party. But with his friends in every camp this seems unlikely. The king was by no means entirely fettered. Burley held his position; Pole's fine was remitted and he was sent to Windsor 'where Burley was his jailer and where the king joined them for Christmas'.

This was no happy augury. It showed the king deeply unwilling to cooperate. During the next year the opposing sides gathered their forces together throughout the country and the storm broke with the battle of Radcot Bridge in Oxfordshire, December 1387, between De Vere's forces, gathered mainly from Richard's royal earldom of Cheshire, always loyal to him, and the rebel lords, Gloucester and the Earls of Arundel and Warwick, now joined by the Earl of Nottingham and no less a person than Gaunt's eldest son, Henry Bolingbroke, Earl of Derby, twenty-one years old, only six months older than Richard. De Vere fled, and the rebel lords marched on London where the aldermen who had refused Richard leave to billet his troops there welcomed them. Richard had to yield and in January 1388 many of his courtiers were sent away and many of his household officials were sacked. Burley lost his lordship of Dover Castle and the wardenship of the Cinque ports.

In February a new Parliament – later called the Merciless Parliament – met in which the rebel lords 'appealed', that is, accused, various of Richard's friends of treason – hence the term, Lords Appellant. Pole and De Vere had fled, and the Archbishop of York (Alexander Neville, brother of Sir William Neville, Chaucer's Lollard friend) saved by his cloth, was translated to St Andrew's in Scotland, next door to outer darkness. The able but arrogant and violent grocer, Brembre, Chaucer's old collector, met the full horrors of the death for treason, while Burley was mercifully granted beheading, as were two other chamber knights. Thomas Usk was executed. The evidence in all these cases was dubious and the punishments cruel, though mainly limited to those regarded as principals. If there was sympathy for the sufferers there was no discernible general movement against the Lords Appellant and in favour of the king.

Could Chaucer have quoted Shakespeare he might have said, 'A plague on both your houses.' He wanted to get on with his own work, and mostly did so, but there were interruptions. He had to go up to Westminster occasionally for matters of business; a commission of inquiry into an abduction with Rickhill in May 1387; collection of his annuities; the winding up of his customs account. Then between June and November 1387, his wife died. Whether they were happy together or not we do not know. In the amusing little poem entitled 'Lenvoy de Chaucer a Bukton', advising Bukton to stay unmarried if he can, and read 'The Wife of Bath' as a warning against marriage, Chaucer refers jestingly to his own freedom. He dare not, he says, write of the sorrow and woe that is in marriage in case he himself falls again into such folly – i.e. marries again. Bukton was probably Sir Peter Bukton of Holderness in Yorkshire, younger than Chaucer (born 1350) but an old friend. After service with Gaunt, including several campaigns, he became one of the king's chamber knights and finally a high official in the Gaunt retinue, receiving a number of favours when Henry Bolingbroke became king. Chaucer's poem was written about 1396 when Bukton was forty-six – rather late to be married for the first time, and for that very reason perhaps a joke. Popular literature is full of the woes of marriage, treated comically more often than not. Yet one does sense a real relief in it. He had felt marriage a gall – and who does not, at times? His jest at the expense of his dead wife is partly a product of that vein of harshness, flippancy and cynicism, that detached heartlessness, which is the other side of his sentiment and sentimentality. Humour arises from detachment in juxtaposition with engagement. Perhaps too that fair-haired sweet girl he married went a bit sour, what with childbirths, separations, travellings, and he really did find her trying. On the other hand, she may well have had a trying husband. Even in 1368, a couple of years after his marriage, he was publicly declaiming, in *The Book of the Duchess*, his eight-year sickness, obviously lovesickness. There is only one physi- cian that can cure him, and she won't. Well, he might have said to his wife, 'I've got to write that sort of thing, it's only a convention. All the best French poets do it. And anyway, as I've said, she won't cure me – she won't have anything to do with me – she doesn't exist – there's nothing in it. All right, I won't do it again.' Any wife might find it rather irritating, especially as in *The Book of the Duchess* Gaunt is represented as so passionately and romantically in love with his dead wife that their marriage and five children are never even mentioned. Chaucer did give up saying that he was languishing unsuccessfully for love. Instead he presented himself in his own person as knowing nothing at all about love, which was hardly complimentary to Philippa. Then there is the strange case of Cecily Champain. Inside many a fat middle-aged man is a randy little thin one trying to get out. Perhaps he sometimes did. The Lollards proclaimed the dangers of vows of chastity for both men and women. A court full of passionate adolescents of both sexes, where love was a frequent topic of conversation, surrounded with sentimentality, and where masculine honour had nothing to do with chastity, seems no likely place for faithful husbands. Yet in the world of courtly imagination, things were different. Love was not a marginal interest but a central passion. In literature the art and craft of fine loving was the supreme art of life for a young man, leading to marriage and perpetual mutual devotion. This art was no mere second-hand imitation or criticism of life, it was in itself a living ideal. And even in the court something like it could happen, as with the devotion of Richard II to his queen. Something of this sweet and ordered feeling, with its recognized rules of decent behaviour, must surely have pervaded Chaucer's own marital life from his poems?

In that troubled late summer and autumn of 1387 it is safe to say that Chaucer had his share of personal sorrows and problems. At the same time he was cogitating the plan of *The Canterbury Tales* and extending his other intellectual interests, while no doubt watching with some anxiety and sympathy the various fates of his friends. The four chamber knights Sturry, Clifford, Neville and Clanvowe who were much more particularly his friends than Simon Burley was, all together with the other Lollard knights, and Vache, seem to have kept their heads down during the period of the Appellants' ascendancy. There is a notable thinness in references to them during this period. Sir William Beauchamp was, of course, on the other side and an active collaborator with the Lords Appellant. Since Chaucer may have gone to Calais with him in July 1387 he was in safe company. probably around this time when Vache, like other chamber knights, could have been in real danger, Chaucer wrote his poem 'Truth' to Vache, telling him to be content with what he had (which was plenty):

> Gret reste stant in litel besinesse . . .

> The wrastling for this world axeth a fal.
> Her is non hoom, her nis but wildernesse . . .

> Therfore, thou Vache, leve thyn old wrecchednesse,
> Unto the world leve now to be thral . . .

It is a deeply religious poem ending with advice to Vache to pray to God. It does not deny the sensible conduct of business affairs, and when we find an enrolment of 1 May 1388 of Chaucer's request to transfer both his annuities to one John Scalby we may guess at a business transaction by which Chaucer was raising a lump sum to improve or extend his property in Kent. About this time are also a couple of actions for debt for a total of around £10 – substantial but not very significant amounts. They might have arisen out of Customs transactions, as a later plea in 1398 arose out of his office as Clerk of Works 1389–91. There is no reason to think that Chaucer in his latter years was a poor man being dunned for debts he could not meet. He was comfortably off, and reasonably content.

Another short Boethian poem of this time may be mentioned apropos the Merciless Parliament: 'Lak of Stedfastnesse', which comments on the vicious instability of the world. Burley's fate might well have inspired such reflections.

What maketh this world to be so variable
But lust that folk have in dissensioun?
For among us now a man is holde unable
But if he can, by som collusioun,
Doon his neighbour wrong or oppressioun . . .

All has gone wrong, truth put down, reason is treated like fiction, virtue is weak, pity exiled, judgment blinded by greed.

The world hath mad a permutacioun
Fro right to wrong, fro trouthe to fikelnesse.

It must be confessed that the poem would suit almost any part of Richard's reign, and indeed almost all the world's history. The final stanza is usually thought to be addressed directly to Richard:

O prince, desyre to be honourable,
Cherish thy folk and hate extorcioun.
Suffre nothing that may be reprevable   [discreditable]
To thyn estat don in thy regioun.
Shew forth thy swerd of castigacioun,   [punishment]
Dred God, do law, love trouthe and worthinesse,
And wed thy folk agein to stedfastnesse.

This is very finely balanced with supremely courtier-like tact. It can be read as both encouragement and admonition. There is a somewhat similar passage against tyranny and describing true kingship in the *Prologue* to *The Legend of Good Women* (*F*, ll. 373ff). The call to 'show forth his sword of punishment', like the reference in the *Prologue* to the queen at Eltham or Sheen, does seem to align Chaucer fairly closely with Richard and the court party; on the other hand the advice to 'hate extorcioun', like the passage in the *Prologue* on cruel tyrants, shows that Chaucer was no mere sycophant. Everybody, including Richard, knew that heavy taxation and oppression by favourites were real grievances.

The Merciless Parliament checked Richard severely and he moved slowly and indirectly, as it proved, to work out a complete revenge nine years later. He also developed some original policies. The first step in recovery was quite soon. On 3 May 1389, at a council, Richard asked the rhetorical question of how old he was, and being twenty-two, was able to claim his right to full independence of rule as king. He allowed the council to continue and recalled Gaunt from Spain, whence he arrived in November 1389 to un- accustomed popularity induced by absence (O stormy people, unsad and ever untrue!); Richard was apparently reconciled to Gloucester. He took as yet no serious revenges, though some officials were dismissed and others appointed.

On 12 July 1389, the warrant for Chaucer's appointment as Clerk of the King's Works was made out, and he had probably been appointed a little before. It is hard to believe that since these appointments were made in response to petitions and depended on grace and favour, Chaucer's own job was not connected with Richard's new assertion of his own independence. Chaucer's

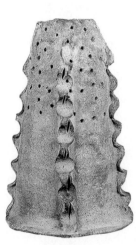

predecessor Roger Elmham was pensioned off with £10 a year having served for two and a half years, while the job itself was worth 2s. a day, which, if Sundays were included, came to £36. 10s. a year, quite a handsome sum. It was an important position, usually held by the kind of clerics who were higher civil servants. There is no reason to think that Elmham was disgraced. He and Chaucer were the only two laymen who held the position in the fourteenth century. He was another king's esquire and went on to the usual set of employments. The extent of Elmham's responsibilities was reduced for Chaucer, while he retained the four very experienced deputies (paid by the Exchequer at 2s. a week), and no doubt the clerks, who served his predecessor and successor and did much of the work. The Clerkship of the Works was not a sinecure, though as always it is difficult to bridge the gap between written formulas and what was actually done. The responsibility was in general managerial and financial – to ensure the employment and payment of workmen, the supply, protection of, and payment for materials, the sale of unwanted wood. Chaucer's responsibilities included the fabric of a number of royal castles and manors, and on 12 July 1390 St George's Chapel, Windsor, was added to these. He took over a fair amount of 'dead stock' in the palace of Westminster, the Tower of London and in the manors at Sheen, Eltham, Kennington, Childern Langley and Byfleet. Some was substantial, and included at Westminster seven stone statues of kings,a couple of winches, a lathe, etc., but some was very small beer. At Byfleet there was only a billhook and a rope. At the Tower were various 'machines', three completely broken wheels, a pair of andirons, a windlass with a worn rod, 'i ramme cum totu apparatu excepta I drawyng-corda que frangitur' (which is broken), one bell called Wyron, 'i fryingpanne', 'i rake', 'i ladel pro officio plumbarii' (for the plumber), and so on – a real junkyard. Perhaps Chaucer solemnly checked it all. The job brought him into contact with the master architect of the age, Henry Yevele (paid 12d. a day – half Chaucer's salary) who designed the nave of Westminster Abbey and Richard II's tomb therein, and was responsible for altering Westminster Hall.

Chaucer's literary interest in appearances may not have made him particularly observant in the ordinary sense of the term, but he must have taken pleasure in the many objects and buildings of beauty with which he was concerned. He was also responsible for ensuring the erection of scaffolds for seating at the great jousts at Smithfield, in May and October 1390. Among the 'dead stock, taken over at the palace of Westminster were '*xii hirdles pro scaffoldes i par de lystis duplicatis continentibus in circuitu xxxii perticatas*'. *Perticata* was a perch, a measure that like most measures in traditional societies was approximate and variable (repetition *with* variation), but was roughly 16 to 18 feet long. The lists were the arena in which knights fought each other in tournaments, and were presumably wooden sections that marked the boundaries of the arena. Those mentioned would give a circuit of about two hundred yards and thus if perfectly round an arena of sixty-six yards in diameter. Chaucer also took over nine small rings for the barriers of the said lists. These were probably for 'tilting at the ring' – trying to catch the ring with a spear while running at it on horseback. The barriers were used for this but also for combats.

OPPOSITE *The magnificen hammerbeam roof of Westminster Hall was designed by Chaucer's colleague Henry Yevele*

They were long wooden fences several feet high which divided the arena. The jousting knights rode at each other from opposite ends of the lists, each with the barrier on his left between them, holding spears in their right hands supported under the right armpit, and pointing the sixteen-foot spear crosswise to the left of and behind the horse's head, over the barrier at the opponent's shield or helmet. The smallish lumbering carthorses cannot have got up a great speed in such a short distance but the sport was dangerous enough sometimes to maim or kill. The Duke of Gloucester, who was interested in these matters, laid down rules for the construction of lists for ordeal combats which Chaucer must have known. In these rules it is stated that the lists must be sixty paces long and forty paces broad, on hard, level, clear ground, with one door to the east and another to the west, each with strong bars at least seven feet high so that a horse may not be able to leap over them. This presupposes an oval shape. Presumably lists for tourna-ments used the same arrangements. The Duke of Gloucester was also the president of the Court of Chivalry during the Scrope-Grosvenor case, which lasted from 1385 to 1390, and before which Chaucer testified on 15 October 1386 during the parliamentary proceedings. Gloucester's persecution of Richard was due to Richard's lack of interest in this kind of thing.

Chaucer's real involvement with day-to-day practicalities, including the erection of lists and scaffolds, probably has a less direct relationship to the vivid realism of his poetry than one might expect. There are some lists described in *The Knight's Tale* with precise detail, but there the circuit is not two hundred yards but one mile, which would give a diameter of five hundred and sixty yards, and a correspondingly immense arena. The seating is not of temporary scaffolding but of stone, sixty paces high arranged in ascending rows so that everyone could see over the heads of the people in front. Something like the vast Colosseum in Rome, or other Roman amphitheatres in Europe that Chaucer could have seen, must be envisaged, but even so the scale is extravagant, and the apparently precise realism is in truth more apparent, at the service of the glorifying imagina-tion, than real. It was Froissart, not Chaucer, who actually described the pageantry of the jousts of Smithfield. Chaucer, like Richard, had a decidedly tempered personal interest in chivalric ceremonial. He was the manager and accountant indeed, who had to deal with the abstractions, the labour, the sport, or war, that occupied most working hours of most people, but as a poet he was concerned with the core of these matters, personal relationships.

The financial aspect of his work led to an unpleasant incident, or incidents, in September 1390. There are records that he was robbed on 3 September, near le foule Ok', of his horse, goods and £20 of the king's money; again on 6 September, at Westminster, of £10; again on 6 September at Hatcham in Surrey of £9. 43*d.* or 44*d.*; and at Hatcham, on an unspecified day, of horse, goods and £20. 6*s*. 8*d.* To be robbed twice in three days is bad luck; four times looks like carelessness. Surely the records have confused the incidents. At least in January 1391 Chaucer was discharged from repaying £20 of the king's money of which he had been robbed on 3 September 1390. He was the victim of a gang, including an Irish cleric and his clerk, and one of whom, Brierley, accused his comrades of a variety of robberies. Even if Chaucer was robbed only once it illustrates the dangers of the times, especially as he had to carry large sums about with him, the equivalent of several thousand pounds today, to pay workmen and suppliers. Being Clerk of the Works was clearly not completely a sinecure.

While Clerk his residence in Kent is further attested by his inclusion on a commission on 12 March 1390, headed by his old friend Sir Richard Sturry, and including several Kentish landowners he already knew from the commission of the peace, to investigate the state of the walls, ditches, etc., on the Thames between Woolwich and Greenwich. There had been a great storm the previous week, on 5 March, which had caused a lot of damage.

After a couple of years as Clerk of the Works it was somebody else's turn, and in June 1391 he gave it up to John Gedney, who already held the rectorship of a church in Norwich and was to go on to be later Constable of Bordeaux. It is hard to think that Chaucer as Clerk was either tremendously zealous or ridiculously incompetent. His experience as an accountant was sufficient, his expenditure as Clerk was about average. It would seem that about this time he was awarded a sub-forestership of the forest of North Petherton, which belonged to Roger Mortimer, Earl of March. Mortimer was a minor and the estate was being farmed by Sir Peter Courtenay, a courtier known to Chaucer. But the records are late and confused, a complicated lawsuit was going on between Courtenay and Mortimer, and we have no means of knowing either Chaucer's duties, if any, or his pay. We presume it was something to be going on with during his last decade, but the Clerkship was Chaucer's last real job. We must assume him to be moderately well off though not averse to any little extra that came his way, and particularly concerned to continue reading and writing. He was living at Greenwich in Kent, though this was only an easy walk of five or six miles from Westminster, and close enough, by foot or horse, to such other royal residences as Eltham and Sheen, and not too far from his friends in London or (as Gower) in Southwark. At times he visited friends in Oxford and Cambridge. He was a successful and famous poet, in favour at court, with many friends in many different walks of life. He was a widower whose two surviving sons were still small, Lewis being about ten in 1391. We might imagine a comfortable house for him, with manservant, a woman to look after the house, a tutor, groom and a couple of boys about the place. He had a study with his books, a small garden, and easy access to the pleasant fields and the manor houses of rich neighbours. With reading, writing, visits to court, to London to see his scribe and to see friends there, visits elsewhere, readings of his poems, visits to him from friends, tolerably good health, supervision of his sons' education, life was agreeable, even if the world was full of wrong and suffering. As he told Vache,

Robbed ... a traveller hastily hands over his purse – but perhaps it is the king's money

Flee fro the prees, and dwelle with sothfastnesse; [crowd; truth]
Suffyce unto thy good, though it be smal ...
Reule wel thyself, that other folk canst rede ... [advise]
Gret reste stant in litel besinesse ...
That thee is sent, receyve in buxumnesse [obedience]
The wrastling for this world axeth a fal.

CHAPTER TWELVE

AND PILGRIMS WERE THEY ALL

I N THE LATE 1380s CHAUCER AS USUAL HAD A PROB-
lem. He was more than ever engaged as poet in 'the intolerable struggle'
with form. His new wine might break the old bottles, but one cannot keep
wine at all without some containers. For a little, perhaps, even the supply of
wine seemed to dry up. He continued to struggle with *The Legend of Good Women*,
but never finished it. Although it had probably been requested, at least playfully,
by the little queen, to 'compensate' for the supposed anti-feminism of *Troilus*, the
emotional impetus was exhausted, and the form, to this most experimental and
virtuoso poet, had become intolerably repetitious and boring. Maybe it was at
such a period that he felt the sentiments expressed in the 'Envoy to Scogan', that
his sleeping muse was rusting in its sheath. Inspiration as both sword and
goddess. The male/female duality of his art was never better imaged.

He probably began to work on *The Canterbury Tales* around 1387 without
consciously giving up the idea of *The Legend of Good Women*. He worked on
different things at different moments, turning from one to another, probably
keeping several works on the go at once. Plans and verses must have run in his
head as he himself rode about, but the Clerkship of Works must have been a
distraction. In 1391 he finished with that and there must have been a burst of
work in the early part of the 1390s, though most of his later works are impossible
to date with any precision. By the time he had finished the first version of the
Prologue to *The Legend* he had also just finished, though not widely circulated,
Palamon and Arcite, which became *The Knight's Tale*. This gathers up his long
interest in romantic love, along with the glory of the court and Boethian reflections on the fickleness of fortune and making the best of things. It shows a new,
more optimistic cast of mind than earlier love poems, since as already quoted the
structure of the story allows one of the two heroes to be eventually successful in
love. There is also a middle-aged flippant worldliness in the poem that goes
perfectly naturally, if inconsistently, with the equally genuine and middle-aged
sententiousness about the inevitable cycle of life and death.

This disengaged flippancy was also attracted by the derisive traditional
humour of the popular comic tales that circulated through Europe in hundreds
of manuscripts and also by word of mouth. They were in part the other side of
the coin of serious, high-minded, passionate courtly romance; in part the normal
interest in gross physical mishap, sexual or stercoraceous; in part the normal

OPPOSITE *'Wel we weren esed atte best . . . | Greet chiere made oure Hoost us everichoon, | And to
the soper sette he us anon. | He served us with vitaille at the beste'*

human reaction against the tensions and structures of what I have called the 'official culture', which represents the good which we seriously think that we and others ought to do and believe, and which is so often what we do not do or believe. Our reaction against the 'official', whether from idleness, selfishness, wantonness, or the desire for freedom and spontaneity, is the 'unofficial culture', which is by no means always bad or merely negative. Medieval comic tales representing the 'unofficial culture, were common to all classes, including the clergy and courtiers. In French they were called *fabliaux*, and French courtly and clerical writers of the thirteenth century, like Boccaccio in the fourteenth, brought these bawdy tales to a pitch of artistic perfection only exceeded by Chaucer. At this stage he had written or was longing to write some.

Then again, he had translated some time before the highly 'official' religious prose tract by the early thirteenth-century Pope Innocent III on the need to despise and reject the world, *De Contemptu Mundi*. If *fabliau* was the other side of the coin from romance, this was different metal entirely. Yet it corresponded with deep human intuitions about the nature of the world, and having done it he didn't want to waste it. It could provide some useful thickening for such a religious folktale as that of the much-tried, well-named Constance.

Folktale was in general increasingly attractive to Chaucer. The comic tales were folktales, but not all folktales are comic, and there are many other types. All traditional stories from the Bible and the Classics onwards have much in common with folktales, and are much more like folktales than novels, but the particular blend of fantasy and realism found in specifically comic tales and religious tales appealed to Chaucer's dual nature and to his poetic virtuosity.

Had he not had genius he might not have noticed the problem of organizing this range of material, and might have simply put the works down either higgledy-piggledy or in some rough classification. There were plenty of manuscript miscellanies. Medieval books were made up of gatherings of leaves of paper or parchment, written on and folded together like a series of pamphlets (as many books still are). Often the separate sections lay about on shelves unbound, as you can sometimes see from the grimy sheen of a page beginning a gathering well within a large book. Chaucer must have had gatherings like that on his shelves containing work he had done. What more natural than to put them together? A mid-fifteenth-century Yorkshire gentleman called Robert Thornton copied out a great variety of secular and religious works that interested him on gatherings of suitable length and eventually had them bound up in exactly this way. This was the most typical kind of late medieval book, a Gothic miscellany. There were also plenty of collections of stories in the Middle Ages. Chaucer himself had started one with *The Legend of Good Women*. Gower was working on another. It is even possible that Chaucer knew the greatest collection so far made, Boccaccio's *Decameron*, and he may have known, as we have seen, the Auchinleck Manuscript, another collection. *The Canterbury Tales* is a Gothic miscellany of romances, bawdy tales, saints' lives, serious tracts in prose, all bound together, but the difference is that they are brought into relation with each other.

Simply to bind up the variety of works together would not have satisfied

Chaucer's need to express his feeling both for the partial breaking down of traditional forms, and for connections, comradeship, and on-going society. The articulation of the stories could also be made to express a fuller humanity that he was almost alone in his time capable of conceiving. In a strange way the stories he knew took on a personality themselves, just as the rumours, news, lies and stories in *The House of Fame* had been like real people, struggling together to get out of the windows. It is as if the tale created the teller. This had happened with the *Troilus*. Translating Boccaccio's *Filostrato* he had changed and re-created the story of Troilus; in so doing the story had re-created him as the teller. Stories are not only about the people in them, they are about the people who tell them. This is so even when the stories are traditional, continually retold and developed by generations of tellers. Each new telling of an old tale expresses both our common humanity and our individual variation of it. The stories Chaucer had in mind generated the idea of people to tell them. The relationships of one story to another become relationships between people; and then relationships between people generated the idea of further stories. The whole plan was fluid from the start, and we can still trace some stages of change as the ideas flowed on. *The Shipman's Tale* for example was designed to be told by a woman, presumably the Wife of Bath, but a better, subtler idea of a story for her came along. This means that the stories still retain a certain independence of their tellers; none is entirely a dramatic expression of the teller's character, and some are merely generally appropriate. Sometimes there are contradictions between teller and tale.

A lecherous couple, reminiscent of Don John and the rich merchant's wife of The Shipman's Tale

There are two collections of material in *The Canterbury Tales*; the pilgrims themselves, described in *The General Prologue* and in the links between tales; and the tales themselves. Altogether they give a remarkable panorama of England in the fourteenth century as reflected in the many facets of Chaucer's mind. To organize this extraordinary variety he devised, with astonishing originality that only now looks obvious, the structure, which is also an anti-structure, of a journey in which people not only tell stories but in which both people and stories relate to each other in a social, dramatic and literary way. The plan offered both firmness and flexibility; the processional form with individual portrayals beloved of Gothic art. It should not be a journey by a fully hierarchical, highly organized, exclusive institution, like a court in transit or an army. A pilgrimage was the thing: purposive yet voluntary, with minimal organization, open to change.

The stories which he had already written, or which he now wanted to write, inevitably expressed the variety of people in the community of England, for traditional stories are the product and the possession of the whole community. The collection of stories had pointed to the collection of people. There was also another miscellaneous body of literary material that described people's characters and nature, equally traditional, rather more learned, which was made up of formal descriptions of persons from top to toe (like that of Blanche), as recommended in handbooks of style; there were also descriptions in encyclopedias and science books; also self-describing confessions put into the mouths of bad characters by writers who wished to satirize them, as in *Le Roman de la Rose*; and there were the satirical descriptions of various classes and types of people in the copious literature of the 'estates'. Chaucer had thus available to him all sorts of stereotypes; ideal knights and parsons, beautiful ladies, hypocritical monks, lecherous friars, as well as medieval and astrological types.

He also had available all sorts of lists that gave him an analysis or 'anatomy' of medieval society. The 'estates' literature provided some; so did the lists of social precedence in hall given in courtesy books, for the marshal in hall (above, p. 54); so did various laws governing clothing allowed to different ranks, or the poll tax. In general, medieval literature had many lists, brief or expanded, from vocabu-laries to encyclopedias. A more profound form of social analysis which gave a vital though submerged framework was the medieval theory of the ideal threefold order of society; knights to fight for all, clergy to pray for all, ploughmen to get food for all. The only characters whom Chaucer approves of among his pilgrims accord with this ideal; the Knight (with his appended Squire perhaps); the Clerk of Oxford and the parson (two aspects of clergy, learning and pastoral care), and the ploughman. Those who do not accord with the ideal are satirized. So here were all sorts of patterns and structures available in Chaucer's mind. Moreover the twelfth-century Anglo-French writer Benoît de Sainte-Maure had a long prologue to his *History of Troy* with formal rhetorical descriptions of the principal characters. Prologues were also a very common medieval form. Why not follow Benoît, but vary the list with portraits of different kinds of people? Thus the ideas of pilgrimage, people, prologues, coalesced.

Once again his genius led him forward. All this miscellaneous literary matter organized his way of seeing life. It was formal and analytical, not unlike the pattern books used by Gothic artists and craftsmen. And just as they, in the fourteenth century, were led by the patterns to try and catch some of the actual living appearances of leaves and faces, so Chaucer too picked up touches of life.

In *The General Prologue*, then is a list, a gathering of people, a simple yet profound idea, an underlying structure that he plays about with in itself, loosened by the touch of life. The portraits are formal in origin, but the order of description is now wilfully arbitrary and fresh, the details often unexpected, trivial, and so more realistic, while some characters had never been described in literature before. The portraits vary a good deal. Of the ideal characters, Knight, Squire and Clerk are the most concretely realized, and nearest Chaucer's own ideal experience of life, but though they recall real people they do not seem to refer to them. The Knight, for example, has fought in Prussia on a crusade, like

While an all-too-familiar pair of lovers fo through the usual courtly rituals, a striped cat and a rat grimly try to outstare each other in the foliage beneath. The marginal decoration of the Ormesby Psalter is full of such realistic details

Henry of Grosmont and his grandson Henry Bolingbroke, who also were both pious men, but the Knight has not once fought in France as had all Chaucer's friends (though the young Squire has). The portrait of the Clerk may honour Chaucer's Oxford friends, but cannot be identified with any of them. True life comes in satire, and then we come closer to an analysis of English society, at least in the representative figures of the middle degrees. The upper nobility, and the great swarm of humble, necessary occupations, cobblers, bakers, wheelwrights, shepherds, swineherds, dairywomen, ditchers and delvers and so forth are given only token representation. The great were too powerful to be represented, the humble were too remote from Chaucer's imaginative experience. In the middle we have vivid pictures that must have been tantalizingly identifiable to Chaucer's immediate circle, probably made up of Sir William Beauchamp, some Lollard knights, and London friends. They would have enjoyed the unquestionably true-life description of Harry Bailly, known to all. They would have relished the broad hints that the Serjeant-of-Law was that Pinchbeck who had annoyed Sir William and was making a lot of money by slightly dubious practice; that the Merchant who was less financially sound than he seemed was that Gilbert Mawfield to whom most of them, including Chaucer, owed money at one time or another, and who eventually died bankrupt. Probably the Doctor was similarly recognizable, and maybe too the Friar called Hubert. It is highly likely that Hodge of Ware the Cook was a well-known London restaurant owner whose food was suspect, and that the skilled, ruthless and not altogether honest Shipman was a well-known rascal. The Prioress came from a well-known convent at Stratford-le-Bow, and her genteel imitation of courtly manners evokes all the snobbish amusement of the courtly in-group at the inappropriate and foredoomed struggles of the inferior outsider. The Franklin has something of the extravagance of a country cousin and may also touch on a Norfolk gentleman associated with Pinchbeck. The Manciple was a sort of butler and is clearly associated with the Inns of Court. Someone like him must have been known, as again with the Norfolk Reeve. The Pardoner comes from the Hospital of the Blessed Mary of Rouncivalle, just by Charing Cross in London, and again surely called a particular person to mind? London was a small town, the court at Westminster of course even smaller, and so many of these characters are specific to well-known places there with limited personnel. Chaucer and his primary audience, whether he still read aloud to them or not, were a well-knit group. He certainly circulated sections of The Canterbury Tales among them – he recommends Bukton in 1396 to read 'The Wife of Bath', and surely The General Prologue was available much earlier. This closeness between the poet and his readers was a powerful social incentive towards realism, and, in such a competitive society, towards satire, though given Chaucer's temperament, of a reflective rather than practical or political kind. The reference to living people in The General Prologue, indisputable in a few cases, highly probable in many more, does not deny the traditional literary structures in the portraits, but shows how Chaucer accepted them, partially broke them down, formed them anew. The people in The General Prologue are so alive because they move between the old-fashioned stereotype and a completely formless arbitrary state which if fully realized would be chaotic, but as glimpsed is freedom and individual potentiality. This 'transition' between form and freedom in art corresponds to the transition offered by pilgrimage. Surely we ourselves live most intensely when in transition. The 'passages' of our lives between one state and another are the extraordinary ones, and the parts of life most full of tension and interest.

Chaucer hits off such feelings of transition in all sorts of ways, often comically, by using his pilgrimage idea. Some of the most vivid and delightful passages (in every sense) are the gaps, or links, between tales, when the pilgrims comment, argue, explain, quarrel, with marvellous vividness. We will never get closer to ordinary fourteenth-century life than in these brilliantly dramatic and interesting episodes. The pilgrimage notion enables Chaucer to free his charac-ters from ordinary social ties, to present them more vividly in themselves, as individuals, with potential for unexpected response and action. It enables him as both a pilgrim-character within the fiction and poet outside it to switch the point of view of narration so that now he seems ignorant, now naïve, now knowing, now sarcastic, and so on. This allows an extraordinary sense of both fixity of object and fluidity of attitude to it, very characteristic of Chaucer and his times.

The idea of pilgrimage is itself both fixed and fluid. A fixed itinerary, London to Canterbury, was established for a recognized religious purpose, to worship at the shrine where Archbishop Thomas Becket had been murdered by Henry II's knights. But holy day has become holiday; the firm religious purpose is surrounded by loose secular varieties and vanities. Chaucer's pilgrimage is very much of this world. There is no reference to the shrines on the way. People's relationships are the chief interest. The idea of pilgrimage (as opposed to just travelling), is almost forgotten en route, easily abandoned at the end.

Chaucer knew the actual road, as he knew the travellers, very well. He did not need to have gone on an actual pilgrimage such as he describes. Indeed it is most unlikely, according to my idea of him, that he had done so. The mixture of simple devoutness, externalized religious observance, vulgar holiday, travel for change and recreation, could never have suited that complex, internalized, sardonic, far-travelled courtier. A holiday for him would have been reading a book at home. He marks the way like a traveller, not a religious tourist, by refer-ences to places one passes: St Thomas's Watering (somewhere in the Old Kent Road), Deptford, Greenwich (where many a scoundrel lives), Dartford, Rochester, Sittingbourne, Ospring, etc. He knew the Tabard Inn in South-wark where he shows the pilgrims gathering to start their journey. He reached it from London or Westminster over London Bridge into Southwark, mixed suburb of houses, gardens, inns, shops, brothels, churches. His friend Gower lived there in the precincts of St Mary Overy's Priory, now Southwark Cathe-dral, in which his handsome Gothic tomb is preserved. Almost opposite St Mary's were some excellent inns including the Tabard (burned down in 1676, but part of whose site is said to be still occupied by an inn of the same name). It has been noted that an innkeeper called Harry Bailly was a prominent citizen of

OPPOSITE *The Pilgrim's Way near Wrotham, Kent*

Southwark in Chaucer's day. Surely he owned the Tabard. Courtiers might laugh at, as well as with, Harry Bailly, but he received what must be the most successful advertisement in the whole world's history for his already popular hotel. Chaucer now passed the inn frequently on his way home to Greenwich, but he had known it for many years before because the way to Canterbury was, and is, the way to Dover, normal port of embarkation for the Continent.

The pilgrims are going to the rich shrine of St Thomas at Canterbury Cathedral, mocked by the Humanist monk Erasmus early in the sixteenth century, looted by Henry VIII a little later. Chaucer abandoned *The Canterbury Tales* before he got to Canterbury, and would probably have felt some sardonic sympathy with Erasmus, and with the Lollards, who condemned pilgrimages. Something of this feeling even gets into the speech of his Parson. The Parson does not tell a real story, but is allocated a devotional prose tract, a 'Meditation', which is the last 'tale' of all. In this the fiction of a story-telling company is abandoned, but in the verses before it the Parson is made to say that he will, on this trip, show his audience the way of 'that perfect glorious pilgrimage that is called heavenly Jerusalem'; i.e. the pilgrimage which is Jerusalem is the religious life advocated by the Parson, which you need not travel to find. This is inconsistent in that the Parson is supposed to be on a pilgrimage, and the inconsistency becomes total and very Gothic when at the end of the Parson's 'tale' Chaucer speaks in his own historical voice, makes no attempt to maintain the fiction, and revokes those of *The Canterbury Tales* that 'tend towards' sin. This shows that Chaucer himself thought of the 'work' as a collection of 'works' of varying type. But this is to anticipate; though the end is significant, the incidents on the journey, of which the stories themselves are chief, are the main source of interest. It is more fun (though not always morally better) to travel than to arrive.

In this worldly yet not exactly irreligious bias Chaucer expresses his own deep attitude, which is deeper, more penetrating, than the Parson's monastically derived moralizing, even though the Parson prevails in the end. The Parson's meditation ultimately derives from religious tracts written for laymen in the early thirteenth century in Latin, which became part of an extensive religious literature spread throughout the languages of western Europe. This literature played a vital part in civilizing Europe, but it was old-fashioned by Chaucer's time, though still immensely powerful. It was being attacked for religious reasons from two sides. On the one side Lollardy attacked it. On the other, the modernist Ockhamist theology undercut it. In the high-powered scientific theology of the fourteenth-century universities, written in Latin, the ordinary 'wayfaring Christian' was referred to as the *viator*, the traveller. He might be good or bad. He was not exactly a pilgrim (*peregrinus*), for he had two possible destinations, not one; either joy or damnation. In the fourteenth century there was now becoming felt by theologians, our greatest authority tells us, 'the intrinsic importance of the life of the *viator* on earth, the value of which was now less exclusively defined in terms of the eternal Jerusalem, the final destination of the viator, and more in terms of the journey itself.' The Parson, whose point of view Chaucer ultimately adopted, does not recognize this, and Chaucer as usual shows within himself the tug-of-war between old and new.

For *The General Prologue* and most of *The Canterbury Tales* we escape from restrictions into the freedom of fictions that are about life itself. At the end of The General Prologue Chaucer makes a genial apology for the realistic reporting which is to follow (he obviously has the bawdy tales in mind) in the name of 'truth'. There is obviously some joking here, just as the realism is obviously limited, but also a real feeling in Chaucer for escape into actual life, especially its 'unofficial', improper, seamy side. He also asks to be forgiven for not setting folk 'in their degree'. Again we have the refreshment of a shake-up and freedom from responsibility. Pilgrimage moves from centre to margin.

The margin, as it turns out, is the best place to see the game. Chaucer's art turns the social activity of poetry into something less socially central, more important, less utilitarian, in which we contemplate all sorts of clashes between the personalities of pilgrims, between stories and between characters in stories, between incompatible values, all gathered up finally in 'the strange moral dialectic of Christianity'. What a rich and varied play of mind and matter we see. The dialectic is especially rich in humour.

It even included Chaucer, in his double character as writer of the whole work, and yet a character inside it who tells what the pilgrims judge to be the worst tale – it is of course the brilliant parody, *Sir Thopas*. Yet the pilgrim Chaucer is also the real Chaucer, if only a part of him. We get a picture of him in the words that the Host of the Tabard addresses to him – a precious glimpse of a physical appearance that cannot have been too far from the truth.

'What man artow?' quod he;   [art thou]
Thou lookest as thou woldest fynde an hare,
For evere upon the ground I se thee stare.
Approche neer, and looke up murily.   [cheerfully]
Now war yow, sires, and lat this man have place!
He in the waast is shape as wel as I:
This were a popet in an arm t'enbrace[puppet]
For any womman, smal and fair of face.
He semeth elvyssh by his contenaunce,   [strangely remote in manner]
For unto no wight dooth he daliaunce.   [friendliness]
                    CT VII, ll. 695–704

There is a real touch of melancholy implicit here. We remember the solemn commonplaces of Egeus the father of Theseus in *The Knight's Tale* at the funeral of Arcite:

This world nys but a thurghfare ful of wo
And we been pilgrymes, passynge to and fro.
                    CT I, ll. 2847–8

This is the consolation at the end of the pilgrimage; but we are still on the way and may accept the more positive consolation of Theseus: the world is bound by a fair chain of love by God who guides all. We must take the rough with the smooth, thank God for all; and after woe let us be merry.

CHAPTER THIRTEEN

FORTH, PILGRIM, FORTH

But al shal passe that men prose or ryme;
Take every man hys turn, as for his tyme.
Envoy to Scogan

HE KNIGHT'S TALE IS THE FIRST AND GRANDEST work of *The Canterbury Tales*. The pilgrims, at Harry Bailly's invitation, are to tell their stories in a competition, the prize to be a free supper at the end of the return journey. Probably The Knight's Tale would have won it. But the pilgrimage moves away from the court, and though Chaucer always remains of the court his gaze, like his lifelong activities, travels further, and shows us further aspects of his life and mind. The Tales themselves begin to proceed by contrast, even hostility. The Knight's Tale is followed in opposition by the aggressively drunken Miller, and he in further hostility by the choleric Reeve. Popular comic tales of quarrelsome deceits that circulated throughout all classes in Europe are attributed by Chaucer to his low and vulgar characters, and located with sharp realism in the university towns of Oxford and Cambridge.

The university world itself is not seen from the inside, though Chaucer shows distinct knowledge of the King's Hall, Cambridge, and of the district. He may have passed through Cambridge on his way to Norfolk to help Sir William Beauchamp administer the Pembroke estates (and incidentally there met the Reeve of Baldswell). There was a Parliament held in Cambridge in 1388 whose members were entertained at King's Hall. A number of Chaucer's colleagues in the royal household had come from the King's Hall, which was a training ground for clerical members of the household and for civil lawyers, and was under special court patronage. Richard Medford, who became Bishop of Salisbury in 1390, was a fellow of the King's Hall from 1352 to 1378, as well as a member of the royal household from 1369 and was a contemporary of Chaucer. King's Hall was the biggest college in Cambridge and had a certain notoriety in the 1370s and 1380s because of bad management. Chaucer's first audience would appreciate a satirical point about the behaviour of the young men.

Oxford is less vividly evoked as a university. We are not told the name of the college of Nicholas, the 'hero' of *The Miller's Tale*. We are told something of his possessions which include an astrolabe and augrim stones (cf. above p. 44), which are notable, since the fellows of Merton themselves had at this period only three astrolabes and one set of augrim stones among them. However, the latter might have been too cheap for the college to bother with, or one made one's own. The miller in *The Reeve's Tale* jests to the Cambridge clerks that since they have learned science they can by arguments make a place twenty foot wide into a

OPPOSITE *Death draws near. The cross is held before the dying man's eyes, friar and nun pray for his soul, a doctor attends, and a member of the family anticipates his inheritance*

mile wide. It is mathematics, and not theology or rhetoric, that Chaucer associates with the universities.

Yet dozens of realistic details suggest that Chaucer knew Oxford town and
its inhabitants better than Cambridge and we cannot deny him even closer
knowledge of the university, or at any rate of people in it. It is likely that his
friend Strode was a fellow of Merton, and Bradwardine, whose name was
known to Chaucer, as *The Nun's Priest's Tale* shows, had been a fellow of Merton
in the early fourteenth century, as well as Walter Burley, influential schoolman,
tutor to the Black Prince and uncle of Sir Simon Burley (above pp. 142–3).
Merton was a large college and particularly distinguished for its part in the great
scientific advances made in Oxford especially in the earlier part of the century.
The interest in astronomy at Merton and Oxford did not fade away in
Chaucer's time. It was usual to base astronomical tables on the Oxford latitude,
and this is what Chaucer himself did with his own work *The Astrolabe*. This
Oxford connection was part of the courtly life, for the friar John Somer who is
referred to in the preface of Chaucer's treatise on the astrolabe was at Oxford
from 1380 to 1395 at least and had an astronomical calendar made for Joan of
Kent. (This still survives as MS. Royal 2 B viii in the British Library.) Joan of
Kent does not normally figure in the history books as an intellectual, but if not
she, at least her circle, which contained so many of Chaucer's friends, took an
intelligent interest in astronomical matters. The Clerk of Oxenford in *The
General Prologue* was probably what we would now call a 'scientist', and Chaucer
sums up the essence of university studies when he writes of him,

> And gladly wolde he lerne and gladly teche.
> *CT* I, l. 308

The compliment to Oxford University is quite explicit.

The Canterbury Tales weave in and out of Chaucer's whole life. The comic
bawdy tales lead us to the universities, to serious learning. Chaucer's *Astrolabe* is
dated around 1391–3 and claims to have been written for his son, little Lewis (cf.
above p. 44). It is a remarkable piece of work: a very early piece of technical
English prose, and a laborious task done for love at a time when one would have
expected Chaucer to be anxious to get on with other things. Nothing better
demonstrates the analytical, and pedagogical, side of his mind. Surely the praise
of the Clerk of Oxenford could well be taken for Chaucer himself.

The astronomical treatise entitled *The Equatorie of the Planetis* has been both
claimed and denied as Chaucer's work. What is important is to recognize the
large place that astronomy held in Chaucer's interests for its own sake in his own
life. This still leads us back to the poetry, for Chaucer also utilizes astronomy for
various purposes, adornment, wit, structure, motivation, even philosophy.
Astronomy cannot be separated from astrology, which attributed to the stars
power to affect events on earth. This was perfectly respectable modern science in
Chaucer's day, though it was recognized as having its dangerous side (as what
science has not?). It was not legitimate to use astrology for prediction, but
doctors, businessmen, clerics, courtiers, all used it for normal working purposes,

such as to discover suitable days for particular enterprises, or to analyse character, or a disease. Chaucer is conscious of all this. He also uses astrology to give new life to his poetic uses of classical mythology. Venus is the shining example; goddess of love in poetry which none believed as fact, but planet also which was thought really to influence our sexual and loving desires. Chaucer wrote a witty account of the astronomical conjunction of the planets Mars and Venus in the form of a love story, full of puns, some a little indecent, probably in the middle 1380s. This is obvious. It has also been argued that *The Squire's Tale* is a more concealed allegory, but of similar type, which is not so sure. More serious and obvious use is made of astrology and astronomy in *Troilus* and *The Franklin's Tale*, where we also find some uncertainty about the legitimacy of the subject.

Venus and her lusty children

This uncertainty is nothing like the downright hostility that Chaucer shows towards alchemy when the topic is introduced in *The Canterbury Tales* by a later development of the plan. Two horsemen catch the pilgrims up on the road. One is a canon of the church and the other his yeoman or servant. The Yeoman in a prologue and a long preamble to his tale reveals the absurd technical practices and failure of his master, so that the Canon flees for shame. What is interesting about it from a personal point of view is that there is an unusual touch of personal vehemence in the Yeoman's condemnation, which may be just a superb dramatic achievement, but which has tempted many critics to feel that Chaucer himself had burned his fingers, if not, like the poor Yeoman, totally discoloured his face and lost all his money, in dabbling with the art. No one can say for sure, but I myself think that Chaucer had a particular dislike for swindling. There is no full portrait of the Canon, but the portrait of the Pardoner in The General Prologue is notably the most severe, with the exaggerated insult that 'I trow he were a gelding or a mare' – 'Either a eunuch or a woman'. Although this is based on a male-dominated society's traditional disgust at sexual ambiguity, it seems to be used to damn the Pardoner because he is such a hypocritical fraud.

It is as impossible to date *The Canon's Yeoman's Prologue and Tale* accurately as it is most of the other *Canterbury Tales* but it seems clear that in this later period Chaucer, at the summit of his art, has no longer the need to work out particular pressures within himself. This is why he turns to the traditional variety of folk tale. What Chaucer now seems ready to do is to take up the varying traditional attitudes he finds and to play with them both for their own sake and for the sense of paradox that their variety gives him and us.

The supreme example of Chaucer's work in this kind is of course the immortal creation of the Wife of Bath, who deserves a eulogy of the kind Dr Johnson addressed to Falstaff. What a gloriously awful woman she is! It is typical of Chaucer at this stage of his life that while he accepts and uses the thousand-year-old tradition of clerical anti-feminism, he so manages it that we end up feeling more sympathy than dislike for the Wife. She represents the 'unofficial' culture of sexual gusto and damn the consequences; of women's triumph over men; of spontaneity, freedom, love. Yet the ending of her tale asserts mutual respect and faithfulness in marriage. And Chaucer in other tales celebrates the very different saintly wives, Constance and Griselda.

It is impossible here to gather up all the 'God's plenty' of the whole *Canterbury Tales*. In them Chaucer came as near to expressing the whole life of a culture as any writer could, for he included serious non-fictional prose along with all the rest, working on the whole collection throughout the 1390s and perhaps releasing them in sections to his friends. He had a scribe called Adam, whom he cursed in a sharp little poem for making so many mistakes in copying *Troilus* and *Boece*, and with Adam's, or his successor's aid, he continued to write new and tinker with his older works. When about 1395 he made some changes to the *Prologue* to *The Legend of Good Women* it was mainly for the sake of improving its earlier rather awkward structure, but he added an item to the list of his prose translations (though no reference to *The Canterbury Tales*), and also the remark that he had sixty books, old and new, full of Greek and Roman stories about women. Would that we had a list of all his books. He also had to remove a refer-ence to Queen Anne, for she had died in 1394, to Richard's great distress.

This note of mortality now calls us back to the world of the court in the last few years remaining to Chaucer. The years from 1389 to 1397 were politically relatively quiet, and represent the summit of the achievement of courtly life as an art in itself. Richard, having dramatically declared his independence at the council meeting of 3 May 1389, was prepared to bide his time in taking revenge for the humiliations of 1386–8. He had his difficulties with the City of London and also with the barons, especially Gloucester, for he pursued an unpopular though to later eyes sensible policy of seeking peace with France.

Although, unlike his father and grandfather, he rarely jousted, he had every intention of enjoying and extending the magnificence that was intrinsic to kingship. Unluckily he was wilfully autocratic, and his intelligence and sensi-bility led him to less popular and more refined pleasures than theirs. He seems, most unusually for a medieval king, not to have been lecherous, and though this led to hostile chroniclers' suspicions of homosexuality, there seem no grounds for that either. While Anne lived he was devoted to her and when she died he fell into paroxysms of grief that recall what seem the extravagances of emotion in Chaucer's poetry. Richard was interested in books and bought beautiful ones, though his taste favoured French. Froissart illustrates this with the story of how he returned to England in 1395 and followed the court around till he eventually caught up with it at Eltham. His old friend Sir Richard Sturry, and Lord Thomas Percy, both friends of Chaucer, presented Froissart to Richard. Richard asked to see the book that he had brought for him. The king was pleased with it, for it was luxuriously bound in crimson velvet, with ten buttons of silver and gilt, and roses of gold in the middle. It was beautifully written and illuminated. The king asked what was the subject, and Froissart said it was 'love', which pleased the king, who read in it in many places, for, Froissart thinks it worth while to tell us, he could speak and read French very well. What is surprising at first sight is that Froissart should not mention Chaucer on this occasion or have sought him out. In all the immense length of his *Chronicles* Froissart mentions Chaucer only once and incidentally, as a member of an embassy, along with Sturry and others, in 1377. If Deschamps could have known Chaucer was a poet, so must have Froissart. Perhaps he was jealous. Probably Chaucer kept himself out of the way. We know of Richard's interest in vernacular English poetry from Gower's proud account at the beginning of his *Confessio Amantis* of how he met Richard on the river, and the king called him into his boat and commissioned the work. Once again we note the absence of such claims in Chaucer's work, and remember the joke in the Prologue to *The Legend* which defends a condemned poem by saying that perhaps it was requested and the poet could not deny it.

Richard was also interested in fine clothes, which were a passion, in fine cooking (his cookery book survives), in jewels and art. To judge from the Wilton Diptych and the fine portrait in Westminster Abbey, his love of painting and his vanity went together. He was also pleased by ceremonial of which he was the centre, though according to a rumour attributed to Sir John Clanvowe he could also behave with undignified frantic childishness when angry, throwing his shoes and cloak out of the window. A splendid occasion that showed how he could be pleased, and is very characteristic of the times, was the procession and celebration that in August 1392 marked his reconciliation with the City of London after a bitter dispute. It was recorded in a Latin poem by the friar, Richard Maidstone. A procession is a characteristically Gothic form of art, though it only came to its full political development in Europe in the seventeenth century. *The Canterbury Tales* is a form of procession. Richard

BELOW The wooden funeral effigy of Anne of Bohemia, made from a death mask. She was plain, but kind, and deserved Richard's devotion

BELOW RIGHT As he grew older and more self-indulgent Richard grew fatter, as even this magnificently idealized tomb effigy shows

approached with his entourage from Westminster. The mayor and aldermen, clad in splendid livery of red and white, met the king, himself radiantly clothed, and surrendered to him the keys of the City. The City streets were decorated with rich cloths and flowers. There was music, singing and shouting, and the conduits in Cheapside ran with wine. Painted allegorical figures, street pageants and plays and formal speeches met the king at various points. Of course this was civic, not royal splendour, but it was designed to please the king, and effectively to match his Coronation procession, to signify a new era.

Since this time Chaucer's own interests, always deeper, had gone beyond the court, it seems that he had rather withdrawn personally from it. Froissart's failure to mention him, the fact that he was still probably living in Greenwich, and, in his fifties, having given up the Clerkship of Works, was in semi-retirement, all encourage this view. Probably he had never been strong and certainly since his campaign never particularly active in body.

Chaucer sounds ill and tired in the so-called 'Complaint of Venus' though it is a highly competent exercise, a free translation from the poems of Sir Otes (or Oton) de Granson, the Savoyard knight in the service of the English king. Chaucer calls Granson 'the flower of those who write poetry in France', a friendly and, it must be admitted, exaggerated remark which might well have irritated Froissart. Granson had written Valentine poems somewhat similar to *The Parliament of Fowls* and Chaucer had probably known him a long time. The 'Venus' ends with a final stanza, an Envoy, beginning either 'princess or 'princes', and asks that the poem be received with good nature,

> For elde, that in my spirit dulleth me   [old age]
> Hath of endyting al the subtilte[composing]
> Wel nygh bereft out of my remembraunce.   [taken]
> *'The Complaint of Venus'* ll. 76–8

There is real pathos in this, and maybe the poem was written late in the decade. It could hardly be after 1397, when Granson was killed in a judicial duel in France, trying to prove his innocence of complicity in a Savoyard conspiracy.

The poems to Scogan and Bukton are also clearly late, but much more amusing and very much better. They are direct, ironical, witty, even though 'Scogan' refers to the poet's age, and says he is 'forgotten in solitary wilderness'. He asks Scogan to make sure his friend is remembered 'where it may be fruitful', which must mean in the king's or some noble's treasury. This poem shows clearly that Chaucer is away from the court. If he were at court he could make his own petitions. On the other hand, we need not take such requests too seriously. They were the small change of a courtier's life. Scogan was a friend and poetic disciple, twenty years younger than Chaucer. He became tutor to the sons of Henry IV. The poem may refer jokingly to the very wet autumn of 1393 as 'the tears of Venus', caused by Scogan's heresy to love,

> That for thy lady sawgh nat thy distresse,
> Therfore thow yave hir up at Michelmesse?   [gave]

The poem to Bukton refers to being captured in Frisia, and since there was an

English expedition there in August-September 1396, was probably written soon after. The old courtier makes one of his rare and typically dismissive references to current political events, but we see him in a more cheerful mood.

He was not entirely forgotten at court, either, for besides whatever he got from the sub-forestership at North Petherton, and his savings, property and annuities, he received £10 in January 1393 and an annuity of £20 in February 1394. It would be agreeable to think that this latter was the result of Scogan's showing the poem he had received to the king. In December 1397 Chaucer received the grant of a butt of wine yearly. He must have paid regular visits to the court and especially to the Exchequer to collect the half-yearly instalments of his annuity. In 1397, however, the political scene had suddenly darkened.

The three last disastrous years of Richard's reign, and almost of Chaucer's life, are no major part of Chaucer's biography. An old tired man, who had always cared little for faction, who had friends in all camps, he may well have looked on with distress and anxiety, but he may equally, and in my opinion more probably, have felt himself detached from these passionate and dangerous worldly concerns. Prudence, old habit, even necessity, as well as love of friends and children, keep him in the circle of the court. His old associations with the house of Lancaster might even be strengthened, now that his sister-in-law, after the death of Constance of Castile, had by papal dispensation become the legitimate wife of John of Gaunt. He received gifts of scarlet robes from Gaunt's son Henry Bolingbroke, now Earl of Derby, eldest son of Blanche the Duchess, at Christmas 1395 and in February 1396 for delivering money to him from the Clerk of the Wardrobe. This renewed association was the result of accident not of extraordinary political foresight. No one could have foreseen at that time the extent of Richard's folly, or of Henry's opportunism. There was a tiresome suit for debt against Chaucer in 1398, arising out of transactions during his Clerkship eight years before, but he was able to get letters of protection against legal action and the case fades out of the records.

'An old tired man'

In 1398 the quarrel between Henry Bolingbroke and Mowbray the Duke of Norfolk resulted in the exile of both. Richard's progressively autocratic behaviour alienated all classes. In 1399 Gaunt died and Richard confiscated the whole of the huge Lancastrian inheritance. He then set sail for Ireland to crush the revolting Irish, thus leaving his base unprotected. This brought Henry back to claim his own inheritance and to find a wave of popular support for him and hatred for Richard that carried Henry to the throne, able swimmer that he was, and sucked Richard under. Richard was deposed and murdered and Henry accepted by parliament on 30 September 1399, as

> conquerour of Brutes Albyon   [Britain]
> Which that by lyne and free eleccion   [descent]
> Been verray king . . .   [true]

The words are Chaucer's and also those of the official proclamation which Chaucer echoes. This last poem of Chaucer's is 'The Complaint of Chaucer to his Purse' a witty petition for reward, the bluntest that survives. It must have

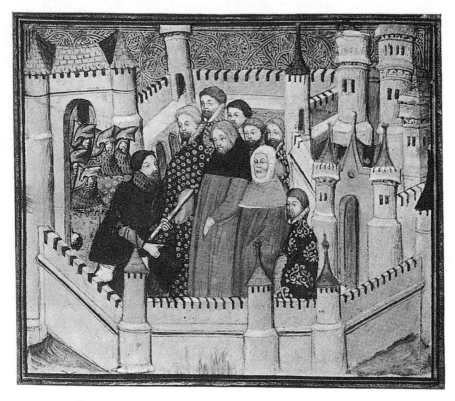

Richard II and Henry Bolingbroke confront each other at Flint Castle in Wales

been written after 30 September 1399 when Henry took over the government. An extra annuity of forty marks was granted to Chaucer on 13 October, in addition, as the record states, to the £20 a year awarded to him by Richard II, which is hereby confirmed. It seems reasonable to suppose that the poem was written and sent during the fortnight between those dates, while the terms of Henry's proclamation were still echoing in people's minds, and that it was promptly rewarded while Henry was consolidating his position, willing to be gracious at small cost to the famous elderly poet and wit, whom he had known all his life, and who was brother-in-law to his stepmother.

Henry was no philistine. He wrote easily in both French and English and could quote Latin tags. He was a skilled musician and lover of music. He was much concerned to have his sons well educated, and their tutor was Chaucer's friend Scogan, whom Chaucer, it will be remembered, had addressed in another jesting poem like 'The Complaint to his Purse', and had asked to keep his friend remembered 'where it might be fruitful'. Henry was keenly interested in books, as well as being a man of action. He was interested in poetry. Gower had switched the dedication of *Confessio Amantis* from Richard to him. Moreover, Gower may have done so after the death of Gaunt on 3 or 4 February 1399, for Henry was not styled as 'of Lancaster' until after the death at that date of his father, John of Gaunt, who was always called Lancaster by contemporaries, after his marriage to Blanche. Henry's intelligence, affability and courtesy were in large part the reason why he was now king. Of course he had many more important things to think of, but a nice little annuity, nothing in comparison with the huge rewards with which he responded to the petitions of barons and politicians (like any medieval king), and obviously in the nature of things not to be long enjoyed by the recipient, would be a very natural answer to Chaucer's elegant poem that amused so many people, and would need no more effort on Henry's part than literally a word to his chamberlain.

Every now and then scholars argue that Chaucer was desperately poor at this period. It is possible that the document recording Chaucer's new annuity was not written out until about 16 February 1400. It has been thought that he was so hard-pressed that he had to seek sanctuary in Westminster Abbey. This is most unlikely. It is indeed quite possible that he had to wait a long time before laying his hands on the cash. While he was waiting (if he did) he also applied to have his earlier grants from Richard formally renewed, on the grounds that the earlier letters patent (i.e. 'open' documents of proof) had been lost. This may well have been true. Chaucer was careless enough to lose a number of works which he mentions in his Retraction. Whether true or not, however, he was not careless about ensuring his finances. In documents referring to October 1399 his earlier annuities of £20 and a tun of wine from Richard are formally renewed.

The political upheaval of Richard's deposition and Henry's accession caused some delay in Exchequer payments, but Henry even made Chaucer a gift of £10 in November to make up the arrears of Richard's annuity, though despite all Chaucer's efforts it seems that he never succeeded in getting quite everything paid to him that he was owed. There was a good deal that was rough-and-ready in fourteenth-century paying and borrowing, as we see from other financial transactions of Chaucer's when perhaps he was more on the credit side, with whatever justice. Nevertheless, even in this last year of his life it seems that the worldly prudence which had ensured unusual success throughout his life, not in acquiring great rewards but in making sure that those he did receive were regularly paid, had by no means deserted Chaucer. It is common experience that as we grow older and nearer to eternity we become more, not less, anxious about money. I imagine that Chaucer was in that respect little different from most other people. He was not poor, and if he had been his well-to-do son Thomas could have helped him. In October 1399 Henry had also confirmed a grant by Richard to Thomas of twenty marks a year, and three days later made him Constable of Wallingford Castle with £40 a year for life. Thomas was well trusted by Henry, for Richard's widowed queen Isabella, whom he had married as a seven-year-old child for political reasons in 1396, was imprisoned at Wallingford. So there was no reason for Chaucer to be desperate. But he was determined to get what was owed to him, and a bit more if possible; not greedy but fussy. In writing the amusingly extravagant 'Complaint to his Purse', with its puns and parody of love, neither his wits nor his wit had failed him. Not only Henry but other people much enjoyed it, for no less than eleven manuscript copies survive. Perhaps Chaucer made a special journey up to court to see and congratulate the new king. But he did not want to stay at court. When he asks his purse, his 'saviour' in this world, to become heavier again, it is in order 'out of this town to help me through your might', and though the meaning is debatable it is perhaps out of the 'town', of the court that he wishes to be helped. Or perhaps he wanted help with moving expenses from the town of Greenwich.

There is no treachery or shameful sycophancy here. The history of the time is full of such changed allegiances, which sometimes even changed back again when Fortune's wheel turned once more, with apparently no hard feelings on either side. Richard had contrived to offend and alarm everybody except his closest favourites and he attracted very little loyalty, though the Lollard Earl of Salisbury tried to lead a revolt in his favour and was killed by the citizens of Cirencester. Practically everybody else, at first, welcomed the change of king.

One more landmark alone of Chaucer's days survives. On 4 December 1399 he took out the lease of a house in the garden of Westminster Abbey for fifty-three years. It is not clear when he left Kent but now he must have planned not only to occupy a more conveniently central house but to have been near the great abbey. In his last days he came decisively to the ancient centre and church. He had never ceased to work on *The Canterbury Tales*, and had occasionally issued or read sections. The plan developed, but the original idea of two stories to be told by each of thirty or so pilgrims on both outward journey and return was hopelessly ambitious, and he cut it short. The prologue to *The Parson's Tale* shows him closing the whole scheme down, though there is no reason to think that the Parson's 'meditation' was necessarily the last thing that he wrote. But this laborious devotional tract must be a late and sincere expression of his views.

His annuity was last drawn on his behalf on 5 June 1400. It was collected for him by Henry Somer and since the distance from his house, in the summery garden of the abbey, to the Exchequer was not far, he may already have been ill. He would have had a housekeeper or nurse and friends from the court could easily have called. One of the chancery clerks was Thomas Hoccleve, who was devoted to his memory and may have known him, since he procured a portrait of him in a manuscript in which he praises Chaucer's work. For by now Chaucer was well-recognized as the 'flower of rhetoric in English', the father of English poetry, who had created a new richness of English speech, had brought learning and sweetness into our tongue. He had always influenced a few friends, like Clanvowe and Scogan and the authors of a number of anonymous poems. With Hoccleve and Lydgate, the monk of Bury, who was about thirty years old in 1400, Chaucer's fame was more widely spread, and the fifteenth century saw poetry in English dominated by his work in both England and Scotland.

> But all shal passe that men prose or ryme.

Chaucer never sought power or influence, poetically or otherwise. He was passion-ately concerned to get the right words, and to get the words right, as his scribe Adam, immortalized by his careless copying, had cause to know, but Chaucer, like Shakespeare, was careless of reputation. As he said of himself in *The House of Fame*,

> Sufficeth me, as I were ded,
> That no wight have my name in honde.
> I wot myself best how y stonde.
>   ll. 1876–8

Now death was drawing near. The change of plan and tone in *The Parson's Tale* was carried a stage further, and in the Retractation, his final word, he actually revokes his secular works and 'those Canterbury Tales that tend to sin'. His pilgrims had wanted either *doctrine* or *mirth*, either *sentence* (serious instruction) or *solace*. Chaucer was interested in solace, in which he included all his secular fictions, the great poems including *Troilus*, which we now cherish, as well as in doctrine. But solace is free, marginal, non-didactic artwork. The serious concern for immortal salvation brought him back to the central concerns of actual life, in which, as he himself says, quoting St Paul, 'All that is written is written for our doctrine' – or at least should be. In some ways it is sad that he should deny so extraordinary an artistic achievement, so remarkable an advance into the secular world, which does not seem, since the Reformation, so irreligious, and which even Ockham's thought might be held to justify. But Chaucer was a poet not a theologian and time was short.

For a poet who was as reflective in both senses as Chaucer it was as natural when dying to revoke his secular works as when in health to write them. As usual he reflects the situation he was in, and the thought and feeling of his age about it. Since from the worldly point of view death is the end it is a closed situation, involuntary and without potential; the opposite of that situation for which and in which he created his merriest tales. Death is the black margin that confines our earthly pleasures and sorrows. Yet Chaucer himself had, especially when young, dwelled on that and other margins. They make up the more interesting parts of experience. It was Chaucer's habit in the end to retreat from margin to centre, from derision to affirmation, disorder to order. In *The Book of the Duchess*, written when young, he returned from death to courtly life. But now he must make another return, from the superficiality of earthly to the centre of spiritual existence. This was the lesson of Boethius when death was close. If death is a margin it is also a passage, a journey, leading to the true centre; Chaucer makes it in proper array, leaving all inappropriate baggage behind.

He prepared for his death, as the Retractation shows. He must have made a will but it does not survive. Taking up residence in the Abbey grounds late in life may well suggest preparation both practical and spiritual for death. According to an inscription once on his tomb he died on 25 October 1400. He was buried in Westminster Abbey near St Benedict's Chapel, a position which Professor Caroline Barron suggested (in a lecture to the New Chaucer Society July 2000) showed his closeness to the monastic tradition. The monks regularly passed by, perhaps walked over, his grave. It was a position both humble and privileged (though moved in the sixteenth century). Its situation reinforces our sense of the genuineness of the Retractation which many modern readers assume to be merely an ironic and insincere way of claiming authorship of the works that he was apparently repenting of. But how could he distinguish those pieces he genuinely regretted from others, more religious, that he was glad to have written, but by listing them? We may accept his 'verray penitence' yet without denying it enjoy even those works which his last stricter thoughts condemned.

BIBLIOGRAPHY

References in the Notes (pp. 195–9) are to the first word or two of the entries below.

COLLECTED EDITIONS OF CHAUCER

Benson, Larry D. (ed.) *The Riverside Chaucer*, 3rd edn. Boston 1987, Oxford 1988.

Skeat (1894) *The Complete Works of Geoffrey Chaucer*, 6 vols. Ed. W. W. Skeat. London

– (1897) *Chaucerian and Other Pieces*. Ed. W. W. Skeat (a supplement to the *Complete Works*). London

Speght (1598) *The Workes of our Antient and Learned English Poet, Geffrey Chaucer*. Ed. T. Speght (for Benham Norton). London

– (1602) (a 2nd edn)

Thynne (1532) *The Workes of Geffray Chaucer*. Ed. W. Thynne. London. Facsimile edn. with material from editions of 1542, 1561, 1598, 1602, ed. D. S. Brewer, Menston. 1969

GENERAL

Ariès, P. (1962) *Centuries of Childhood*. Trans. R. Baldick. London and New York

Armitage-Smith, S. (1904) *John of Gaunt*. London

Ashmole, E. (1672) *The Institution, Laws and Ceremonies of the most Noble Order of the Garter*. Facsimile edn, London 1971

Auerbach, E. (1965) *Literary Language and its Public in Late Latin Antiquity and in the Middle Ages*. Trans. R. Manheim. London and Princeton, N.J.

The Autobiography of Guibert, Abbot of Nogent-sous-Coucy. Trans. C. C. Swinton-Bland. London and Philadelphia, Pa. (n.d.)

Barnie, J. (1974) *War in Medieval Society: Social Values and the Hundred Years War 1337–99*. London and Princeton, N.J.

Bartholomaeus Anglicus (1976) *Batman vppon Bartholome His Booke De Proprietatibus Rerum* 1582. With an Introduction and Index by Jürgen Schäfer. *Anglistica and Americana* (161). Hildesheim and New York

Baxandall, M. (1972) *Painting and Experience in Fifteenth-Century Italy: A Primer in the Social History of Pictorial Style*. London and New York

Beltz, G. F. (1841) *Memorials of the Most Noble Order of the Garter*. London

Bennett, J. A. W. (1969) 'Chaucer's Contemporary' in *Piers Plowman: Critical Approaches*. Ed. S. S. Hussey. London; New York 1970

– (1974) *Chaucer at Oxford and Cambridge*. Oxford

Berners *Sir John Froissart's Chronicles*. Trans. John Bourchier, Lord Berners, 2 vols 1523–5; reprinted 1812. Ed. W. P. Ker, Tudor Translations, 6 vols 1901–3. Ed. and abridged G. C. Macaulay, Globe Edn 1895. London

Bishop, M. (1964) *Petrarch and his World*. London and Bloomington, Ind.

Blake, N. F. (1972) *Middle English Religious Prose*. York Medieval Texts. London and Evanston, Ill.

Bowden, M. (1948) *A Commentary on the General Prologue to the Canterbury Tales*. New York; reprinted 1967

Brewer, D. S. (1954a) 'Chaucer's *Complaint of Mars*', *Notes and Queries* (I) 462–3

– (1954b) 'Love and Marriage in Chaucer's Poetry', *Modern Language Review* (49) 461–4

– (1955) 'The Ideal of Feminine Beauty in Medieval Literature', *Modern Language Review* (50) 257–69

– (1958) *Proteus: Studies in English Literature*. Tokyo and Folcroft, Pa.

– (1960) *The Parlement of Foulys*. Ed. D. S. Brewer. London; revised and reprinted, Manchester 1972

– (1963) *Chaucer in his Time*. London (reissued 1973); New York 1973

– (1964) 'Children in Chaucer', *A Review of English Literature* (V) 52–60

– (1966a) *Chaucer and Chaucerians*. Ed. D. S. Brewer. London and Birmingham, Ala.

– (1966b) 'The Relationship of Chaucer to the English and European Traditions' in Brewer (1966a) 1–38

– (1966c) 'Images of Chaucer 1386–1900, in Brewer (1966a) 240–70

– (1968a) 'The Fabliaux' in *Companion* (1968) 247–67

– (1968b) 'Class Distinction in Chaucer', *Speculum* (XLIII) 290–305

– (1969) *Geoffrey Chaucer. The Works 1532 With Supplementary Material from the Editions of 1542, 1561, 1598 and 1602*. Facsimile edn with Introduction by D. S. Brewer. Menston, Yorkshire

– (1970) '*Troilus and Criseyde* in *The History of Literature in the English Language*, Vol. I *The Middle Ages*. Ed. W. F. Bolton. London. 195–228

– (1971) '*The Reeve's Tale* and the King's Hall, Cambridge', *The Chaucer Review* (5) 311–17

– (1972) 'The Ages of Troilus, Criseyde and Pandarus', *Studies in English Literature* (Tokyo) English Number, 3–15

– (1973a) *Chaucer*, 3rd Supplemented Edn; first published 1953. London

– (1973b) 'Honour in Chaucer', *Essays and Studies of the English Association* 1973. Ed. J. Lawlor. London

– (1974a) *Geoffrey Chaucer (Writers and their Background)*. Ed. Derek Brewer. London; reprinted Woodbridge and Rochester, N.Y., 1991

– (1974b) 'Gothic Chaucer' in Brewer (1974a) 1–32

– (1974c) 'Some Metonymic Relationships in Chaucer's Poetry', *Poetica* (I) 1–20

– (1974d) 'Some Observations on the Development of Literalism and Verbal Criticism', *Poetica* (2) 71–95

– (1975) *The Thornton Manuscript (Lincoln Cathedral MS. 91)*. Facsimile edn with Introduction by D. S. Brewer and A. E. B. Owen. Menston, Yorkshire

– (1976) The Interpretation of Dream, Folktale and Romance with special Reference to *Sir Gawain and the Green Knight*', *Newphilologische Mitteilungen* (LXXVII) 569–81

– (1977a) *Chaucer: The Critical Heritage*. London and Boston, Mass.

– (1977b) Review of Kelly (1975) in *The Review of English Studies*

– (1984) *An Introduction to Chaucer*. London

– (1998) A New Introduction to Chaucer, London, Addison Wesley Longman

Chadwick, D. (1922) *Social Life in the Days of Piers Plowman*. Cambridge; reprinted New York 1969

Chambers, E. K. (1903) *The Medieval Stage*, 2 vols. London and New York

Chandos Herald (1910) *Life of the Black Prince*. Ed. M. K. Pope and E. C. Lodge. Oxford

Chaucer Life-Records (1966). Ed. M. M. Crow and C. C. Olson. Oxford; Austin Tex., 1972. (See also *Life Records* 1900)

Chaytor, H. J. (1945) *From Script to Print*. Cambridge; reprint of 1966 edn, Folcroft, Pa., 1974

Cipolla, C. M. (1967) *Clocks and Culture* 1300–1700. London

– (ed.) (1972) *The Fontana Economic History of Europe: The Middle Ages*. London and New York

Clanvowe See Scattergood (1975)

Cohn, N. (1957) *The Pursuit of the Millennium*. London and New York

Clark, P. and Slack, P. (eds.) (1972) *Crisis and Order in English Towns 1500–1700*. London and Toronto

Collis, M. (1958) *The Hurling Time*. London

Companion to Chaucer Studies (1968). Ed. Beryl Rowland. Toronto

Coulton, G. G. (1918) *Social Life in Britain from the Conquest to the Reformation*. Cambridge; reprinted Philadelphia, Pa., 1971

– (1938) *Medieval Panorama: The English Scene from Conquest to Reformation*. Cambridge; paperback New York 1974

– (1940) *Europe's Apprenticeship*. London and Toronto

Cunningham, J. V. (1952) 'The Literary Form of the Prologue to the *Canterbury Tales*', *Modern Philology* (XLIX) 172–81

Dobson, R. B. (1970) *The Peasants' Revolt of 1381*. London and New York

Donaldson, E. T. (1970) *Speaking of Chaucer*. London and New York

Douglas, M. (1966) *Purity and Danger: An Analysis of Concepts of Pollution and Taboo*. London and New York

– (1973) *Natural Symbols: Explorations in Cosmology*, 2nd edn. London and New York

Du Boulay, F. R. H., and Barron, C. M. (eds) (1971) *The Reign of Richard II*. London

Du Boulay, F. R. H. (1974) 'The Historical Chaucer' in Brewer (1974a) 33–57

Duby, G. (1968) 'The Diffusion of Cultural Patterns in Feudal Society', *Past and Present* (39)

Early English Lyrics (1907). Ed. E. K. Chambers and F. Sidgwick. London; reprinted 1947

Eliade, M. (1960) *Myths Dreams and Mysteries*. London. Reprinted in The Fontana Library of Theology and Philosophy. London and New York 1968

Elliott, R. W. V. (1974) *Chaucer's English*. London

Emden, A. B. (1963) *A Biographical Register of the University of Cambridge to 1500*. Cambridge and New York

English Historical Documents 1327–1485 (1969). Ed. A. R. Myers. London and New York

The Equatorie of the Planetis (1955). Ed. D. J. Price, with a linguistic analysis by R. M. Wilson. Cambridge and New York

Fanfani, A. (1951) 'La préparation intellectuelle et professionelle à l'activité économique en Italie du XIVe au XVIe siècle', *Le Moyen Age* (LVII) 327–46

Fisher, J. H. (1965) *John Gower: Moral Philosopher and Friend of Chaucer*. London and New York

Fortescue, Sir J. (1561) *De Laudibus Legum Angliae* (for the Company of Stationers). London

– (1942) *De Laudibus Legum Angliae*. Ed. S. B. Chrimes. Cambridge and New York

Fowler, K. (1969) *The King's Lieutenant*. London and New York

Fox, D. (1966) 'The Scottish Chaucerians' in Brewer (1966) 164–200

Frank, R. W., Jr (1972) *Chaucer and the Legend of Good Women*. Cambridge, Mass.

Frye, N. (1957) *Anatomy of Criticism*. Princeton, N.J. and Oxford

Gairdner, J. (1908) *Lollardy and the Reformation in England*, Vol. I. London; reprinted New York 1965

Gower, J. (1900) *The English Works of John Gower*, 2 vols. Ed. G. C. Macaulay. Early English Text Society, E.S. (LXXXI). London and New York

Harbert, B. (1974) In Brewer (1974a) 137–53

Hardy, B. C. (1910) *Philippa of Hainault and her Times*. London

The Harley Lyrics (1948). Ed. G. L. Brook. Manchester; 3rd reprint 1964

Harvey, J. H. (1944) *Henry Yevele*. London and New York

– (1948) *Gothic England: A Survey of National Culture 1300–1500*, 2nd edn. London and New York

Henderson, G. (1967) *Gothic*. Harmondsworth and New York

Hill, R. (1971) `A Chaunterie for Soules: London Chantries in the Reign of Richard II' in Du Boulay and Barron (1971) 242–55

Holmes, G. (1962) *The Later Middle Ages 1272–1485*. London; paperback New York 1966

Hornsby, J. A. (1988) *Chaucer and the Law*, Norman, Oklahoma

Howard, D. R. (1976) *The Idea of the Canterbury Tales*. Los Angeles and London

Hulbert, J. R. (1912) *Chaucer's Official Life*. Doctoral dissertation. Chicago, Ill.; reprinted New York 1970

Illustrations of Chaucer's England (1918). Ed. D. Hughes. London; reprint of 1919 edn, Folcroft, Pa., 1972

Julian of Norwich (1966) *Revelations of Divine Love*. Trans. C. Wolters. Harmondsworth

Jusserand, J. J. (1889) *English Wayfaring Life in the Middle Ages*. London; many later reprints incl. Boston, Mass., 1973

Kane, G. (1965) *The Autobiographical Fallacy in Chaucer and Langland Studies*, Chambers Memorial Lecture, University College, London. London

Kelly, H. A. (1975) *Love and Marriage in the Age of Chaucer*. Ithaca. N.Y., and London

King Horn (1901). Ed. J. J. Hall. Oxford

Kittredge, G. L. (1903) 'Chaucer and Some of his Friends', *Modern Philology* (I) 1–18

Knowles, D. (1961) *The English Mystical Tradition*.London and Naperville, Ill.

Langland, W. (1886) *Piers the Plowman and Richard the Redeless*, 2 vols. Ed. W. W. Skeat. London and New York

– (1975) *Piers Plowman: the B Version*. Ed. G. Kane and E. T. Donaldson. London and New York

Le Goff, J. (1972) In Cipolla (1972)

Lewis, C. S. (1964) *The Discarded Image*. Cambridge and New York

Life Records of Chaucer (1900). Ed. R. E. G. Kirk. London

Life-Records (1969) (See *Chaucer Life-Records*)

Little John of Saintré (1931). By Antoine de la Salle trans. into English by I. Gray. London

Loomis, L. H. (1962) *Adventures in the Middle Ages*. New York

Love, N. (1908) *The Mirrour of the Blessed Lyf of Jesu Christ*. Ed. L. F. Powell. Oxford

McFarlane, K. B. (1972) *Lancastrian Kings and Lollard Knights*. Oxford and New York

McKisack, M. (1959) *The Fourteenth Century 1307–1399*. Oxford and New York

Magoun, F. P., Jr (1961) *A Chaucer Gazetteer*. Stockholm and Chicago, Ill.

Manly, J. M. (1926) *Some New Light on Chaucer*. London; reprinted Gloucester, Mass., 1959

Mann, J. (1973) *Chaucer and Medieval Estates Satire: The Literature of Social Classes and the General Prologue to the Canterbury Tales*. Cambridge and New York

Manners (1868) *Manners and Meals in Olden Time*. Ed. F. J. Furnivall. Early English Text Society, O.S. (32). London

Manzalaoui, M. (1974) 'Chaucer and Science' in Brewer (1974a) 224–61

Martindale, A. (1967) *Gothic Art*. London and New York

Mathew, G. (1968) *The Court of Richard II*. London and New York

Medieval Comic Tales (1973). Trans. P. Rickard and others. Cambridge and Totowa, N.J.

Meiss, M. (1952) *Painting in Florence and Siena after the Black Death*. Oxford; Icon Edn, New York 1973

The Minor Poems of the Vernon MS (1901), Part II. Ed. F. J. Furnivall. Early English Text Society, O.S. (117). London

Morris, G. C. (1971) 'The Plague in Britain', *The Historical Journal* (XIV) 205–24

Muscatine, C. (1957) *Chaucer and the French Tradition*. Berkeley, California, and Cambridge

– (1963) 'Locus of Action in Medieval Narrative', *Romance Philology* (XVII) 115–22

–(1972) *Poetry and Crisis in the Age of Chaucer*. Notre Dame, Ind., and London

North, J. D. (1969) 'Kalenderes Enlumyned Ben They: Some Astronomical Themes in Chaucer', *The Review of English Studies*, N.S. (XX) 129–54; 257–83; 418–44

Oberman, H. A. (1967) *The Harvest of Medieval Theology*, revised edn. Grand Rapids, Mich.

Orme, N. (1973) *English Schools in the Middle Ages*. London and New York

Palmer, J. N. (1974) 'The Historical Context of *The Book of the Duchess*: A Revision', *The Chaucer Review* (8) 253–61

Pantin, W. A. (1955) *The English Church in the Fourteenth-Century*. Cambridge and New York

Parks, G. B. (1949) 'The Route of Chaucer's First Journey to Italy', *ELH, A Journal of English Literary History* (XVI) 174–87

The Paston Letters 1422–1509 (1900–1), 4 vols. Ed. J. Gairdner. London

Pearsall, D. A. (1966) 'The English Chaucerians' in Brewer (1966) 201–39

– (1970) *John Lydgate*. London

– (1992) *The Life of Chaucer*, Oxford, Blackwell

Peristiany, J. G. (ed.) (1966) *Honour and Shame: The Values of Mediterranean Society*. London

Phythian-Adams, C. (1972) In Clark and Slack

Pierce the Ploughman's Crede (1906). Ed. W. W. Skeat. Oxford

Platt, C. (1976) *The English Medieval Town*. London and New York

Plimpton, C. A. (1935) *The Education of Chaucer*. London and New York

Pratt, R. A. (1949) 'Geoffrey Chaucer, Esq., and Sir John Hawkwood', *ELH, A Journal of English Literary History* (XVI) 188–93

Rickert, E. (1913) 'Thou Vache', *Modern Philology* (XI) 209–17

– (1948) *Chaucer's World*. Ed. C. C. Olson and M. M. Crow. New York

Robertson, D. W., Jr (1968) *Chaucer's London*. New York

Robson, J. A. (1961) *Wyclif and the Oxford Schools*. Cambridge and New York

Russell, J. C. (1972) 'Population in Europe 500–1500' in Cipolla (1972) 25–70

Salter, E. (1974) 'Nicholas Love's *Myrrour of the Blessed Lyf of Jesus Crist*', *Analecta Cartusiana* (10). Salzburg

Scattergood, V. J. (1968) 'Two Medieval Book Lists', *The Library* (XXIII) 236–9

– (1975) *The Works of Sir John Clanvowe*. Cambridge and Totowa, N.J.

Selections from John Gower (1968). Ed. J. A. W. Bennett. Clarendon Medieval and Tudor Series. Oxford and New York

The Sermons of Thomas Brinton, Bishop of Rochester 1373–89 (1954). Ed. Sister Mary Aquinas Devlin. Camden Third Series (LXXXV), The Royal Historical Society

Shepherd, G. T. (1970) *The Nature of Alliterative Poetry in Late Medieval England*. Sir Israel Gollancz Memorial Lecture. *Proceedings of the British Academy* (LVI)

–(1974) 'Religion and Philosophy in Chaucer' in Brewer (1974a) 262–89

Shrewsbury, J. F. D. (1970) *A History of Bubonic Plague in the British Isles*. Cambridge and New York

Sir Launfal (1960). Ed. A. J. Bliss. London

Skelton, J. (1931) *The Complete Poems of John Skelton*. Ed. P. Henderson. London and New York

Smith, D. E. (1923) *History of Mathematics*, 2 vols. Boston, Mass.

Sources and Analogues of Chaucer's Canterbury Tales (1941). Ed. W. F. Bryan and G. Dempster. Chicago, Ill.

Spearing, A. C. (1976) *Medieval Dream-Poetry*. Cambridge

Spurgeon, C. F. E. (1925) *Five Hundred Years of Chaucer Criticism and Allusion 1357-1900*, 3 vols. Cambridge; illus. edn, New York 1960

Stanley, A. P. (1854) *Historical Memorials of Canterbury*. London

Steel, A. (1941) *Richard II*. Cambridge and New York

Stevens, J. (1961) *Music and Poetry in the Early Tudor Court*. London and New York

Strutt, J. (1838) *The Sports and Pastimes of the People of England*. Ed. W. Hone. London; latest edn, Detroit, Mich., 1968

Takano, H. (1972) 'The Audience of *Troilus and Criseyde*', *Bulletin of the Faculty of Humanities*, Seikei University (8) 1-9

Thrupp, S. L. (1948) *The Merchant Class of Medieval London*. Ann Arbor, Mich.; Cambridge 1949

Thynne, F. (1875) *Animaduersions 1598*. Ed. F. J. Furnivall. Chaucer Society, Second Series (13). London and New York

Tout, T. F. (1920-33) *Chapters in the Administrative History of Medieval England*. 6 vols. London

– (1929) 'Literature and Learning in the English Civil Service', *Speculum* 4, 365-89

Tuck, A. (1973) *Richard II and the English Nobility*. London; New York 1974

Turner, V. W. (1969) *The Ritual Process*. New York and London; paperback, 1974

– (1974) *Dramas Fields and Metaphors*. Ithaca, N.Y., and London

Vocabularies (2 vols 1872, 1873). Ed. T. Wright. A Library of National Antiquities. Privately printed

Wesencraft, A. (1975) 'Derivations', *University of London Bulletin* (26) 12-13

Wickham, G. (1959) *Early English Stages 1300 to 1660: Volume One 1300 to 1576*. London and New York

Wilkins, E. H. (1949) 'Cantus Troili' *ELH, A Journal of English Literary History* (XVI) 167-73

Wimsatt, J. I. (1974) 'Chaucer and French Poetry' in Brewer (1974) 109-36

Wordsworth *The Poetical Works of William Wordsworth* (1940-9), 5 vols. Ed. E. de Selincourt. Oxford

Wright, T. (1862) *A History of Domestic Manners and Sentiments in England During the Middle Ages*. London

Wyatt *The Collected Poems of Sir Thomas Wyatt* (1949). Ed. with an Introduction by K. Muir. London; Cambridge, Mass., 1950

Wyclif, J. (1921) 'The Translation of the Bible' in *Fourteenth-Century Verse and Prose*. Ed. K. Sisam. Oxford; New York 1937

NOTES

References are to the Bibliography pp. 216–218. Page references are only used where strictly necessary.

Page INTRODUCTION

2 The mirth . . . Early English Lyrics 241
  You cannot . . . CT V 57; BD 411; CT IV
  2140; TC III 351–2
3 There was . . . Pierce the Plowman's Crede
  420–42
4 In 1339 . . . Jusserand 86
  In some towns . . . Platt 48
  One paved road . . . Jusserand 84–5
5 Fourteenth-century . . . Platt 49
  Ladies might . . . Jusserand 95–6
6 The covered wagon . . . Jusserand 99
  The two-and-a-half . . . Magoun
  There is a . . . Medieval Comic Tales 60ff.
7 Chaucer on . . . Jusserand 131
  On entering . . . Rickert 280 Langland . . . B V
  340ff.
8 The towns . . . Russell 30ff.
  London had . . . Platt 40
9 Once past . . . Platt 27ff.
  In Bristol . . . Platt 51
13 Centres of . . . Turner (1974) 166ff.

CHAPTER ONE

15 Even Henry IV . . . McFarlane 13, 161
  Among the Pastons . . . Paston Letters (1900–1)
  Introd. XXXII
16 Sir Richard . . . Rickert (1948) 147ff.
18 Chaucer seems . . . Life Records of Chaucer
  (1900) vi–vii
19 The powers . . . Platt 21
  Noblemen readily . . . Thrupp
21 Even the charitable . . . McKisack 95
23 The only carpet . . . Platt 72–3
  A rich Southampton . . . Platt 74
24 Along Thames Street . . . Robertson
25 Foreign merchants . . . Le Goff; Holmes 153ff.

CHAPTER TWO

27 In the upper . . . Brewer (1963) Chapter V
  He was washed . . . Bartholomaeus VI, 5
  The adjectives . . . Brewer (1964)
28 St Augustine . . . Autobiography of Guibert.
  Coulton (1918) 60
  Another image . . . Brewer (1954b)
29 He would not . . . Bartholomaeus VI, 15
  The story of . . . Brewer 1977a
30 City families . . . Le Goff
  The priest . . . Coulton (1918)
  From then on . . . Phythian-Adams
31 His notable . . . Brewer (1972)
  There is a string . . . Manners 1ff.
32 There is a famous . . . Loomis 131ff.
33 Chaucer's early . . . Brewer (1966a)

The Auchinleck . . . Brewer (1963) Chapter V
  'To read' . . . Chaytor 10ff.
  Such games . . . Rickert (1948)
35 Some of them . . . Chambers (1903) I, 1ff.
  He could play . . . Wesencraft
36 The course . . . Shrewsbury; Morris; Coulton
  (1938)
  The great medieval . . . Morris 207
37 Italy is . . . McKisack 333
38 Before he . . . Orme 138
39 Thus the basic . . . Fanfani
  From this general . . . Baxandall
  From early . . . Thrupp 158. Rickert (1948) 111
40 On arrival . . . Orme 119ff.
  From about . . . Orme 124
  He first . . . Plimpton
41 The effect of . . . Brewer (1966a). Davies 1974.
  Elliott
  In Aquitaine . . . Berners II, CCXXXII
42 At school . . . Orme 120
  After the English . . . Orme 88
  It is not . . . Coulton (1940)
  An earlier schoolmaster . . . Rickert (1948)
43 Chaucer's knowledge . . . Harbert
  A little more . . . Smith
44 The interest in . . . Coulton (1918) 60
  As late as . . . Manners xlvii
45 There were plenty . . . Manners liv

CHAPTER THREE

46 The record . . . Illustrations 164–5. Vocabu-
  laries s.v.
47 Geoffrey's older . . . Coulton (1918) 84ff.
  The young widow . . . Little John of Saintré 33
50 Guibert says . . . Autobiography of Guibert 67
52 The King's chief . . . King Horn l. 233ff.
  The notable work . . . Manners 115ff.
55 At first . . . Donaldson (1970).
  An hendy . . . Harley lyrics
  In the huge . . . Minor poems 479ff; TC I 171
  In any big . . . Chandos Herald
56 It was high . . . Barnie
  From the point . . . Peristiany; Brewer (1973a)
  (1973b)
57 In 1359 . . . Barnie 127; McKisack 248
  Whereas the . . . McKisack 237ff.
61 The name of . . . Sir Launfal 15
62 But the drawing . . . CT I 2087–8

CHAPTER FOUR

64 The evidence . . . Manly 1ff; Workes Speght
  (1598); Brewer (1977b)
65 In his Mirour . . . Fisher 57

The notable fifteenth-century . . . Fortescue
  (1942) 117–19
  It was expensive . . . Brewer (1973a); Rickert
  (1948) 111
  Less than . . . Fortescue (1942) Chapter 48
  The expense . . . Fortescue (1942) Chapter 49
66 Geoffrey knew . . . Loomis 160; LG W Pro G
  273
67 This view . . . Brewer (1969)
  The group of . . . Tout III 201–2
68 The neighbouring . . . Holmes 197
69 There is no sign . . . Auerbach
  Spain, including . . . Magoun
72 Constance was . . . Armitage-Smith 357

CHAPTER FIVE

75 It was Edward's . . . Barnie 111
  He was the first . . . Hardy 67–8
77 According to . . . Berners II, CXXX
78 In April 1331 . . . Fowler 28
  Still more . . . Berners II, LXXVII
79 One of the many . . . Fowler 104
80 The traditional attitude . . . Wyatt xv
81 The making of . . . The Times, London 21
  December 1976
84 At the same time . . . Brewer (1974b); Turner
  (1974)
  'Government was' . . . Holmes 68
85 But most esquires . . . Hulbert
  The recreational . . . Brewer (1973a)
86 The normal way . . . Hulbert 35
  In one case . . . Hulbert 42–3
88 In the court . . . Chaucer Life-Records (1966)
  86
  If Romantic . . . Brewer (1958)

CHAPTER SIX

90 On September . . . Life Records of Chaucer
  (1900) 172
  But it now . . . Palmer
92 Most directly . . . Brewer (1966a)
  His dependence . . . Wimsatt
  Wordsworth composed . . . Wordsworth II, 517
  Only three . . . Brewer (1975)
94 In romances . . . Brewer (1977a)
95 Another aspect . . . Brewer (1974d)

CHAPTER SEVEN

98 Though both . . . Wilkins
99 Chaucer's personal . . . Parks
101 A few years . . . Usk
103 For example the . . . Baxandall
105 Giotto who . . . Meiss
106 So forms . . . Meiss 96

107   St Catherine . . . Emden
108   This book was . . . Salter; Love
109   Petrarch, the most . . . Bishop

CHAPTER EIGHT

111   In May . . . Hulbert 80ff.
      The uncertainty is . . . Du Boulay (1974) 49ff.
112   Even the requirement . . . Hulbert 87
115   Professor Manly . . . Manly 181ff; Rickert (1948)
      185ff.
116   At any rate . . . Fisher
118   The publicity of . . . Brewer (1963) 206–13
      The arguments were . . . Shepherd (1974)
119   When warned . . . Collis 194ff. is very vivid
      He was doing . . . Langland (1886) B Prologue
      191
121   Since his gildsmen . . . Bowden 184–5
122   The betrayed lady . . . Brewer (1954b); (1958)
      176ff.
124   In paradise . . . Eliade 58
      They express . . . Turner (1974)
      In a valey . . . Early English Lyrics 151

CHAPTER NINE

126   It has been devised . . . Robertson 99–100
127   The legal historian . . . Chaucer Life-Records
      (1966) 345–7
      K. B. McFarlane . . . McFarlane (1972) 183
128   Incidentally, it . . . Dobson 107–11
129   A league . . . Bartholomaeus XIX 132
      Ball was . . . Cohn
      Then, 'with Ball' . . . McKisack 408
131   So I do not . . . Dobson 97–8, 387–8
132   But one of the aldermen . . . Dobson 217
      This accusation . . . Dobson 212–13
136   Though most of the . . . Dobson 303
137   I earlier called . . . Brewer (1958)
138   There are a number . . . Brewer (1960) 5
      There had been . . . Robertson 87–8
      In the fourteenth . . . Stevens 154–202

CHAPTER TEN

140   At almost every . . . Muscatine (1972)
      There were many . . . Shepherd (1974)
      Lollardy was . . . Du Boulay (1974)

141   God's purpose . . . Shepherd (1974) 275
      There were a number . . . Knowles; Pantin
143   This may be so . . . Henderson 35–7
      It could be seen . . . Brewer (1964) 208ff.
      Wyclif himself . . . Shepherd (1974) 281ff.
144   A total of . . . McFarlane 139ff.
      Clifford, born . . . Kittredge; Brewer (1977b)
145   Gaunt and . . . Complaint of Venus l. 82;
      Robinson Works 538
146   Deschamps in . . . Kittredge 7, 11
147   The apparent contradictions . . . Scattergood
      (1975)
148   The first obviously . . . Gairdner I 45–6
      Sir William . . . Hulbert 71ff.
149   Sir Philip . . . Rickert (1913)
      A curate would . . . Hill 242–4
151   Although Chaucer . . . Robson 39
      Wyclif's emphasis . . . Wyclif
      Many lay people . . . Robson 33
153   He enriched . . . Brewer (1970)
      Besides these . . . Brewer (1972)
154   Troilus is . . . Kelly; Brewer (1977c)
155   It has plenty . . . Frank; Brewer (1973)

CHAPTER ELEVEN

157   Moreover, the relatively . . . Turner (1974) 231ff.;
      Brewer (1974b) 17ff.
      The Prologue . . . Takano
158   The busy and very rich . . . Du Boulay (1974)
      42
      Sir Simon . . . Scattergood (1968)
160   Chairborne warriors . . . Du Boulay (1974) 53ff.
      There is no reason . . . Brewer (1964) 161–2.
      Berners II, CCII
161   Richard withdrew . . . Steel 121
      Burley maintained . . . McKisack 446
165   The job brought . . . Harvey (1944)
      These were probably . . . Strutt III, 1, Sect. XII
166   In these rules . . . Strutt III, 1, Sect. XXIII

CHAPTER TWELVE

169   Although it had . . . LGW Pro F 366–7
      This disengaged . . . Medieval Comic Tales
170   In French . . . Brewer (1968a)
      A mid-fifteenth . . . Brewer (1975)

171   The plan offered . . . Muscatine (1957) 167ff.
172   Chaucer had thus . . . Mann
      The 'estates' . . . English Historical Documents
      1153, 166
      In general . . . Vocabularies
      A more profound . . . Brewer (1968b)
173   They would have . . . Manly 192
174   This variable . . . Donaldson (1970) 1–12
      Chaucer's pilgrimage . . . Howard
      Chaucer knew . . . Magoun 48ff.
175   It has been . . . Manly 77
202   The pilgrims . . . Stanley; Brewer (1963)
      The Parson's . . . Sources and Analogues.
      Blake
      In the fourteenth . . . Oberman 39, 214
176   Chaucer's art . . . Auerbach 322, 327; Mann 198;
      Brewer (1974b)

CHAPTER THIRTEEN

178   The university world . . . Bennett; Brewer (1971)
      We are told . . . Bennett 33
179   It was usual . . . Bennet 75ff.
      Chaucer's Astrolabe . . . North 432; Manzal-
      aoui 233ff.
      The astronomical treatise . . . Price; North 433–
      6
180   Chaucer wrote . . . Brewer (1954); Manzalaoui
      It has also . . . North 257–62
182   Richard was . . . Mathew 22
      The King was . . . Berners II. CXCVII
      He was also pleased . . . English Historical
      Documents
      Richard approached . . . Rickert (1948) 35ff.
183   Granson had . . . Brewer (1960) Appendix I
186   The history of . . . Du Boulay (1974) 52
187   For by now . . . Brewer (1977b)
      With Hoccleve . . . Fox; Pearsall (1966) (1970)
188   One could imagine . . . CT I 2822–6; IV 2364–
      5; LGW Pro 1ff.
      In dying . . . CT I 3042–3
      Here is no home . . . Truth 17–19
      His spirit . . . CT I 2809–12
      Like Troilus . . . Troilus V 1821–7

NOTES ON THE ILLUSTRATIONS

Abbreviations used are:

BL   By permission of The British Library
BN   cliché Bibliothèque nationale de France
        Paris
RMN   Agence photographique de la réunion des
        musées nationaux

JACKET FRONT Ms. Cod. Marc. Lat. I 99 f.8v,
Biblioteca Nazionale Marciana, Venice.   Photo
Scala, Florence

COLOUR PLATES

REVERSE OF FRONTISPIECE A Portrait of
Chaucer from Hoccleve's De Regimine Principum,
Ms. Harl. 4866, f.88 min BL

FRONTISPIECE CCC MS 61, fr., by kind permission of the Master and Fellows of Corpus Christi
College, Cambridge

Facing page

16   Ms. Add. 27695, f.14r, BL
17   Ms 2617, f.53 Oesterreichische Nationalbibli-
     othek, Vienna
64   Arras tapestry, Musée des Arts Décoratifs,
     Paris. Photo Laurent-Sully Jaulmes
65   Ms. Royal 18 D II f.148, BL
80   Ms. Amb. 317 2°, f.10r, Stadtbibliothek
     Nürnberg

81 Copyright Sonia Halliday and Laura Lushington
120 Alb apparel, detail, V & A Picture Library
CENTRE SPREAD Palazzo Publico, Siena. Photo Scala, Florence
121 Ms lat. 1173, f.1v, 2v, 5, BN
160 Ms. Cod. Marc. Lat. I 99 f.2v, Biblioteca Nazionale Marciana, Venice. Photo Scala, Florence
161 Ms. Cod. Marc. Lat. I 99 f.8v, Biblioteca Nazionale Marciana, Venice. Photo Scala, Florence
176 © National Gallery, London
177 © The British Museum

BLACK AND WHITE ILLUSTRATIONS
Page
6 Ms. Holkham 311, f.41v, reproduced by permission of Lord Leicester
9 Cambridge University Aerial Photography, © Crown Copyright/MOD. Reproduced with the permission of the Controller of Her Majesty's Stationery Office
10 Ms. Royal 2 B VII f.171, BL
11 V & A Picture Library
12 Ms. 9242, f.48v, copyright Brussels, Royal Library of Belgium
14 Ms. Rh. 15 f.54r, Zentralbibliothek, Zürich
15 Edwin Smith
18 TOP LEFT Ms. Add. 19720 f.165, BL
TOP RIGHT Courtesy of the Museum of London
20 © Crown Copyright. National Monuments Record
21 Edwin Smith
23 © Crown Copyright. National Monuments Record
24 TOP Conway Library, Courtauld Institute of Art
BOTTOM Ms. Bodl. 264, f.173r, The Bodleian Library, University of Oxford
27 J C D Smith
30 Courtesy of the Museum of London
33 Edwin Smith
36 © Crown Copyright. National Monuments Record
37 BOTH PICTURES © The British Museum
39 From E J Burford *The Orrible Synne*, 1973
40 Ms. nouv. acq. lat. 1673, f.66, BN
43 National Museum of Ireland
44 BOTH PICTURES J C D Smith
46 J C D Smith

47 Ms. Douce 6, f.99r, The Bodleian Library, University of Oxford
48 Ms. Bodl. 264, f.130v, The Bodleian Library, University of Oxford
49 Ms. Bodl. 264, f.54v, The Bodleian Library, University of Oxford
51 Conway Library, Courtauld Institute of Art
52 Alinari/Art Resource, NY
53 Lincoln Cathedral Library
55 The Roudnice Lobkowicz Library, Nelahozeves Castle, Czech Republic
56 J C D Smith
57 Ms. Add. 28162 f.9v, BL
59 V & A Picture Library
61 © The British Museum
62 © The British Museum
63 Ms lat. 14284, f.63, BN
67 V & A Picture Library
68 Chansonnier dit de Montpellier, H 196 f.88r, Bibliothèque universitaire de Médecine, Montpellier
71 The Wallace Collection, London
74 National Monuments Record. © The Warburg Institute, London
75 Paris, Musée National du Moyen Age – Thermes et Hôtel de Cluny. Photo RMN
79 BOTH PICTURES Musée du Louvre, Département des Arts Graphiques. Photo RMN
82 Chansonnier dit de Montpellier, H 196 f.63v, Bibliothèque universitaire de Médecine, Montpellier
84 © The British Museum
87 Ashmolean Museum, Oxford
88 Musée du Louvre. Photo RMN
90 Ms. fr. 1586, f.56, BN
94 Conway Library, Courtauld Institute of Art
97 Ms. Royal 20 C VII f.41v, BL
99 Edwin Smith
100 Musée du Louvre. Photo RMN
102 V & A Picture Library
104 © Dean and Chapter of Westminster
106 Ms. Royal 2 B VII f.72v, BL
107 Ms. Cotton Nero D VII f.7r, BL
109 Courtesy of the Museum of London
110 By courtesy of the National Portrait Gallery, London
113 10 B 23, f.2, Museum of the Book/Museum Meermanno-Westreenianum
118 The Pierpont Morgan Library, New York, II, 75
123 Ms. lat. 4802, f.132 v°, BN
125 Palazzo Publico, Siena. Photo Scala, Florence
129 © National Gallery, London

130 The Pierpont Morgan Library, New York, MS M.917, p.149
132 Ms. 927. f.145r, Rouen, Bibliothèque Municipale. Lauros-Giraudon
135 © Copyright The British Museum
137 Ms. nouv. acq. lat., 1673, f.95, BN
140 The Warburg Institute, London
144 Ms. lat. 1173, f.6v°, BN
148 Alfred Lammer
151 LEFT Courtesy of the Museum of London
RIGHT Ms. Add. 47682 f.6, BL
152 From The Hidden World of Misericords by Dorothy and Henry Kraus (Michael Joseph, 1976). © 1975 Dorothy and Henry Kraus
157 Ms. Add. 28162 f.10v, BL
162 Ms. 2617 f.76b, Oesterreichische Nationalbibliothek, Vienna
163 Ms Vat Pal Lat 1071, © Biblioteca Apostolica Vaticana
164 © National Gallery, London
167 Ms. Douce 366, f.109r, The Bodleian Library, University of Oxford
169 Ms. nouv. acq. fr. 5243, f.34, BN
172 Courtesy of the Museum of London
175 TOP V & A Picture Library
BOTTOM © Copyright The British Museum
178 BOTH PICTURES Bildarchiv Foto Marburg
180 CT447 Book of Hours, V & A Picture Library
185 Ms. Cod. 2 761, f.38, Oesterreichische Nationalbibliothek, Vienna
189 BOTH PICTURES © Copyright The British Museum
191 Edwin Smith
193 Ms. Ee.3.59, f.4r, by permission of the Syndics of Cambridge University Library
194 Bayerisches Landesamt für Denkmalpflege, München
197 Staatliche Museen zu Berlin - Bildarchiv Preussischer Kulturbesitz, Skulpturensammlung, Friedrich, 1964
198 Ms. Douce 366, f.131r, The Bodleian Library, University of Oxford
201 Edwin Smith
202 Courtesy of the Museum of London
203 Courtesy of the Museum of London
204 The Pierpont Morgan Library, New York. MS M.917, p.180
207 © Kunstsammlung der Fürsten zu Waldburg-Wolfegg
209 LEFT © Dean and Chapter of Westminster
RIGHT A F Kersting
211 © Crown Copyright. National Monuments Record
212 Ms. Harley 1319 f.50 BL

INDEX